ASSASSIN'S
CREED
ORIGINS

TITAN
COMICS

Assassin's Creed Origins

EDITOR: TOM WILLIAMS
SENIOR DESIGNER: ANDREW LEUNG

Managing & Launch Editor: Andrew James
Titan Comics Editorial: Jonathan Stevenson, Dan Boultwood
Senior Production Controller: Jackie Flook,
Production Supervisor: Maria Pearson
Production Controller: Peter James
Art Director: Oz Browne
Circulation & Sales Manager: Steve Tothill
Press Officer: Will O'Mullane
Marketing Manager: Ricky Claydon
Commercial Manager: Michelle Fairlamb
Head of Rights: Jenny Boyce
Publishing Manager: Darryl Tothill
Publishing Director: Chris Teather
Operations Director: Leigh Baulch
Executive Director: Vivian Cheung
Publisher: Nick Landau

9781782763086

Published by Titan Comics
A registered trademark of Titan Publishing Group Ltd.
144 Southwark St.London SE1 0UP

A CIP catalogue record for this title is available from the British Library

First edition: Octobe 2018

10 9 8 7 6 5 4 3 2 1

Printed in China.

WWW.TITAN-COMICS.COM

Follow us on Twitter @ComicsTitan
Visit us at facebook.com/comicstitan

For rights information contact: jenny.boyce@titanemail.com

ACKNOWLEDGEMENTS:
Many thanks to Aymar Azaïzia, Anouk Bachman, Richard Farrese,
Raphaël Lacoste, Antoine Ceszynski, Caroline Lamache and Clémence Deleuze.

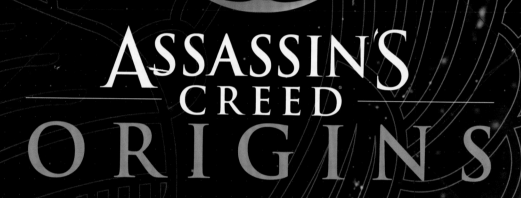

ASSASSIN'S CREED
ORIGINS

< STORY CONCEPT BY >
< ANNE TOOLE & ANTHONY DEL COL >

< WRITER >
< ANTHONY DEL COL >

< STORY CONSULTANT >
< ANN LEMAY >

< ARTIST >
< PJ KAIOWA >

< COLORS >
< DIJJO LIMA >

< LETTERS >
< COMICRAFT >

< COLLECTION COVER >
< STEPHEN MOONEY & TRIONA FARREL >

LOADING MEMORY...

Egypt – the turbulent final years of
the Ptolemaic period.

Succeeding in their mission of vengeance, Bayek of
Siwa and his wife Aya eliminated those responsible
for the death of their son. But their quest for
retribution led them to uncover the secretive Order
of the Ancients, and its plans to control all of Egypt
– and beyond.

Aware of the magnitude of the threat the Order
poses toward the freedom of all people, Bayek
and Aya parted ways to dedicate their lives toward
building a brotherhood to resist the power of the
Order. Known as the Hidden Ones, they work from
the shadows to assassinate those who would seek
to control the free will of the people.

With the city of Rome as her new base of
operations, Aya has already enlisted the help of a
number of like-minded individuals to set her sights
on a new target: the increasingly power-hungry
dictator Julius Caesar...

CHAPTER 1

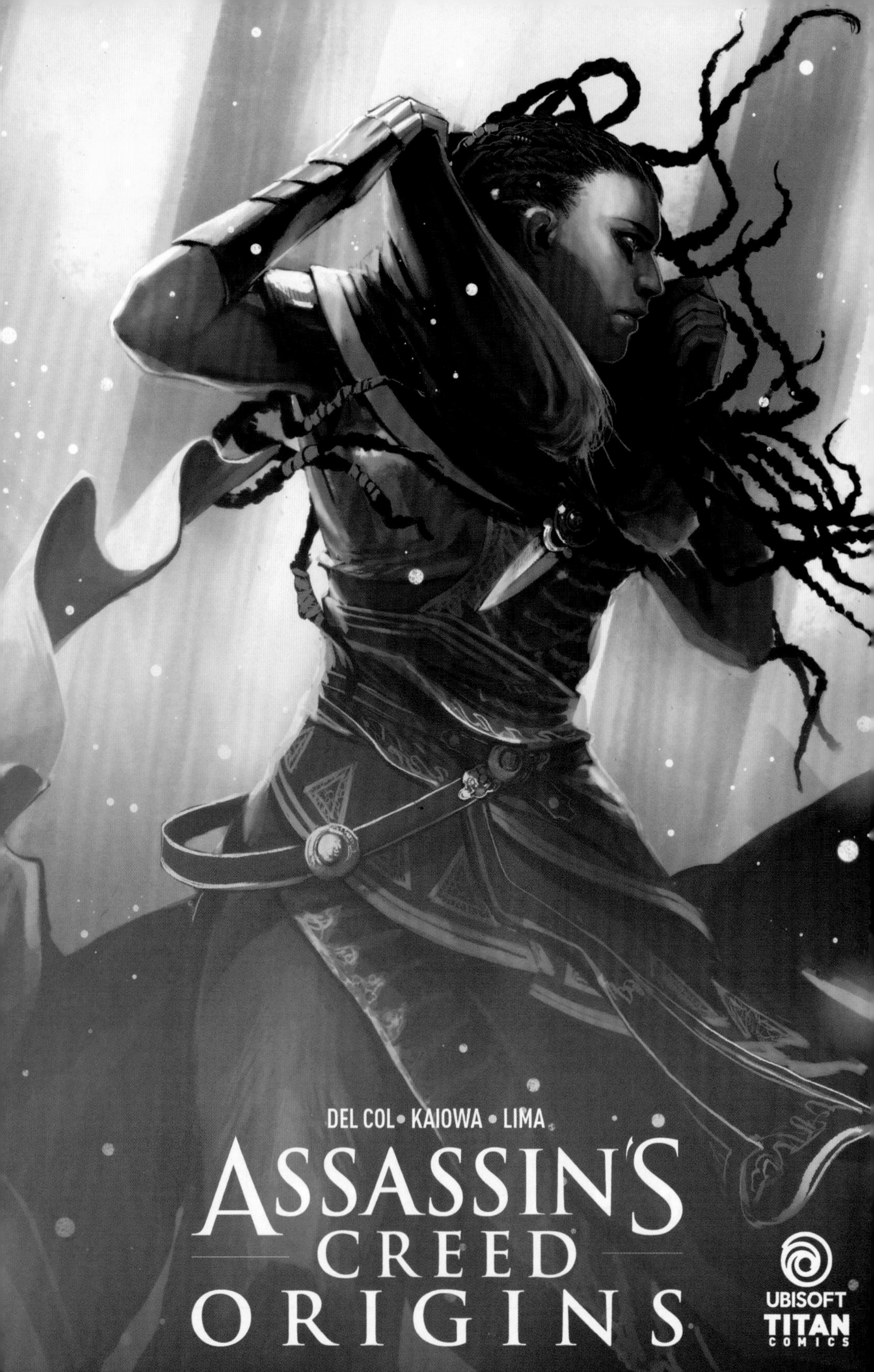
DEL COL • KAIOWA • LIMA
ASSASSIN'S CREED ORIGINS
UBISOFT
TITAN COMICS

> #1 COVER A / STEPHANIE HANS

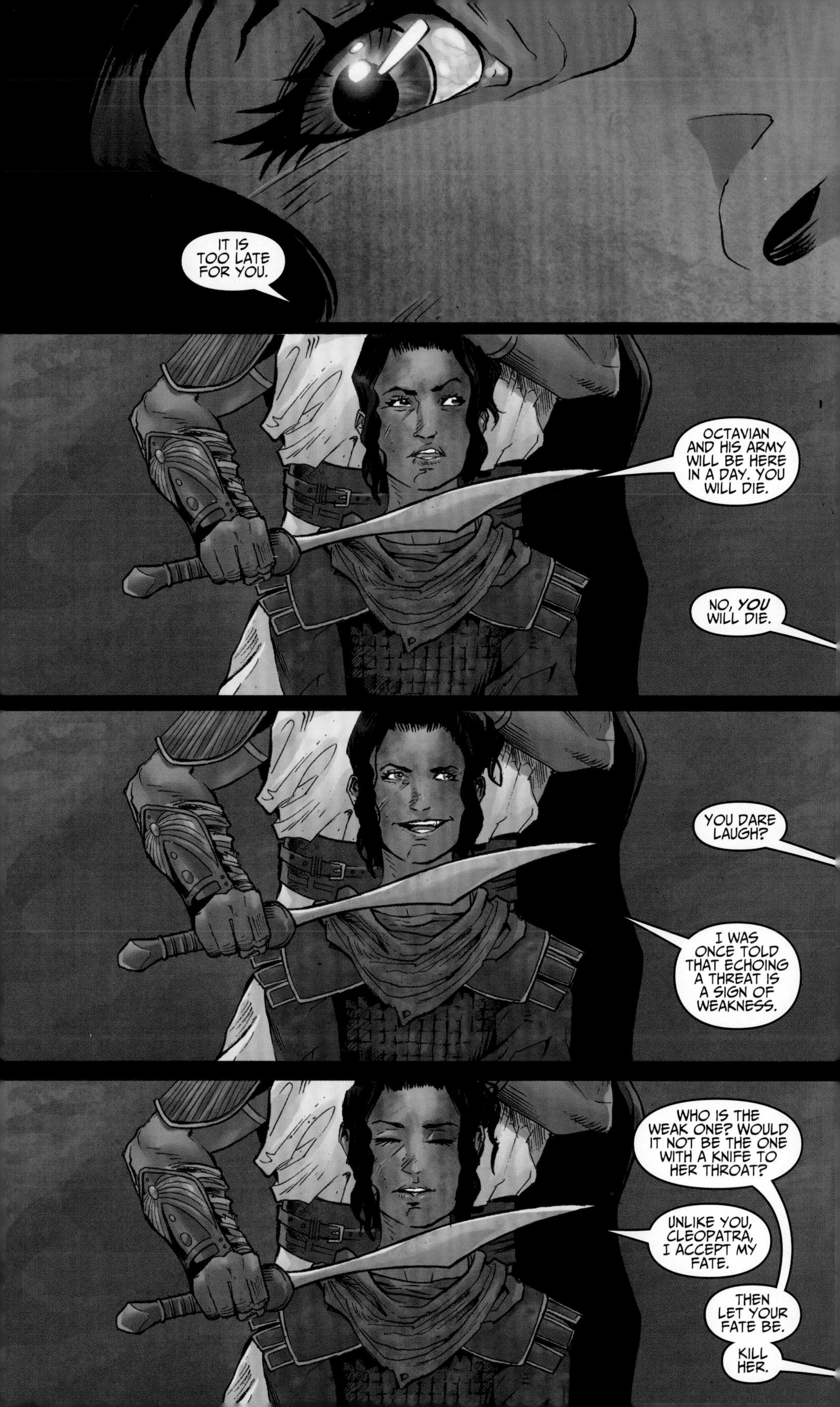

IT IS TOO LATE FOR YOU.
OCTAVIAN AND HIS ARMY WILL BE HERE IN A DAY. YOU WILL DIE.
NO, *YOU* WILL DIE.
YOU DARE LAUGH?
I WAS ONCE TOLD THAT ECHOING A THREAT IS A SIGN OF WEAKNESS.
WHO IS THE WEAK ONE? WOULD IT NOT BE THE ONE WITH A KNIFE TO HER THROAT?
UNLIKE YOU, CLEOPATRA, I ACCEPT MY FATE.
THEN LET YOUR FATE BE.
KILL HER.

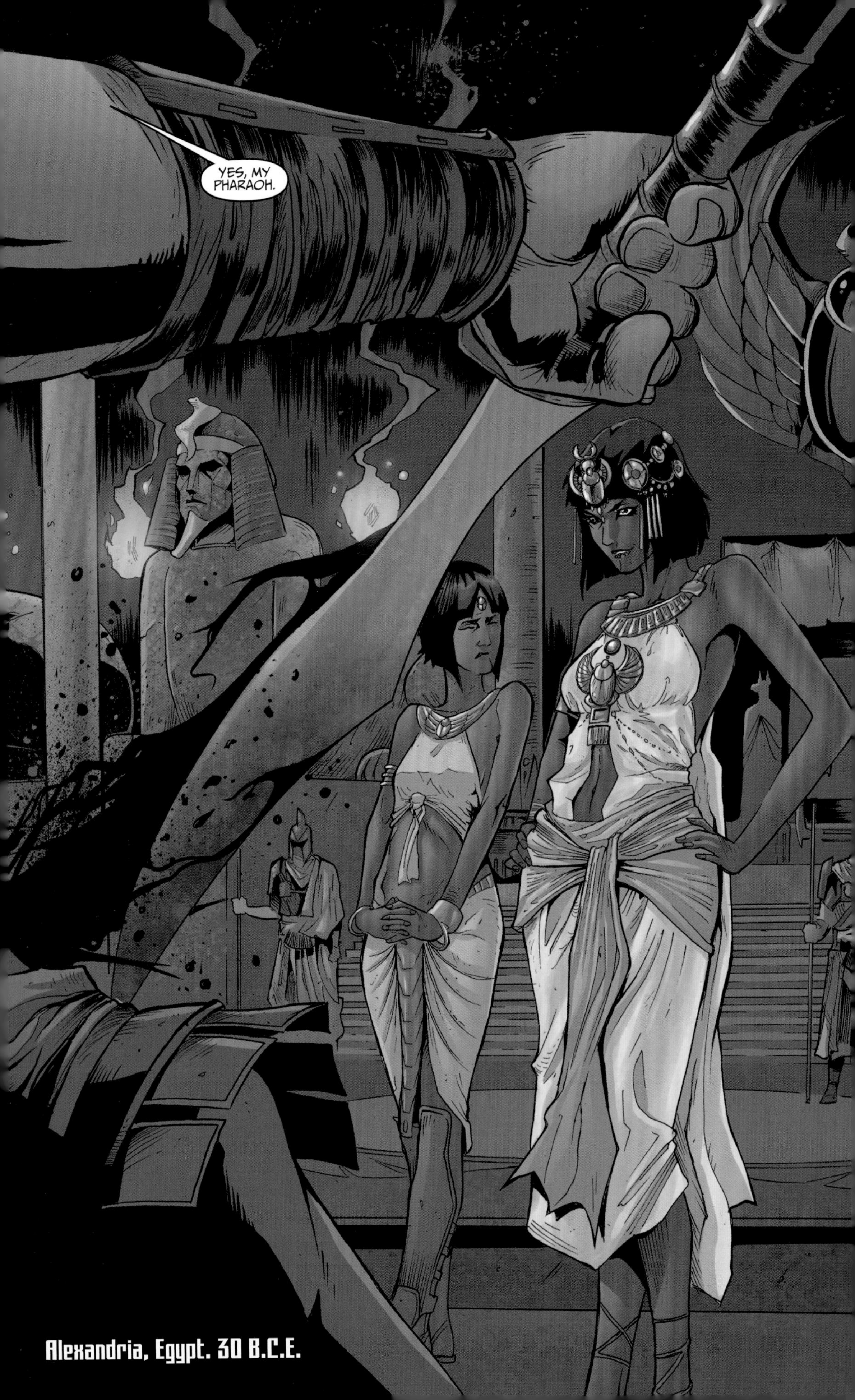
YES, MY PHARAOH.
Alexandria, Egypt. 30 B.C.E.

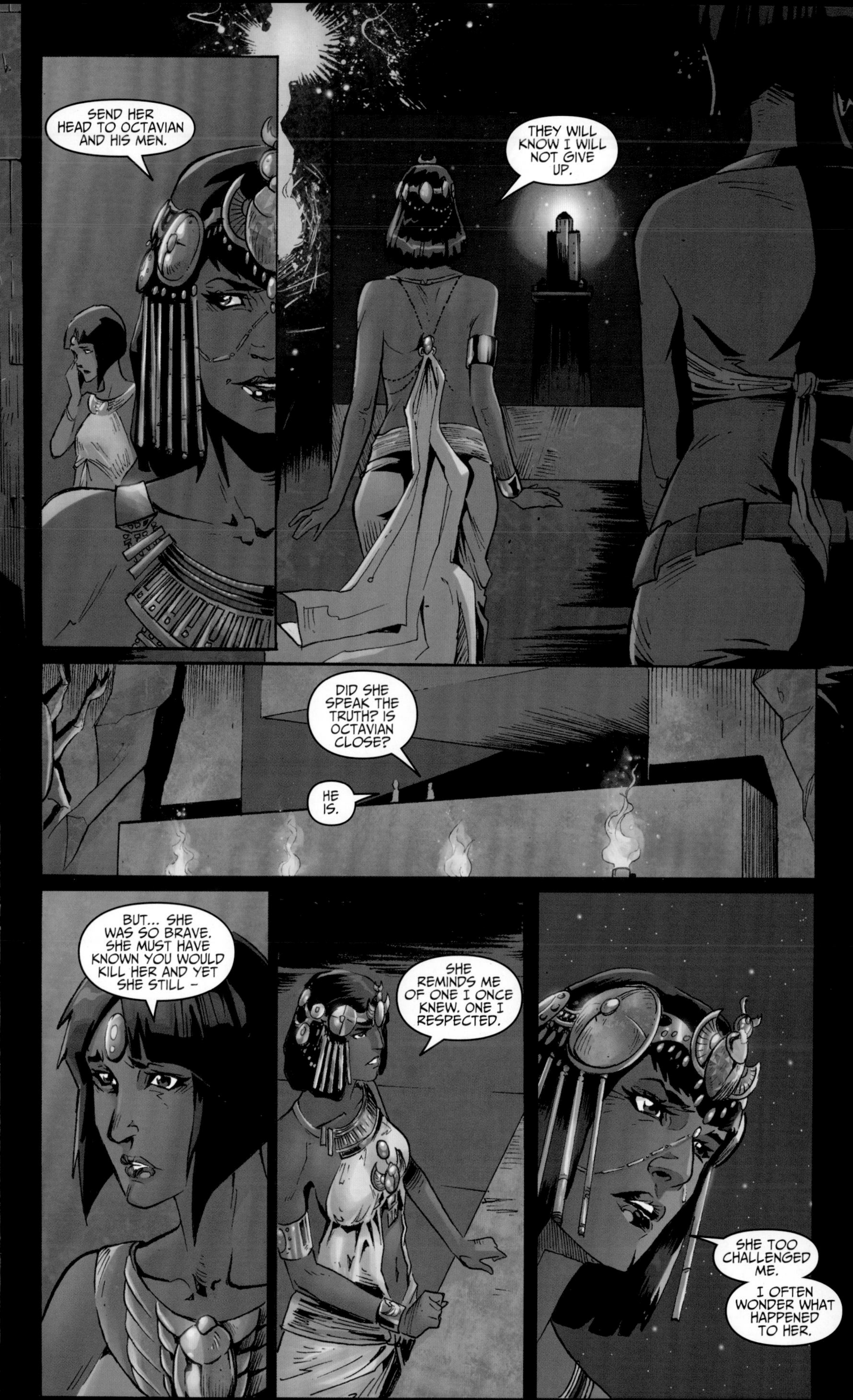
SEND HER HEAD TO OCTAVIAN AND HIS MEN.
THEY WILL KNOW I WILL NOT GIVE UP.
DID SHE SPEAK THE TRUTH? IS OCTAVIAN CLOSE?
HE IS.
BUT... SHE WAS SO BRAVE. SHE MUST HAVE KNOWN YOU WOULD KILL HER AND YET SHE STILL -
SHE REMINDS ME OF ONE I ONCE KNEW. ONE I RESPECTED.
SHE TOO CHALLENGED ME.
I OFTEN WONDER WHAT HAPPENED TO HER.

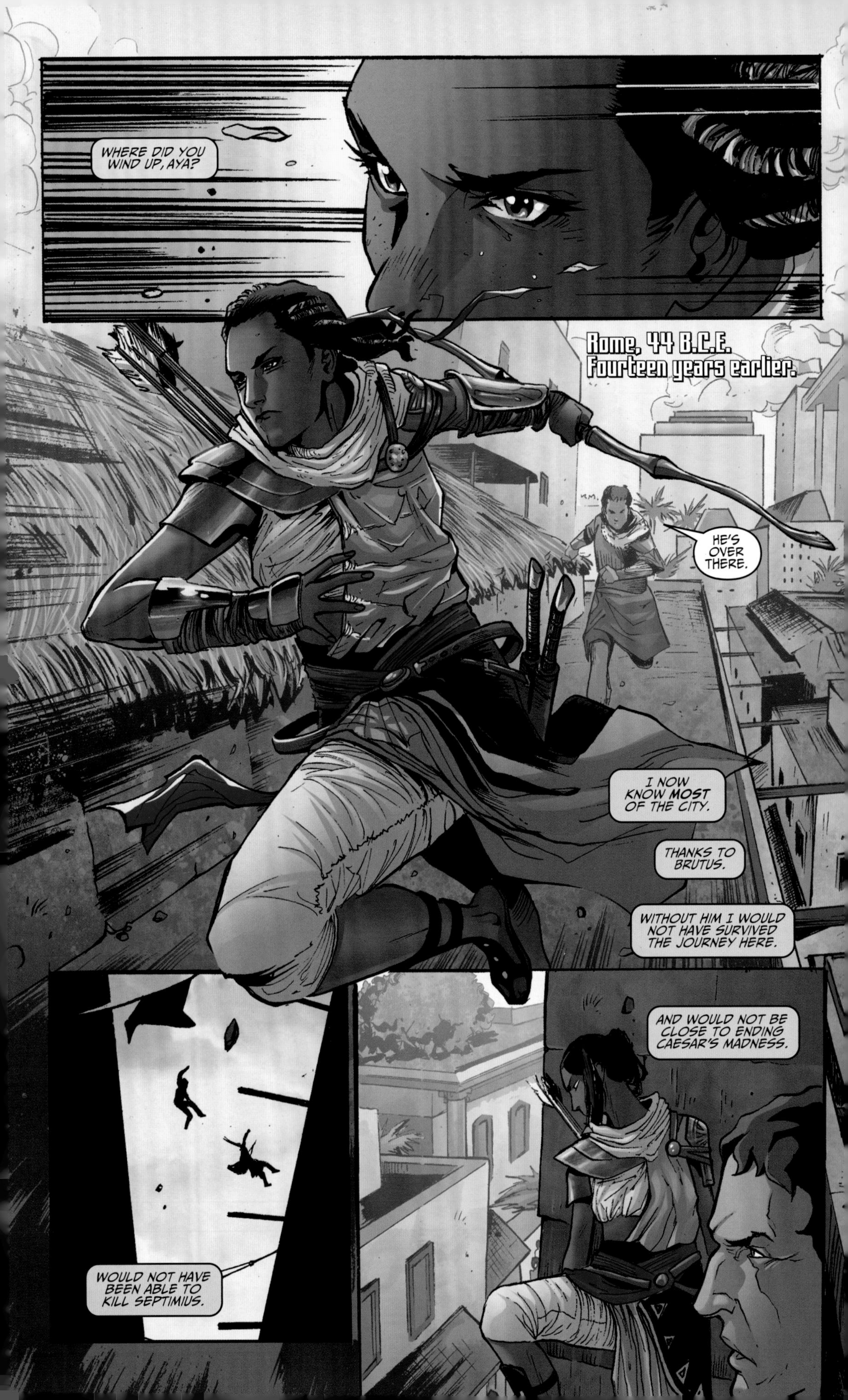
WHERE DID YOU WIND UP, AYA?
Rome, 44 B.C.E. Fourteen years earlier.
HE'S OVER THERE.
I NOW KNOW MOST OF THE CITY.
THANKS TO BRUTUS.
WITHOUT HIM I WOULD NOT HAVE SURVIVED THE JOURNEY HERE.
WOULD NOT HAVE BEEN ABLE TO KILL SEPTIMIUS.
AND WOULD NOT BE CLOSE TO ENDING CAESAR'S MADNESS.

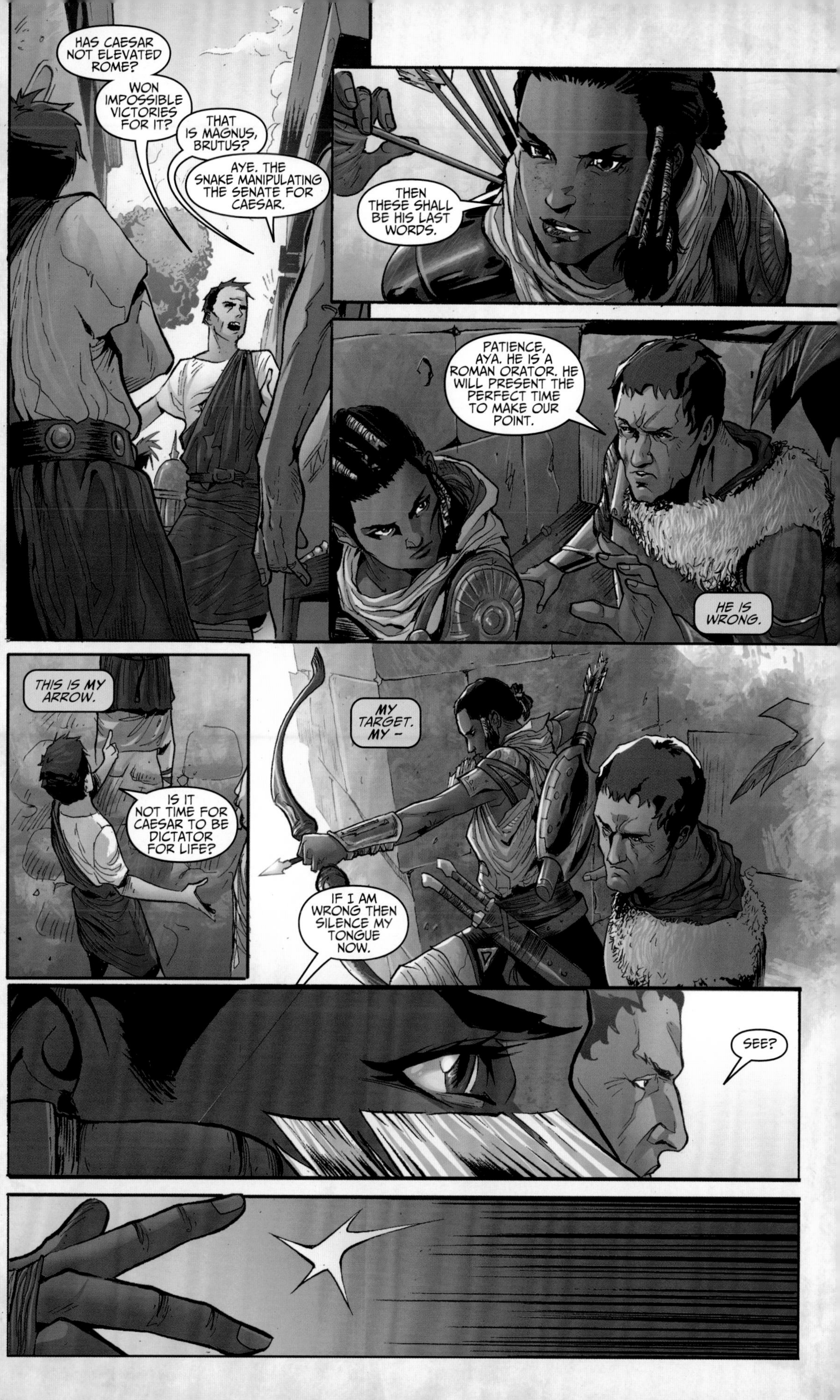
HAS CAESAR NOT ELEVATED ROME?
WON IMPOSSIBLE VICTORIES FOR IT?
THAT IS MAGNUS, BRUTUS?
AYE. THE SNAKE MANIPULATING THE SENATE FOR CAESAR.
THEN THESE SHALL BE HIS LAST WORDS.
PATIENCE, AYA. HE IS A ROMAN ORATOR. HE WILL PRESENT THE PERFECT TIME TO MAKE OUR POINT.
HE IS WRONG.
THIS IS MY ARROW.
MY TARGET. MY –
IS IT NOT TIME FOR CAESAR TO BE DICTATOR FOR LIFE?
IF I AM WRONG THEN SILENCE MY TONGUE NOW.
SEE?

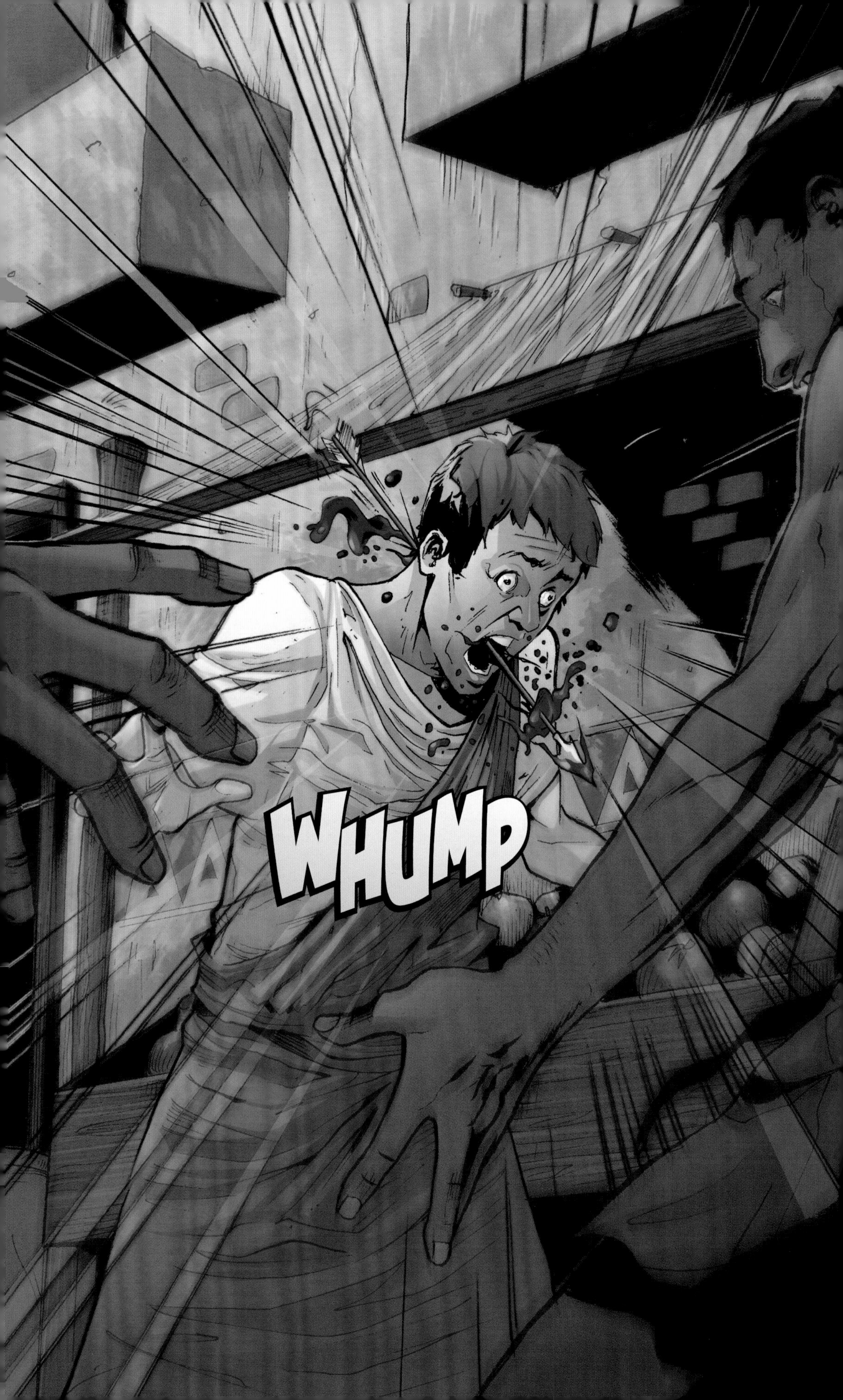
WHUMP

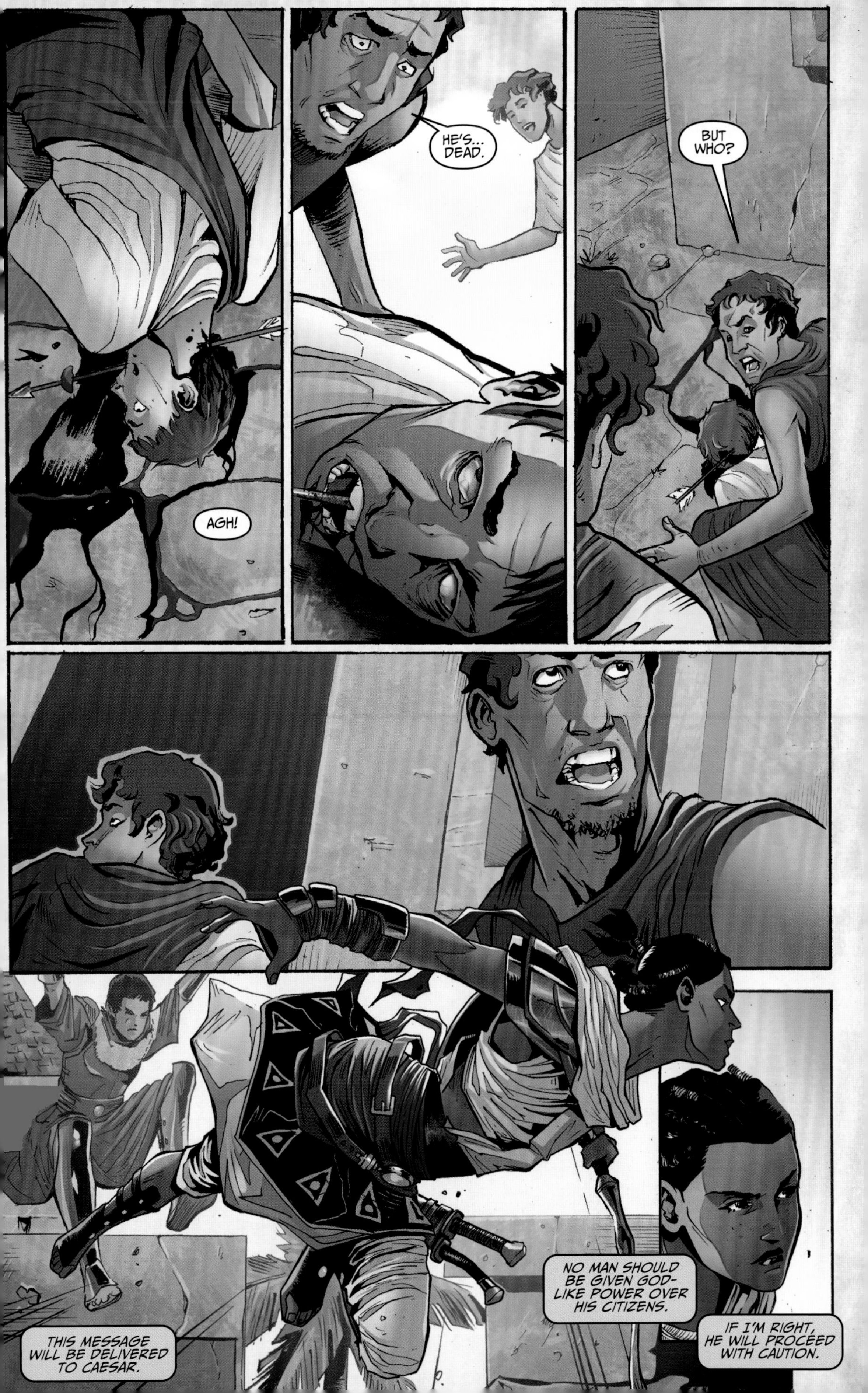
AGH!
HE'S... DEAD.
BUT WHO?
THIS MESSAGE WILL BE DELIVERED TO CAESAR.
NO MAN SHOULD BE GIVEN GOD-LIKE POWER OVER HIS CITIZENS.
IF I'M RIGHT, HE WILL PROCEED WITH CAUTION.

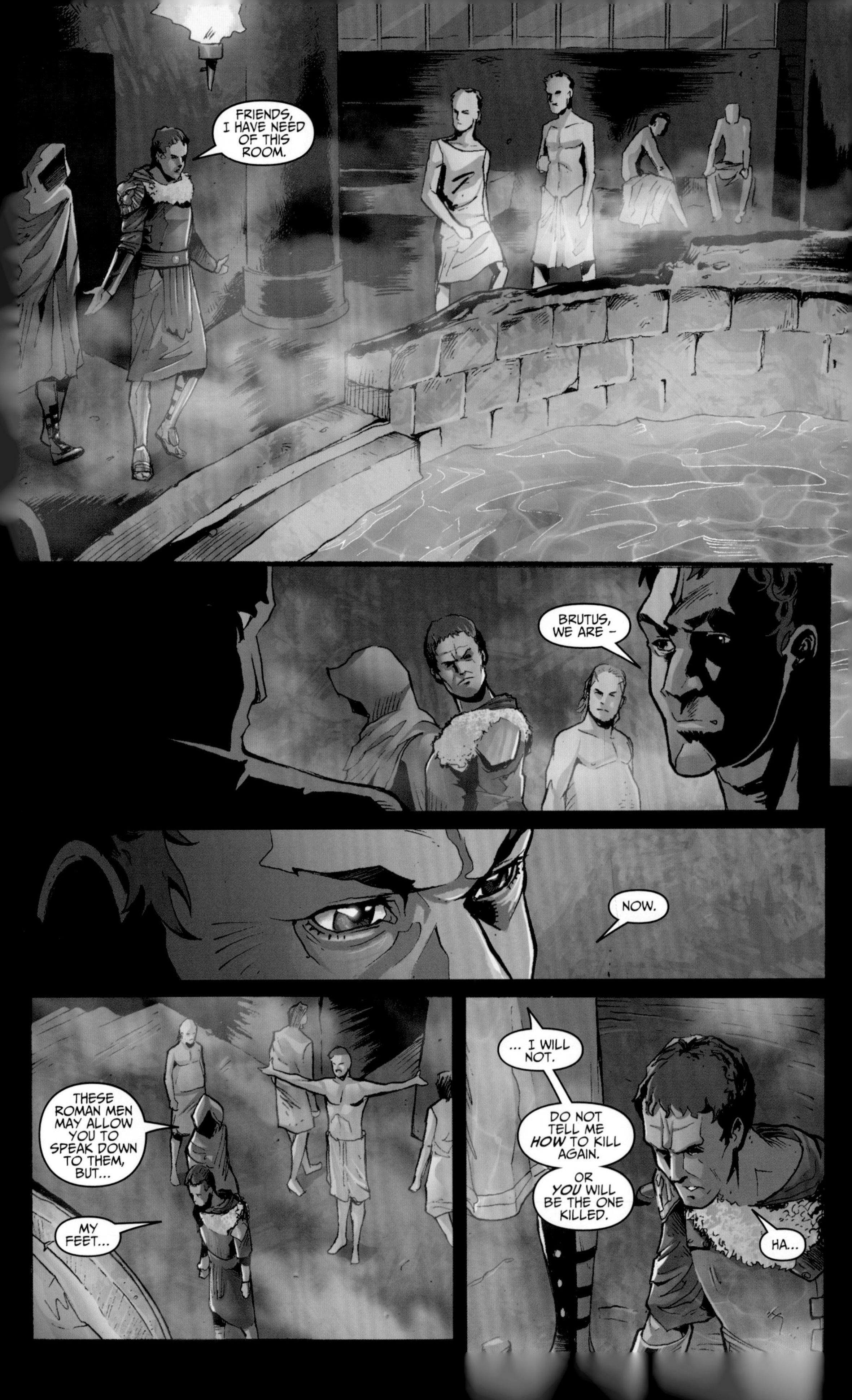
FRIENDS, I HAVE NEED OF THIS ROOM.
BRUTUS, WE ARE -
NOW.
THESE ROMAN MEN MAY ALLOW YOU TO SPEAK DOWN TO THEM, BUT...
MY FEET...
... I WILL NOT.
DO NOT TELL ME *HOW* TO KILL AGAIN.
OR *YOU* WILL BE THE ONE KILLED.
HA...

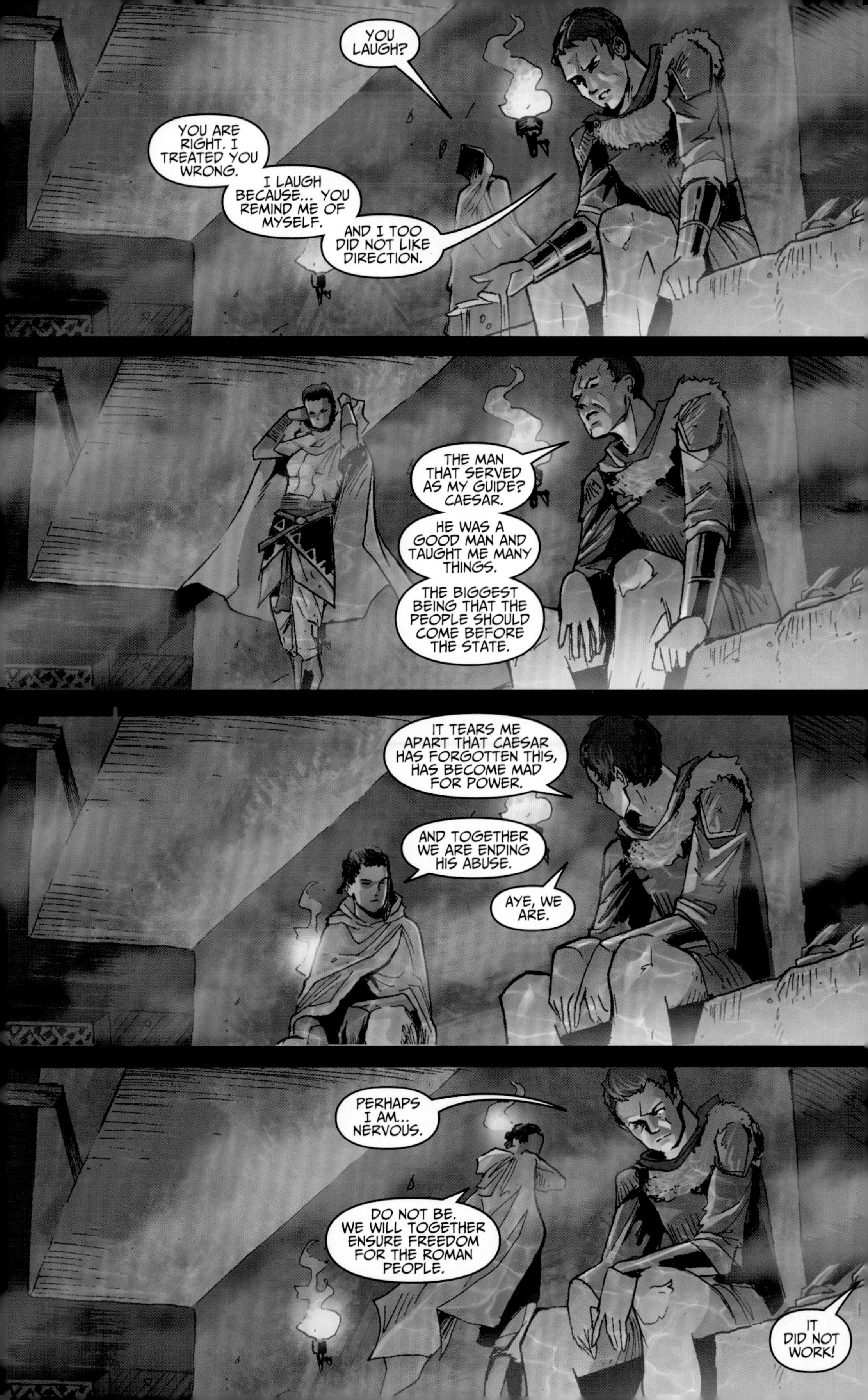
YOU LAUGH?
YOU ARE RIGHT. I TREATED YOU WRONG.
I LAUGH BECAUSE... YOU REMIND ME OF MYSELF.
AND I TOO DID NOT LIKE DIRECTION.
THE MAN THAT SERVED AS MY GUIDE? CAESAR.
HE WAS A GOOD MAN AND TAUGHT ME MANY THINGS.
THE BIGGEST BEING THAT THE PEOPLE SHOULD COME BEFORE THE STATE.
IT TEARS ME APART THAT CAESAR HAS FORGOTTEN THIS, HAS BECOME MAD FOR POWER.
AND TOGETHER WE ARE ENDING HIS ABUSE.
AYE, WE ARE.
PERHAPS I AM... NERVOUS.
DO NOT BE. WE WILL TOGETHER ENSURE FREEDOM FOR THE ROMAN PEOPLE.
IT DID NOT WORK!

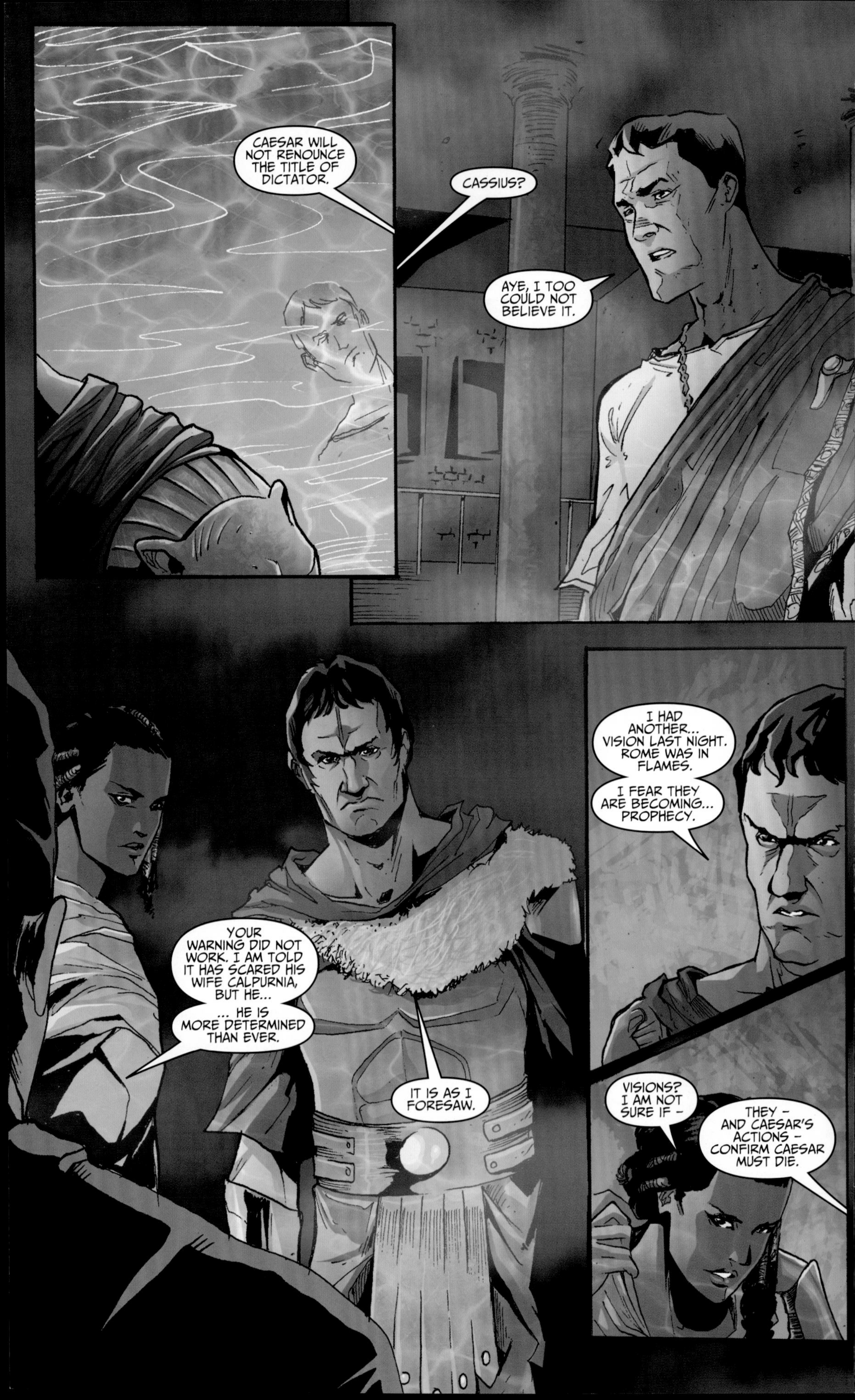
CAESAR WILL NOT RENOUNCE THE TITLE OF DICTATOR.
CASSIUS?
AYE, I TOO COULD NOT BELIEVE IT.
YOUR WARNING DID NOT WORK. I AM TOLD IT HAS SCARED HIS WIFE CALPURNIA, BUT HE...
... HE IS MORE DETERMINED THAN EVER.
IT IS AS I FORESAW.
I HAD ANOTHER... VISION LAST NIGHT. ROME WAS IN FLAMES.
I FEAR THEY ARE BECOMING... PROPHECY.
VISIONS? I AM NOT SURE IF –
THEY – AND CAESAR'S ACTIONS – CONFIRM CAESAR MUST DIE.

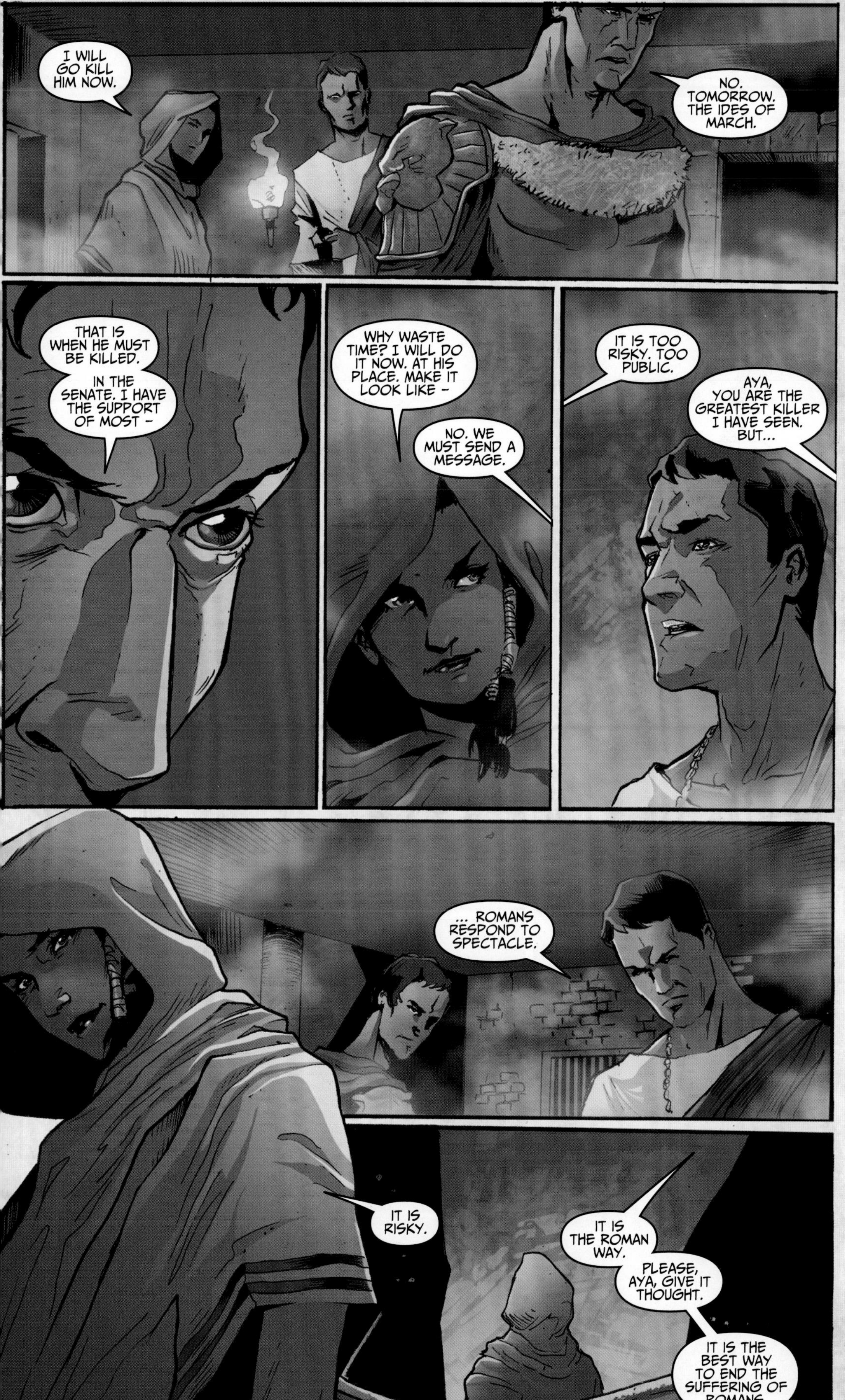
I WILL GO KILL HIM NOW.
NO. TOMORROW. THE IDES OF MARCH.
THAT IS WHEN HE MUST BE KILLED.
IN THE SENATE. I HAVE THE SUPPORT OF MOST -
WHY WASTE TIME? I WILL DO IT NOW. AT HIS PLACE. MAKE IT LOOK LIKE -
NO. WE MUST SEND A MESSAGE.
IT IS TOO RISKY. TOO PUBLIC.
AYA, YOU ARE THE GREATEST KILLER I HAVE SEEN. BUT...
... ROMANS RESPOND TO SPECTACLE.
IT IS RISKY.
IT IS THE ROMAN WAY.
PLEASE, AYA, GIVE IT THOUGHT.
IT IS THE BEST WAY TO END THE SUFFERING OF ROMANS.

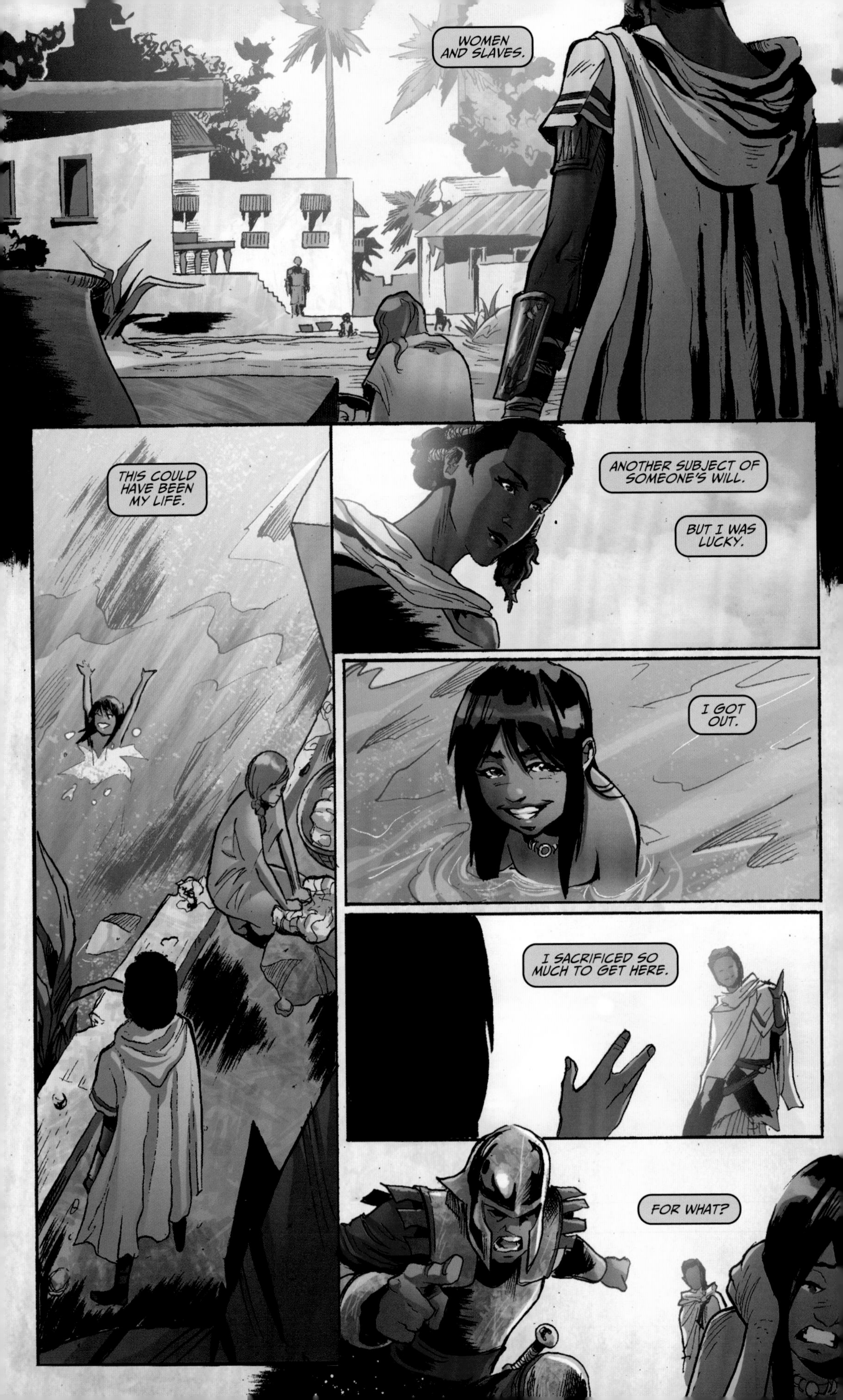
WOMEN AND SLAVES.
THIS COULD HAVE BEEN MY LIFE.
ANOTHER SUBJECT OF SOMEONE'S WILL.
BUT I WAS LUCKY.
I GOT OUT.
I SACRIFICED SO MUCH TO GET HERE.
FOR WHAT?

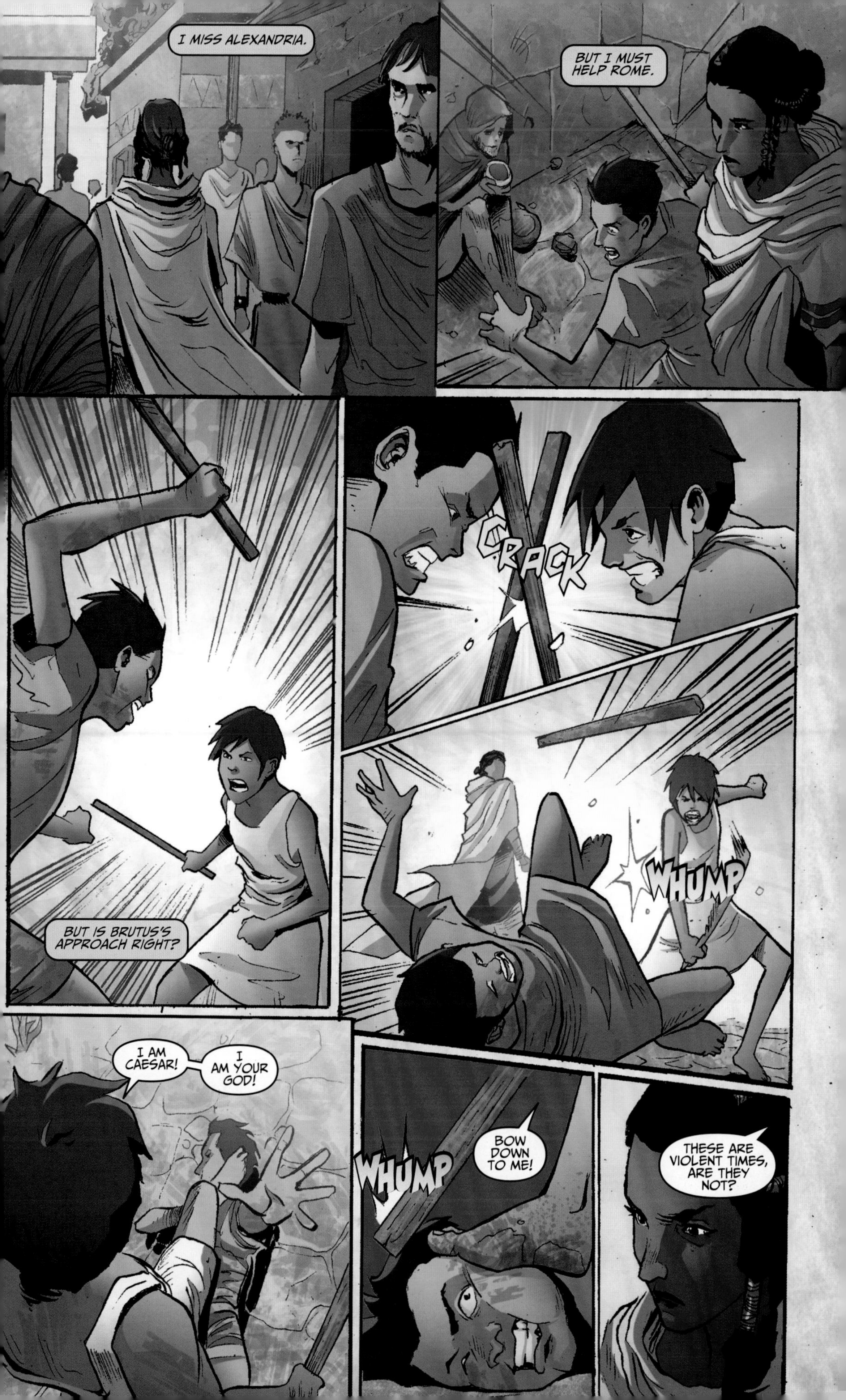
I MISS ALEXANDRIA.
BUT I MUST HELP ROME.
BUT IS BRUTUS'S APPROACH RIGHT?
CRACK
WHUMP
I AM CAESAR!
I AM YOUR GOD!
WHUMP
BOW DOWN TO ME!
THESE ARE VIOLENT TIMES, ARE THEY NOT?

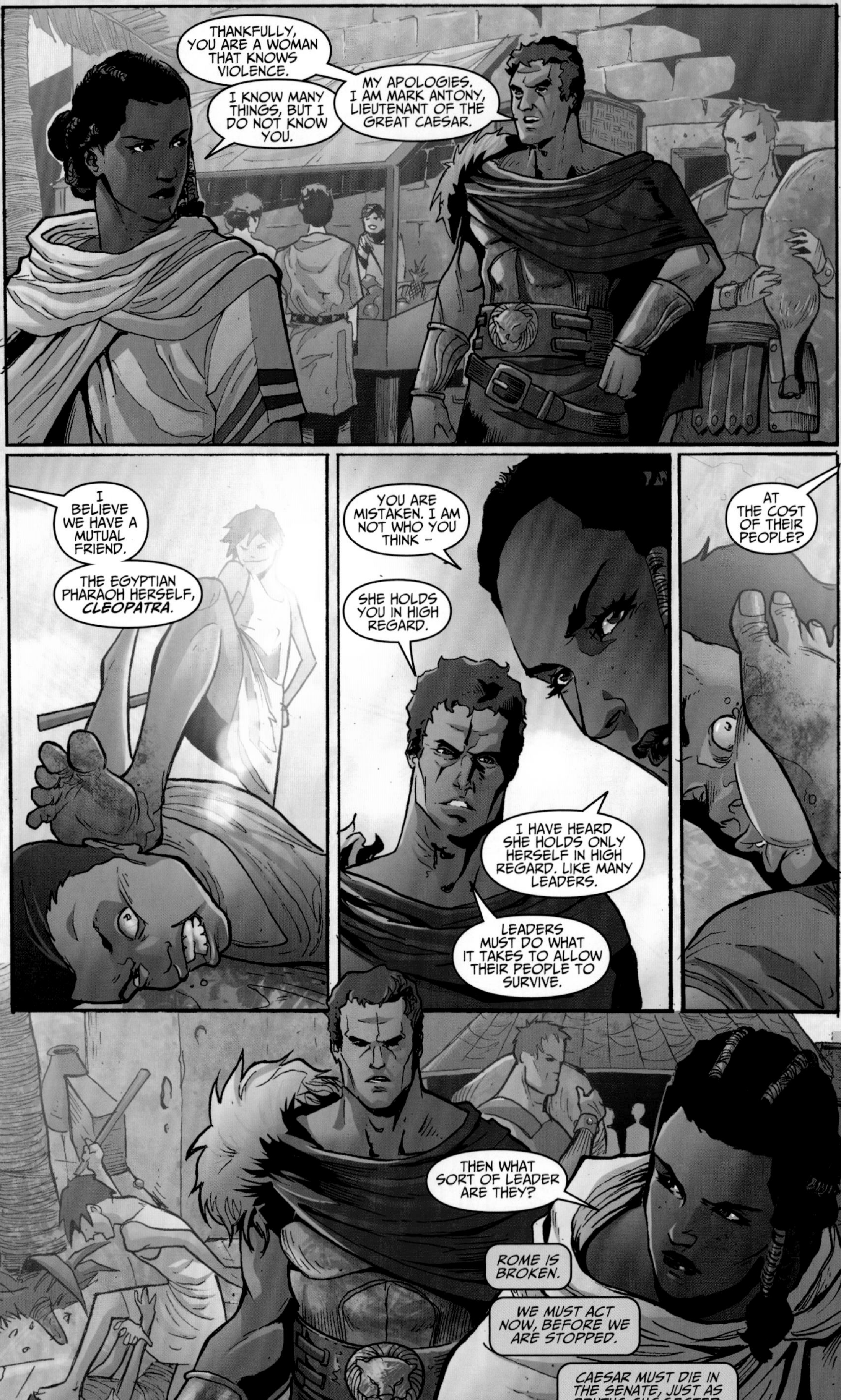
THANKFULLY, YOU ARE A WOMAN THAT KNOWS VIOLENCE.
I KNOW MANY THINGS, BUT I DO NOT KNOW YOU.
MY APOLOGIES. I AM MARK ANTONY, LIEUTENANT OF THE GREAT CAESAR.
I BELIEVE WE HAVE A MUTUAL FRIEND.
THE EGYPTIAN PHARAOH HERSELF, *CLEOPATRA*.
YOU ARE MISTAKEN. I AM NOT WHO YOU THINK –
SHE HOLDS YOU IN HIGH REGARD.
I HAVE HEARD SHE HOLDS ONLY HERSELF IN HIGH REGARD. LIKE MANY LEADERS.
LEADERS MUST DO WHAT IT TAKES TO ALLOW THEIR PEOPLE TO SURVIVE.
AT THE COST OF THEIR PEOPLE?
THEN WHAT SORT OF LEADER ARE THEY?
ROME IS BROKEN.
WE MUST ACT NOW, BEFORE WE ARE STOPPED.
CAESAR MUST DIE IN THE SENATE, JUST AS BRUTUS SUGGESTED.

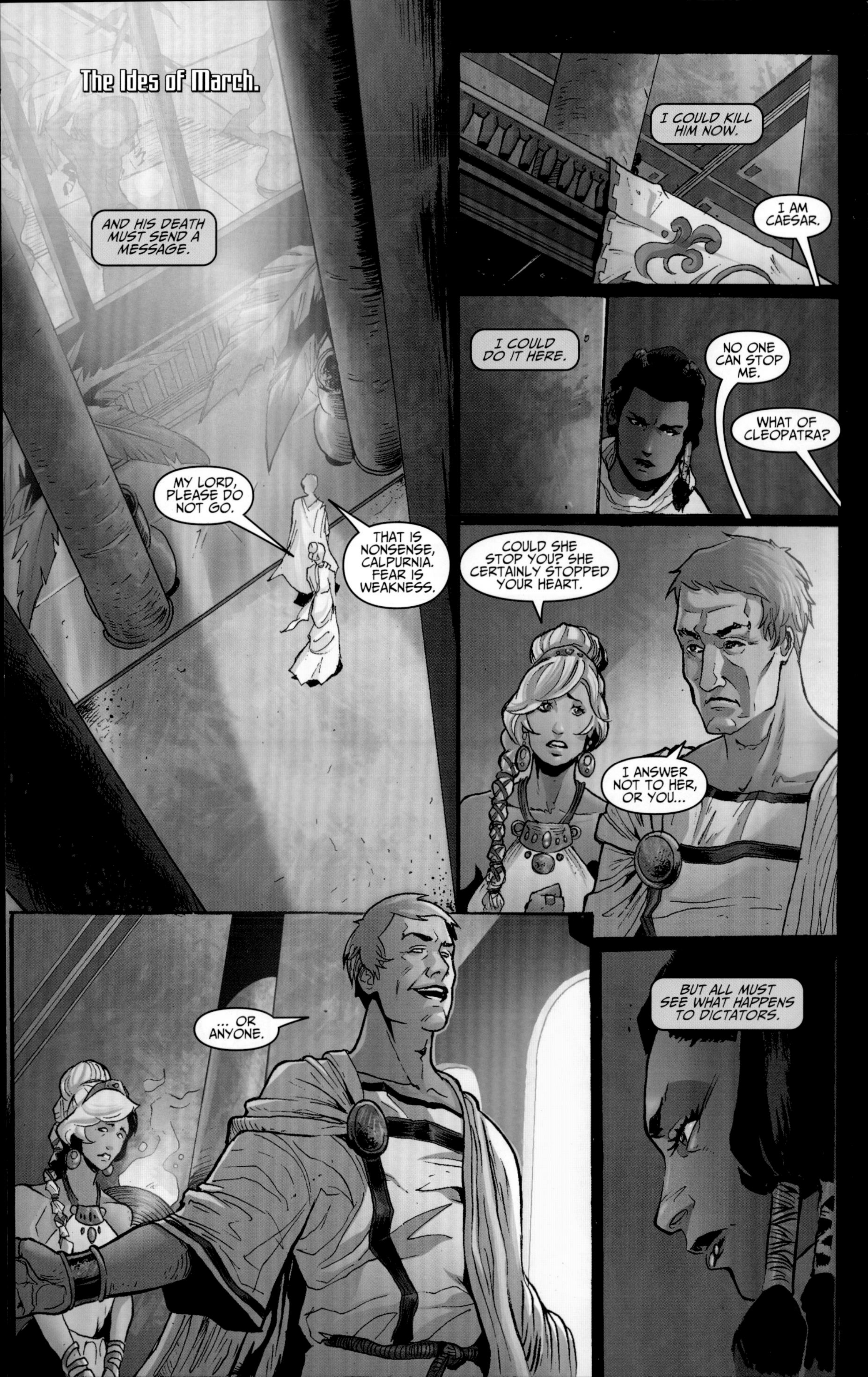
The Ides of March.
AND HIS DEATH MUST SEND A MESSAGE.
MY LORD, PLEASE DO NOT GO.
THAT IS NONSENSE, CALPURNIA. FEAR IS WEAKNESS.
I COULD KILL HIM NOW.
I AM CAESAR.
I COULD DO IT HERE.
NO ONE CAN STOP ME.
WHAT OF CLEOPATRA?
COULD SHE STOP YOU? SHE CERTAINLY STOPPED YOUR HEART.
I ANSWER NOT TO HER, OR YOU...
... OR ANYONE.
BUT ALL MUST SEE WHAT HAPPENS TO DICTATORS.

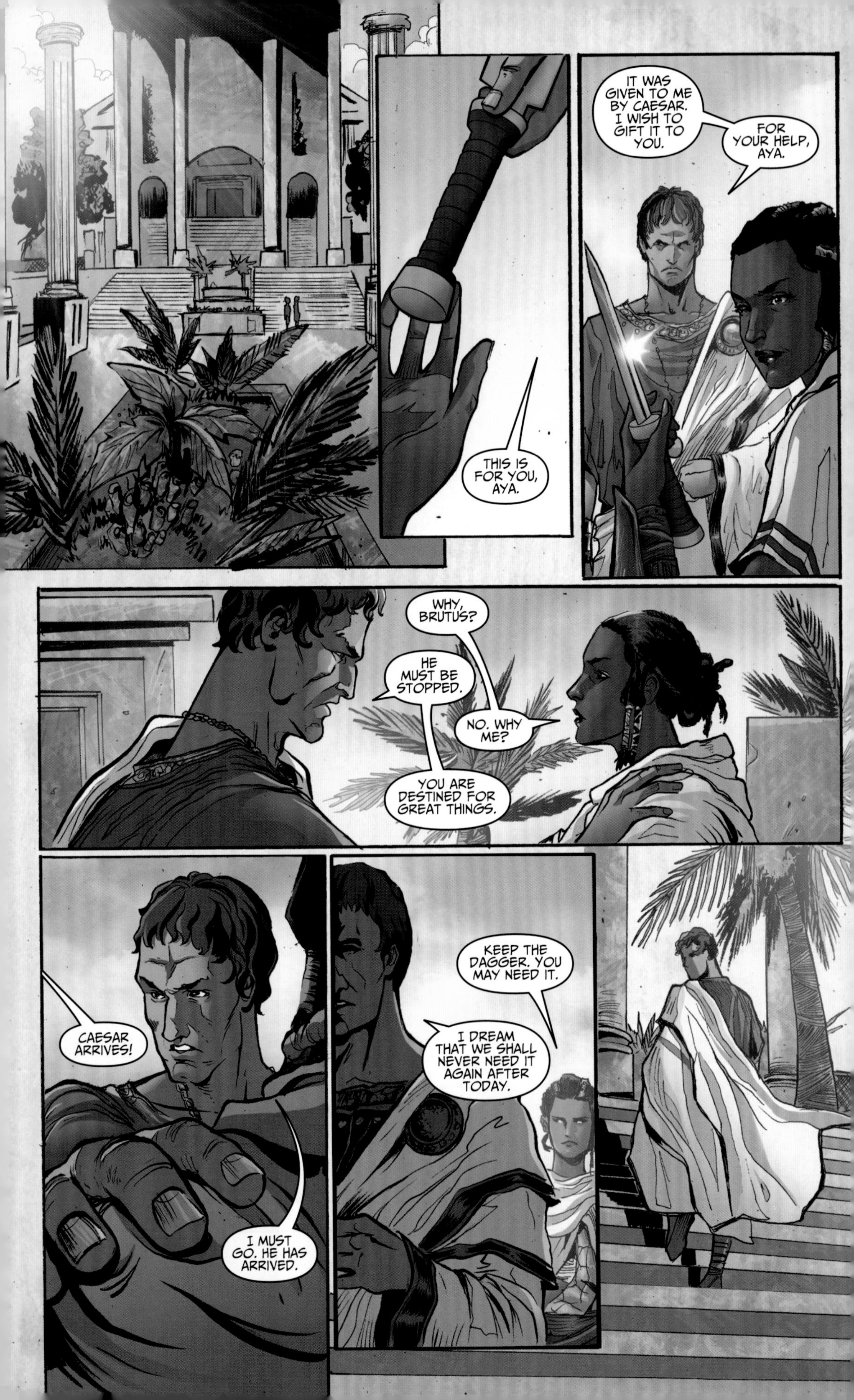
THIS IS FOR YOU, AYA.
IT WAS GIVEN TO ME BY CAESAR. I WISH TO GIFT IT TO YOU.
FOR YOUR HELP, AYA.
WHY, BRUTUS?
HE MUST BE STOPPED.
NO. WHY ME?
YOU ARE DESTINED FOR GREAT THINGS.
CAESAR ARRIVES!
I MUST GO. HE HAS ARRIVED.
KEEP THE DAGGER. YOU MAY NEED IT.
I DREAM THAT WE SHALL NEVER NEED IT AGAIN AFTER TODAY.

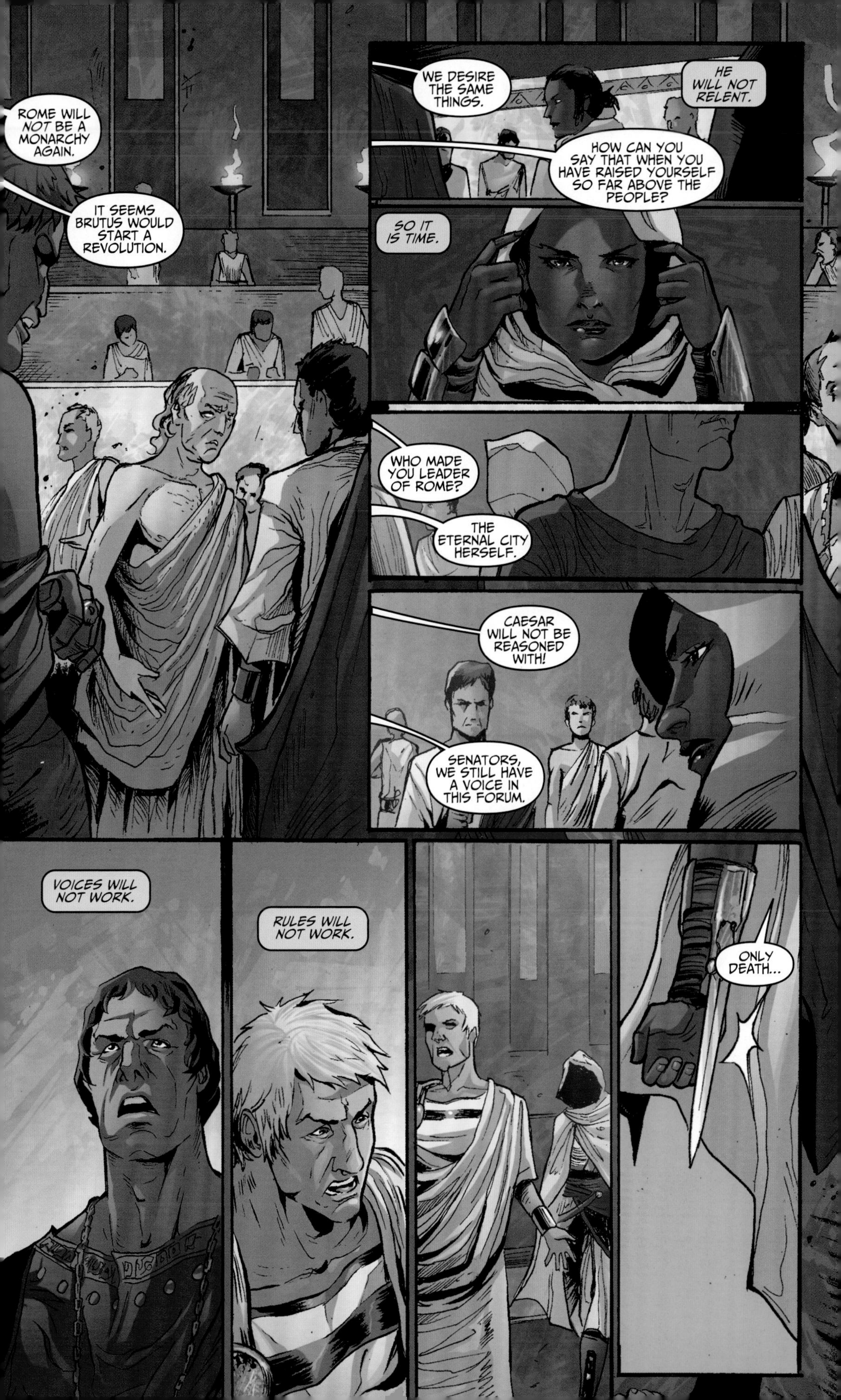

ROME WILL NOT BE A MONARCHY AGAIN.
IT SEEMS BRUTUS WOULD START A REVOLUTION.
WE DESIRE THE SAME THINGS.
HE WILL NOT RELENT.
HOW CAN YOU SAY THAT WHEN YOU HAVE RAISED YOURSELF SO FAR ABOVE THE PEOPLE?
SO IT IS TIME.
WHO MADE YOU LEADER OF ROME?
THE ETERNAL CITY HERSELF.
CAESAR WILL NOT BE REASONED WITH!
SENATORS, WE STILL HAVE A VOICE IN THIS FORUM.
VOICES WILL NOT WORK.
RULES WILL NOT WORK.
ONLY DEATH...

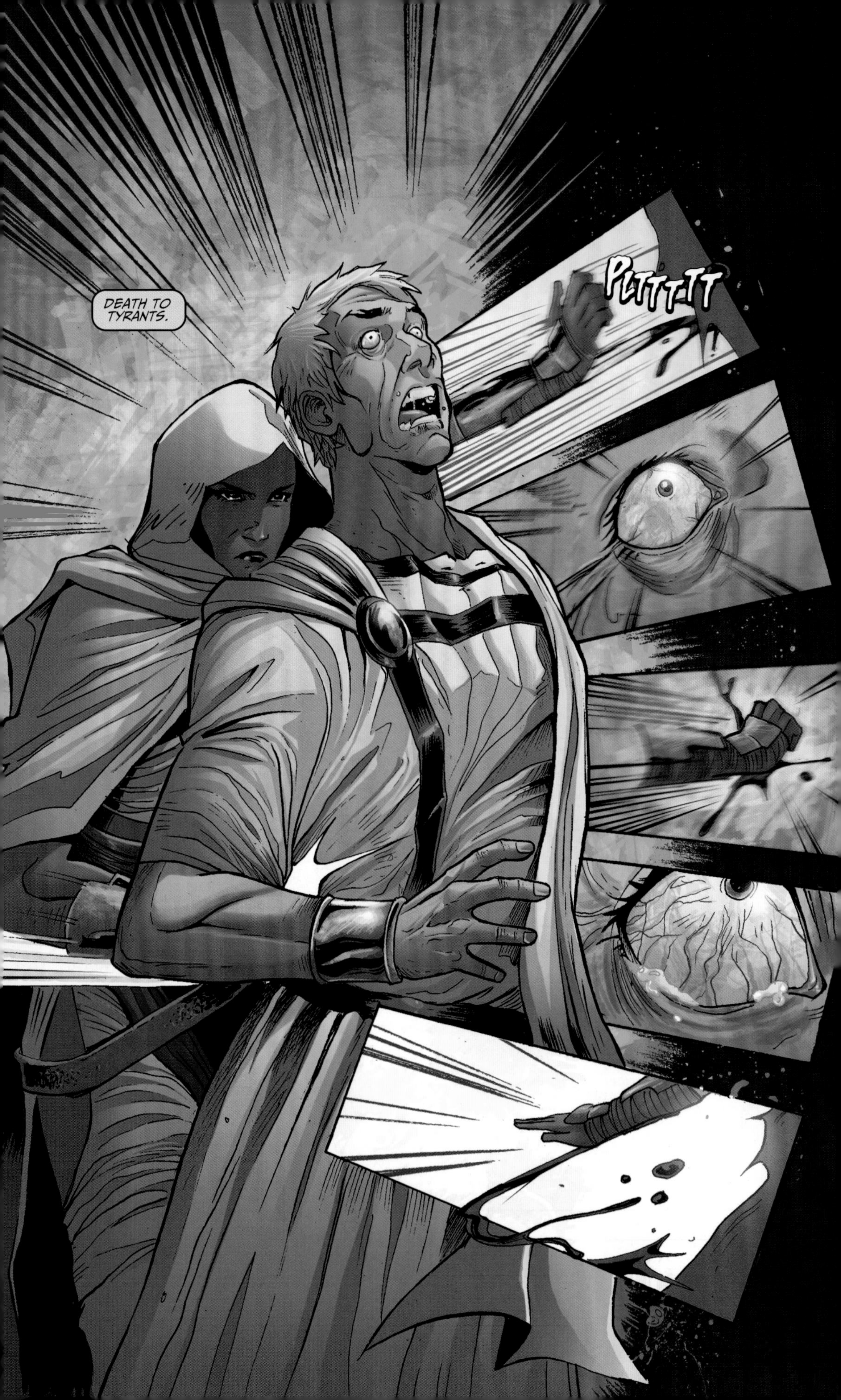
DEATH TO TYRANTS.
PLTTTTT

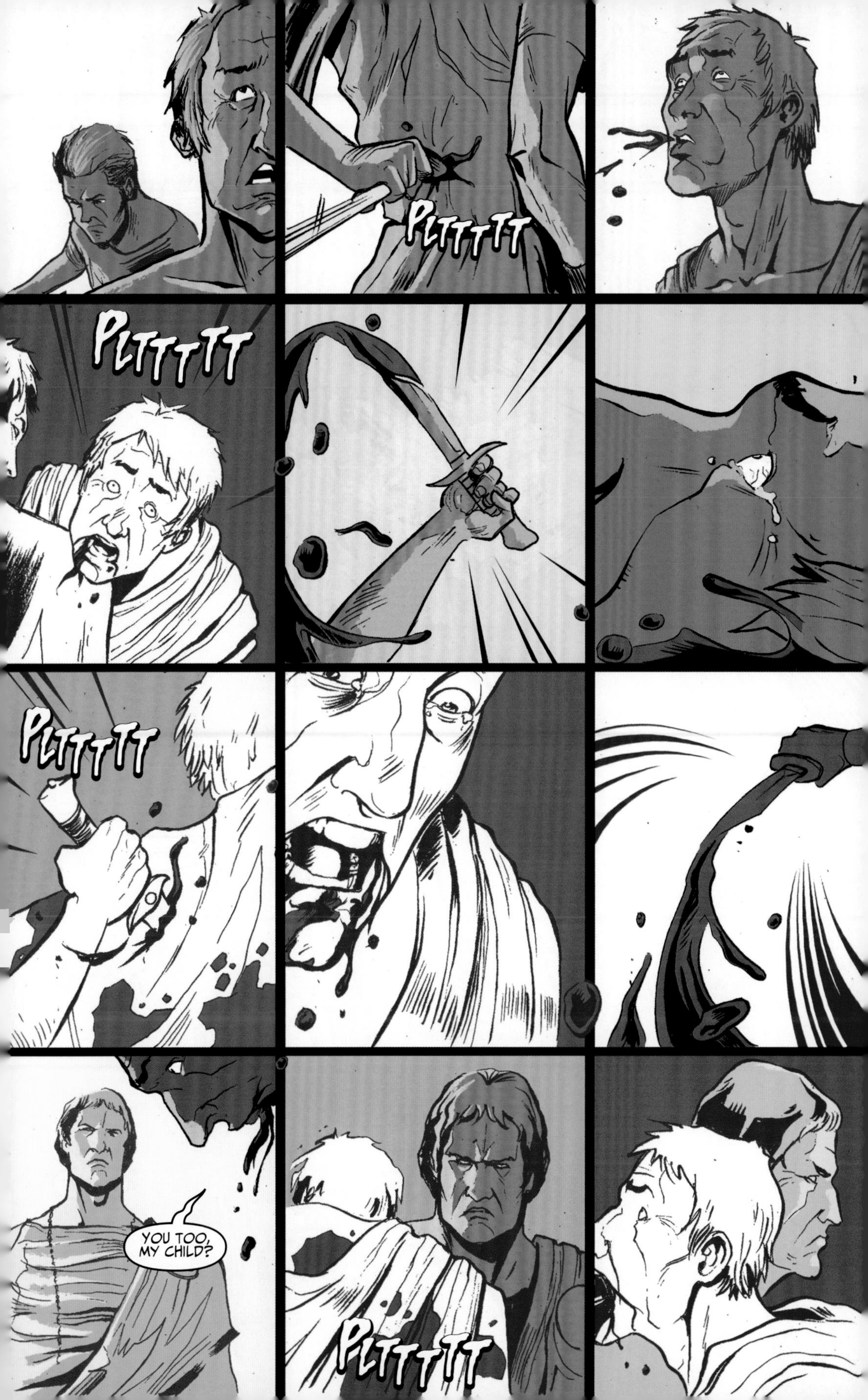
PLTTTTT
PLTTTTT
PLTTTTT
YOU TOO, MY CHILD?
PLTTTTT

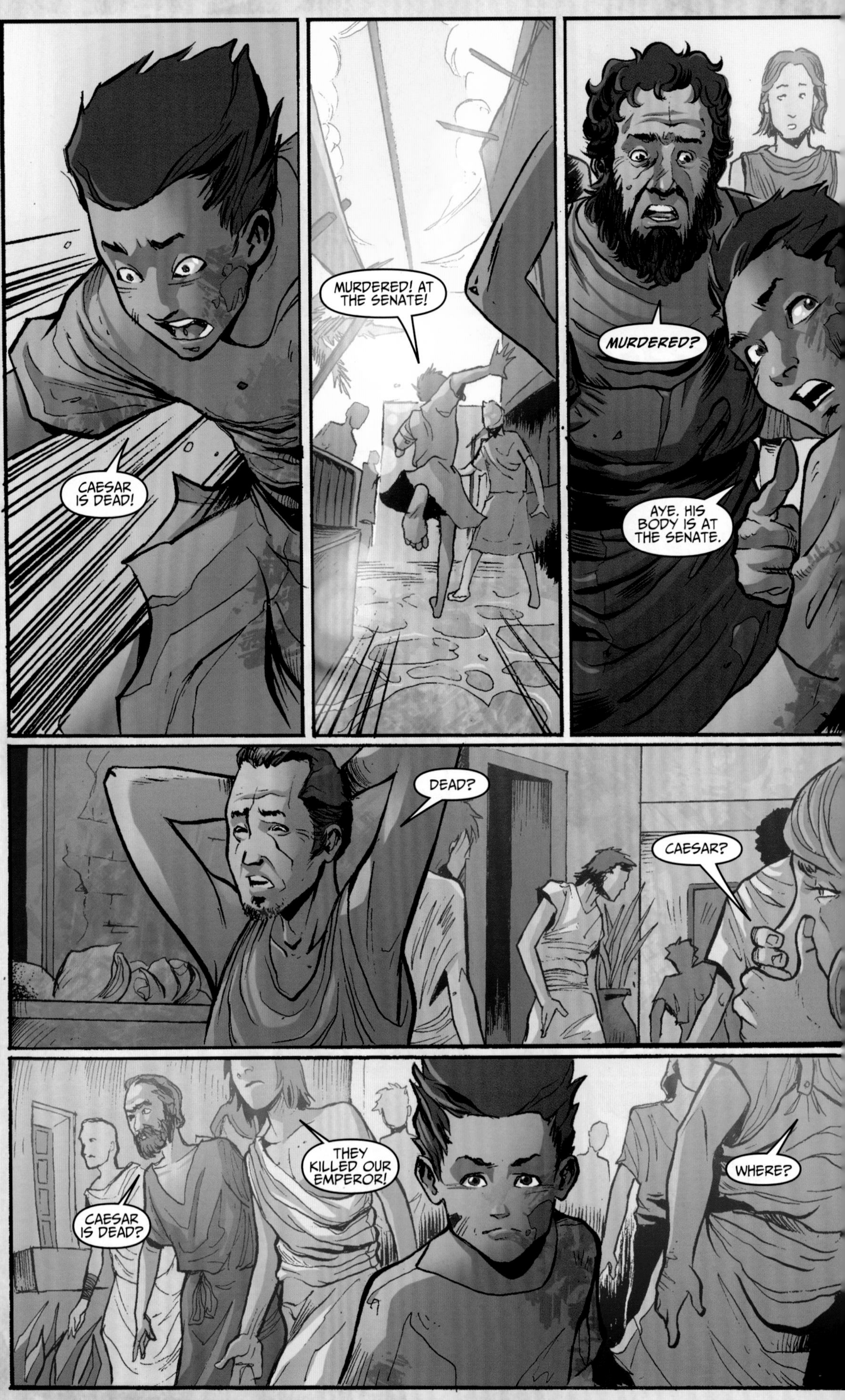
CAESAR IS DEAD!
MURDERED! AT THE SENATE!
MURDERED?
AYE. HIS BODY IS AT THE SENATE.
DEAD?
CAESAR?
CAESAR IS DEAD?
THEY KILLED OUR EMPEROR!
WHERE?

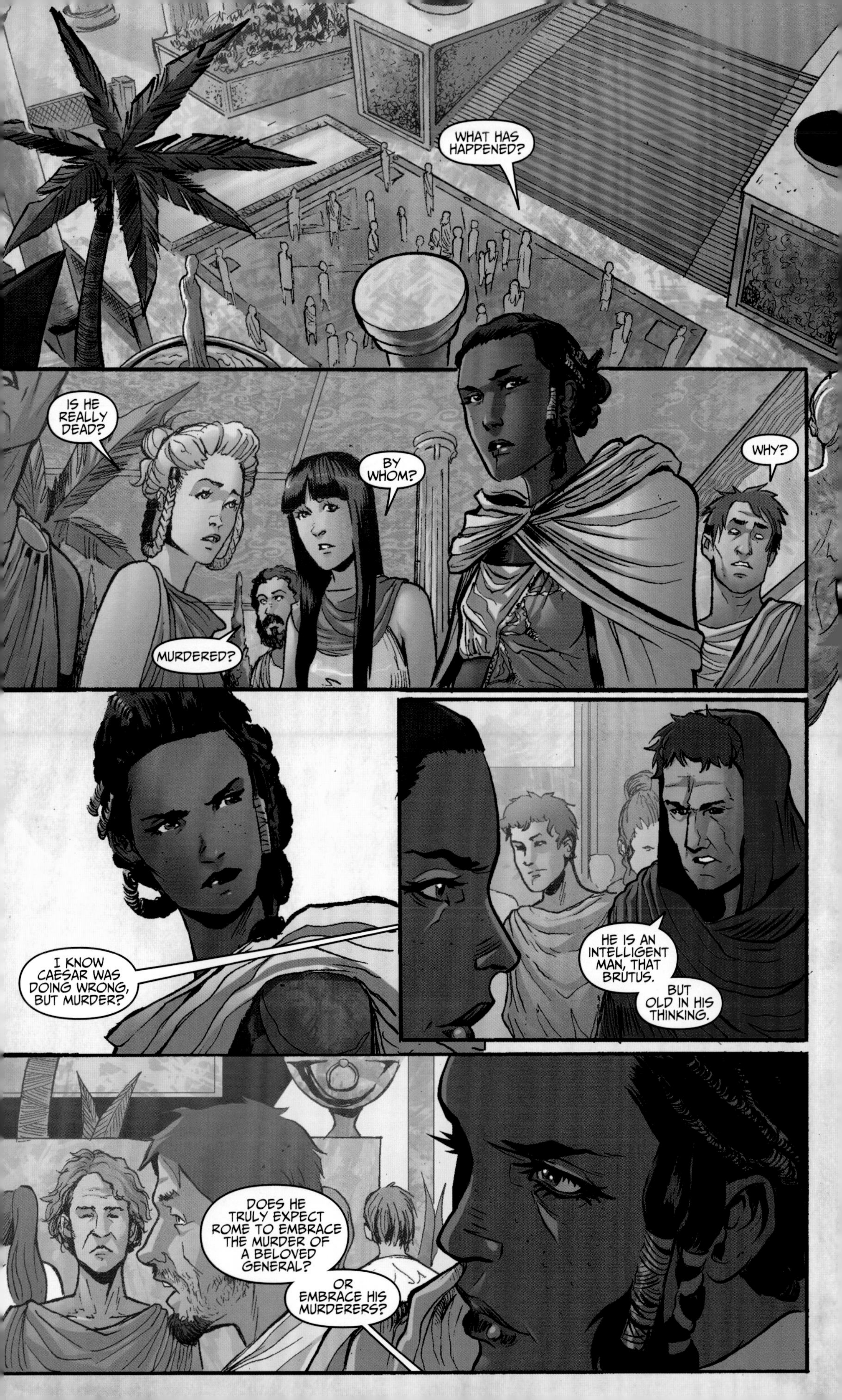
WHAT HAS HAPPENED?
IS HE REALLY DEAD?
BY WHOM?
WHY?
MURDERED?
I KNOW CAESAR WAS DOING WRONG, BUT MURDER?
HE IS AN INTELLIGENT MAN, THAT BRUTUS.
BUT OLD IN HIS THINKING.
DOES HE TRULY EXPECT ROME TO EMBRACE THE MURDER OF A BELOVED GENERAL?
OR EMBRACE HIS MURDERERS?

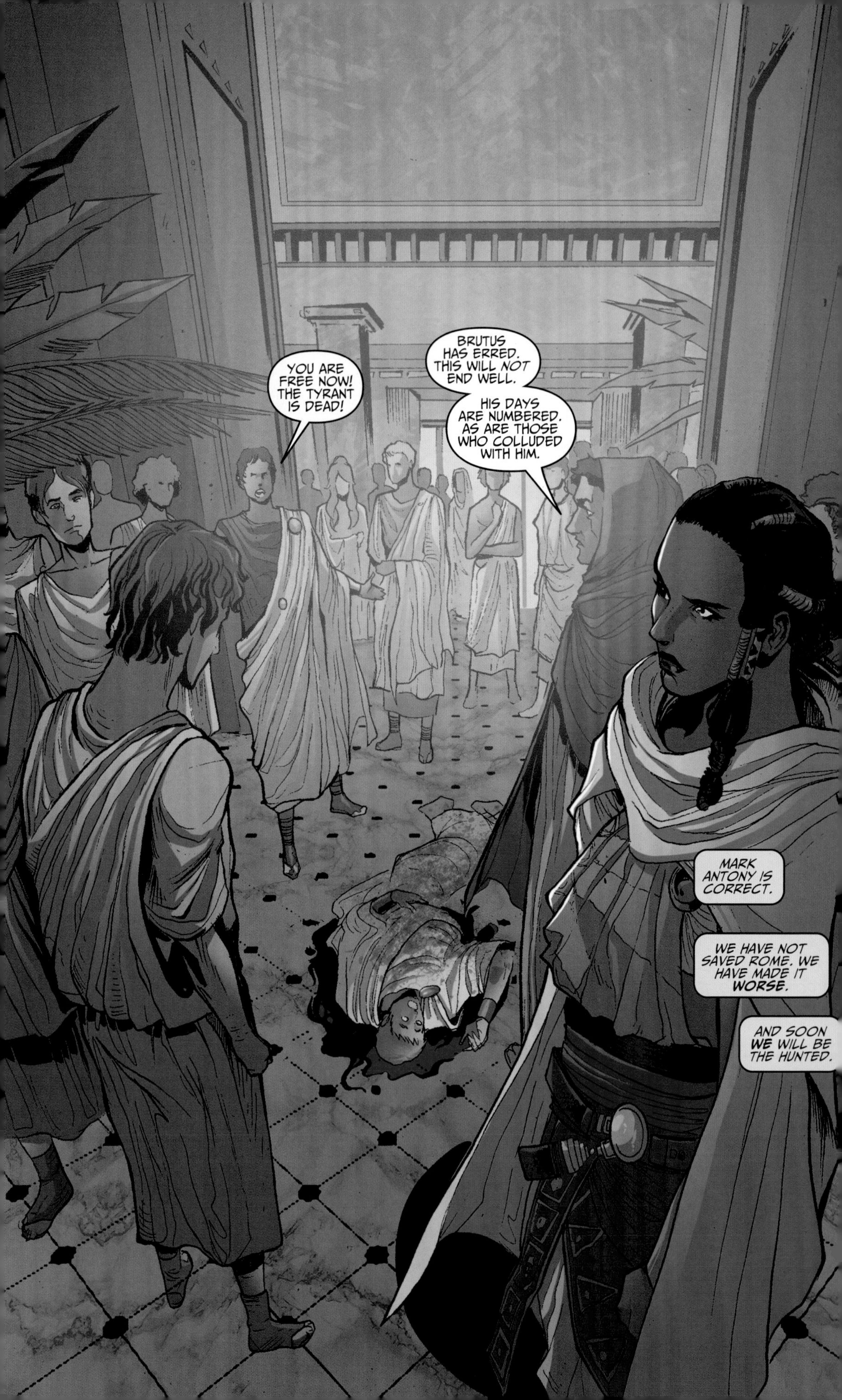
YOU ARE FREE NOW! THE TYRANT IS DEAD!
BRUTUS HAS ERRED. THIS WILL *NOT* END WELL.
HIS DAYS ARE NUMBERED. AS ARE THOSE WHO COLLUDED WITH HIM.
MARK ANTONY IS CORRECT.
WE HAVE NOT SAVED ROME. WE HAVE MADE IT **WORSE**.
AND SOON **WE** WILL BE THE HUNTED.

CHAPTER 2

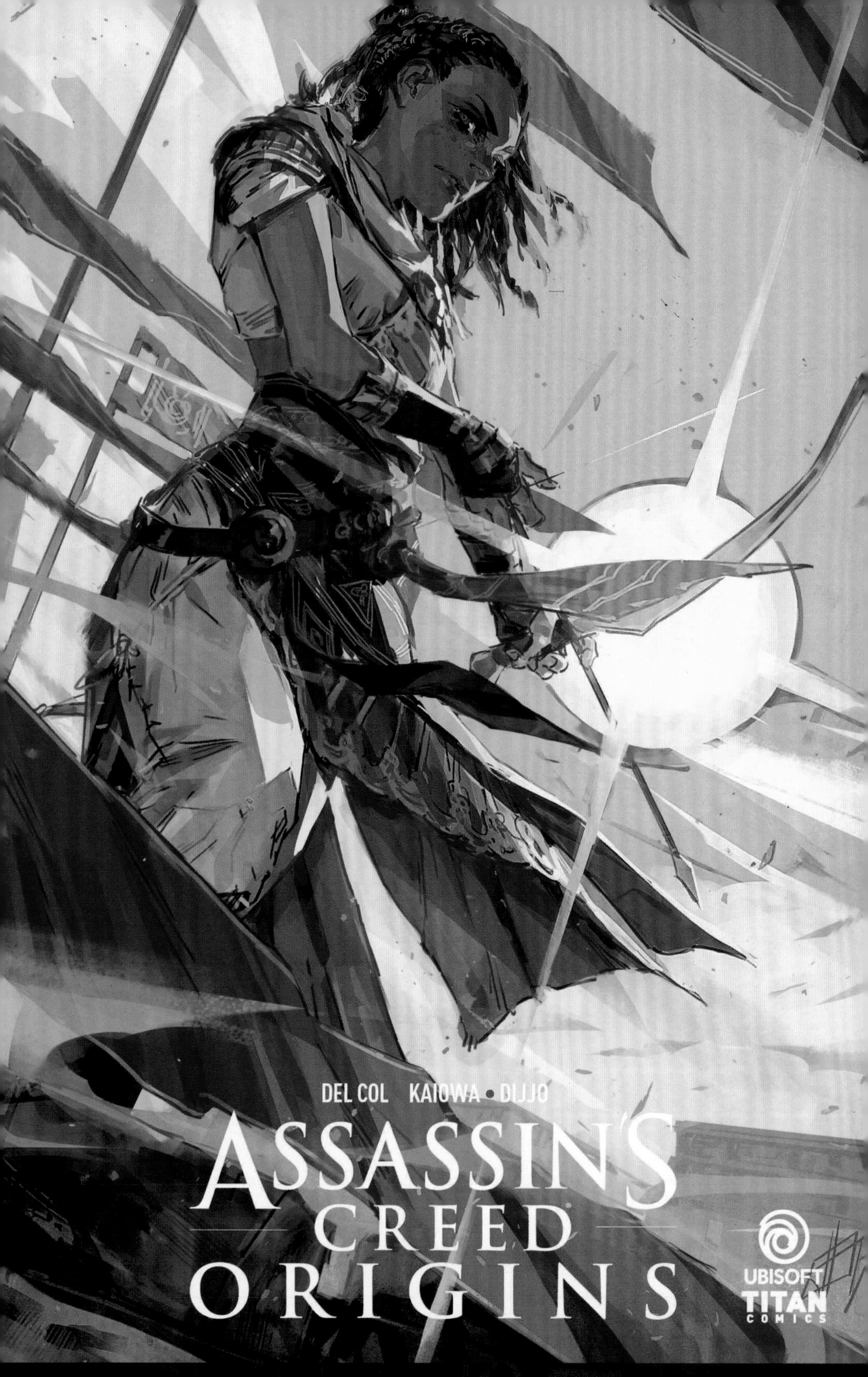
DEL COL KAIOWA • DIJJO
ASSASSIN'S CREED ORIGINS
UBISOFT
TITAN COMICS

> #2 COVER A / TONI INFANTE

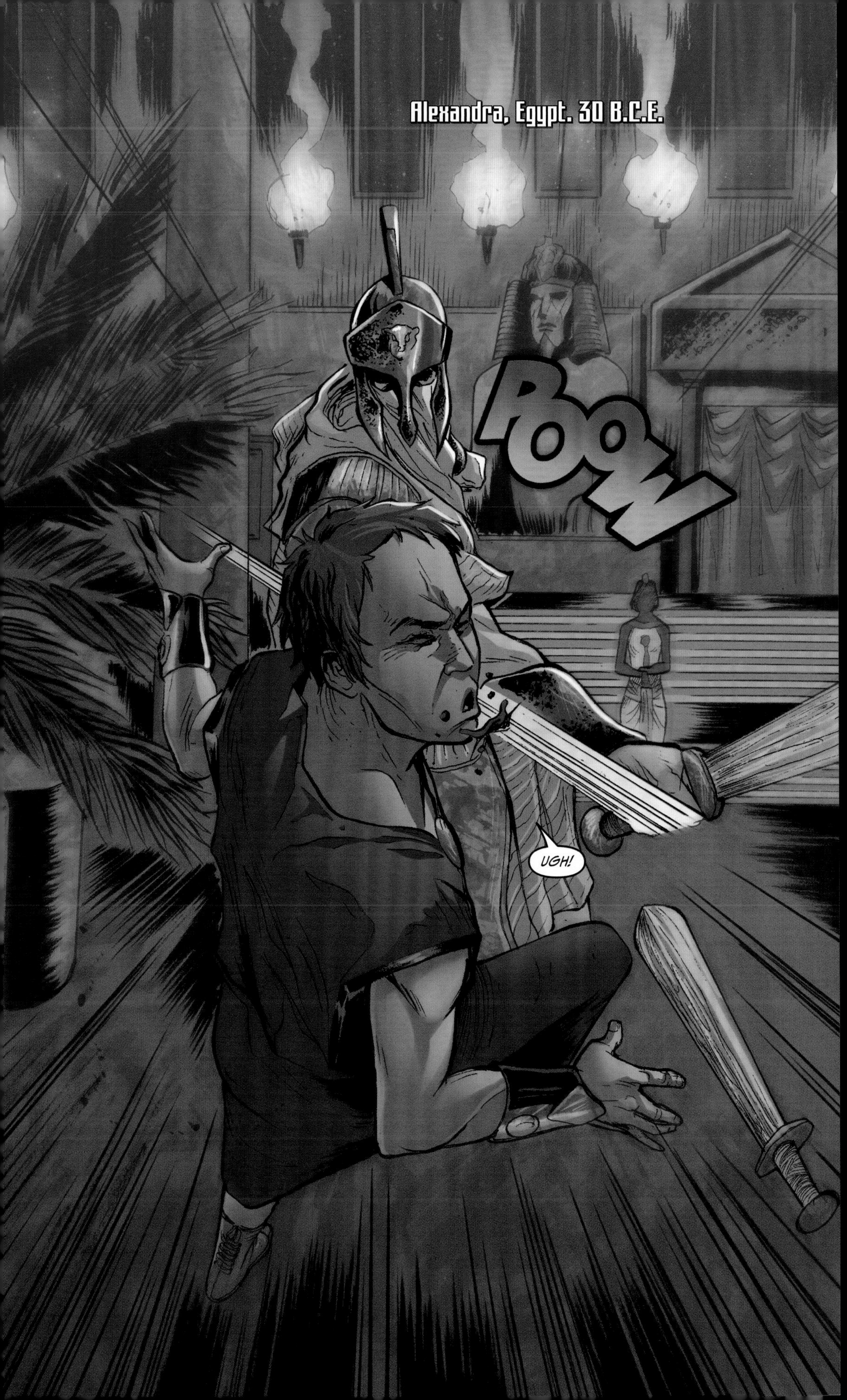
Alexandra, Egypt. 30 B.C.E.
POOW
UGH!

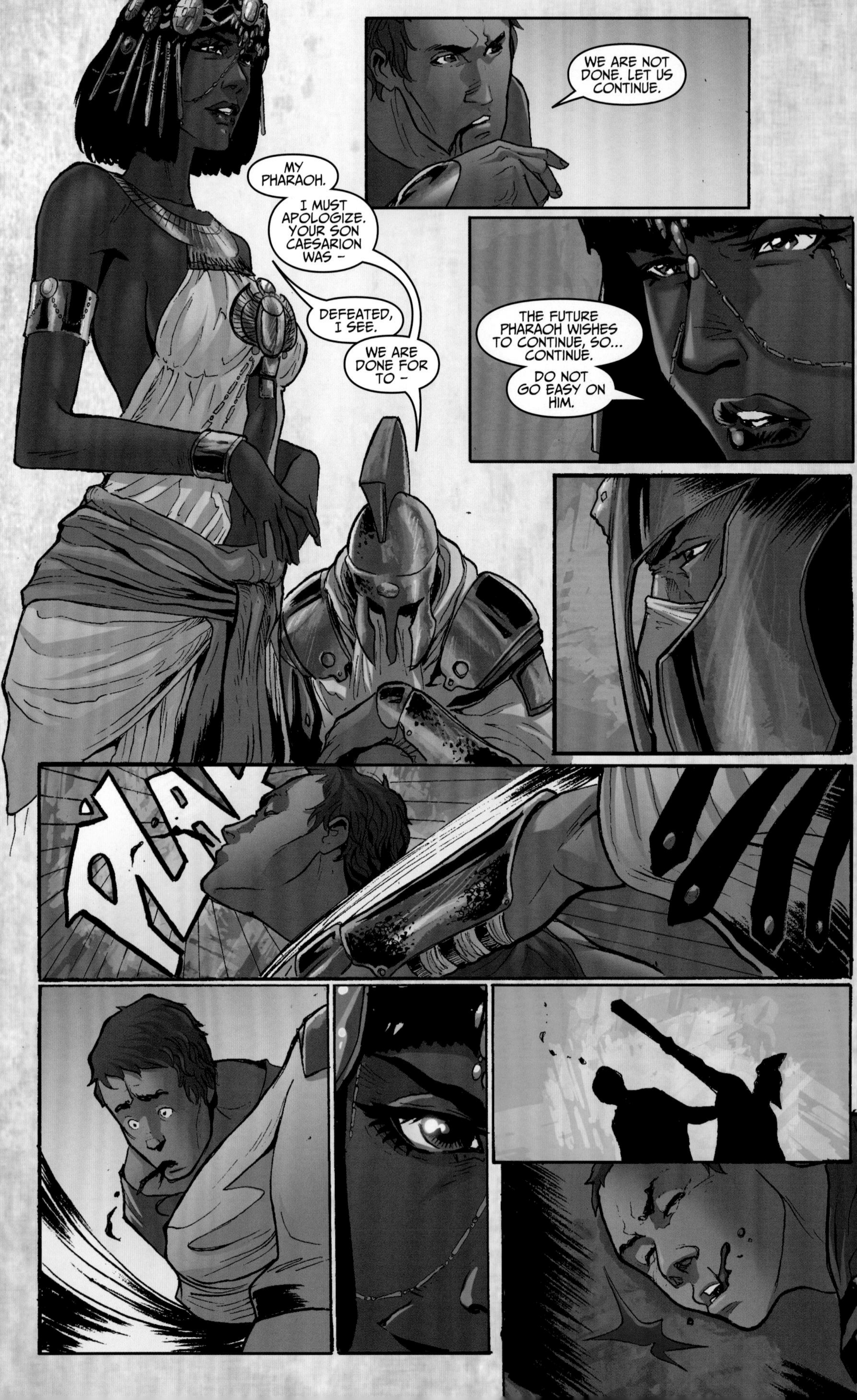
WE ARE NOT DONE. LET US CONTINUE.
MY PHARAOH.
I MUST APOLOGIZE. YOUR SON CAESARION WAS –
DEFEATED, I SEE.
WE ARE DONE FOR TO –
THE FUTURE PHARAOH WISHES TO CONTINUE, SO... CONTINUE.
DO NOT GO EASY ON HIM.

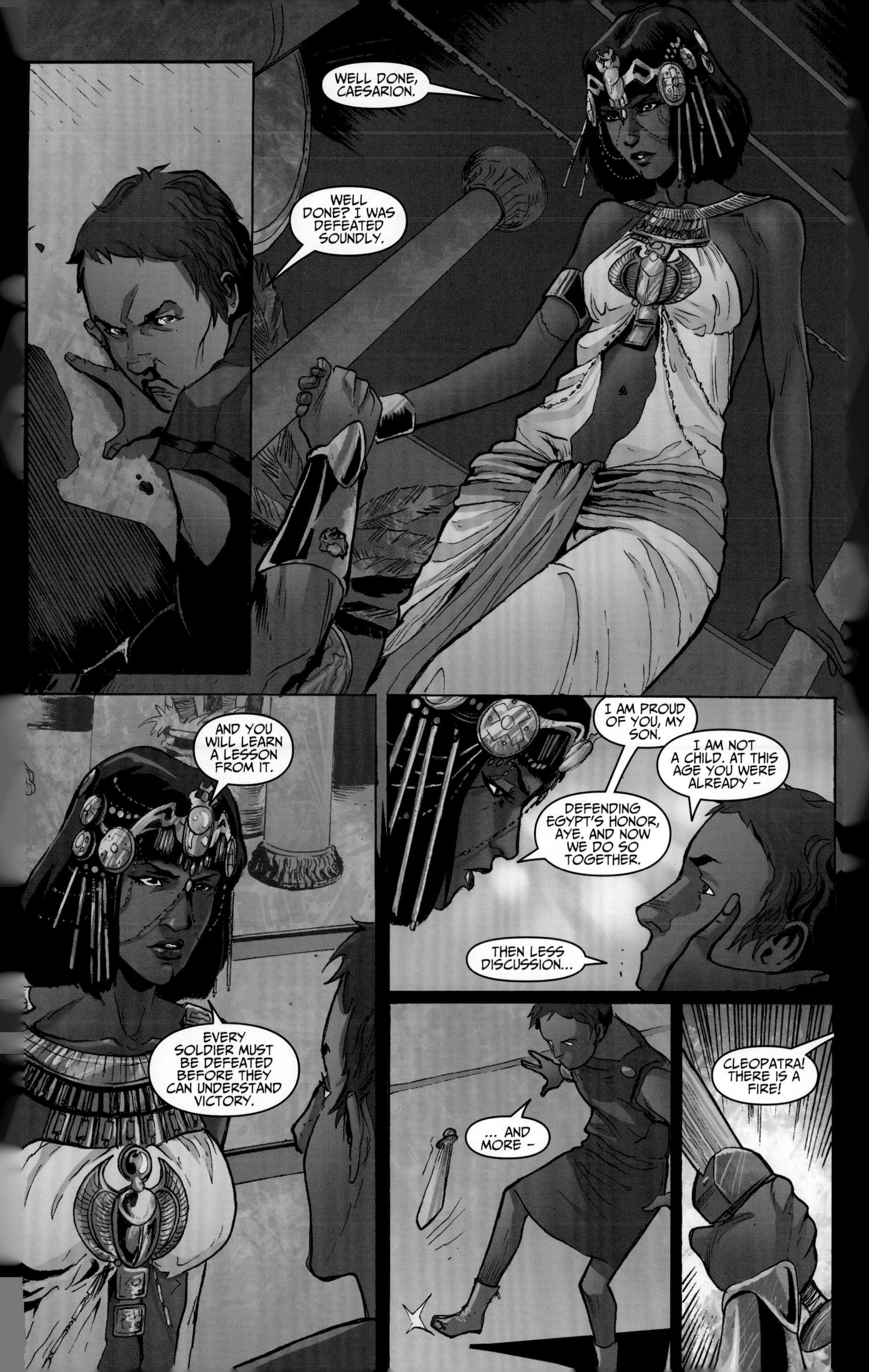
WELL DONE, CAESARION.
WELL DONE? I WAS DEFEATED SOUNDLY.
AND YOU WILL LEARN A LESSON FROM IT.
EVERY SOLDIER MUST BE DEFEATED BEFORE THEY CAN UNDERSTAND VICTORY.
I AM PROUD OF YOU, MY SON.
I AM NOT A CHILD. AT THIS AGE YOU WERE ALREADY –
DEFENDING EGYPT'S HONOR, AYE. AND NOW WE DO SO TOGETHER.
THEN LESS DISCUSSION...
... AND MORE –
CLEOPATRA! THERE IS A FIRE!

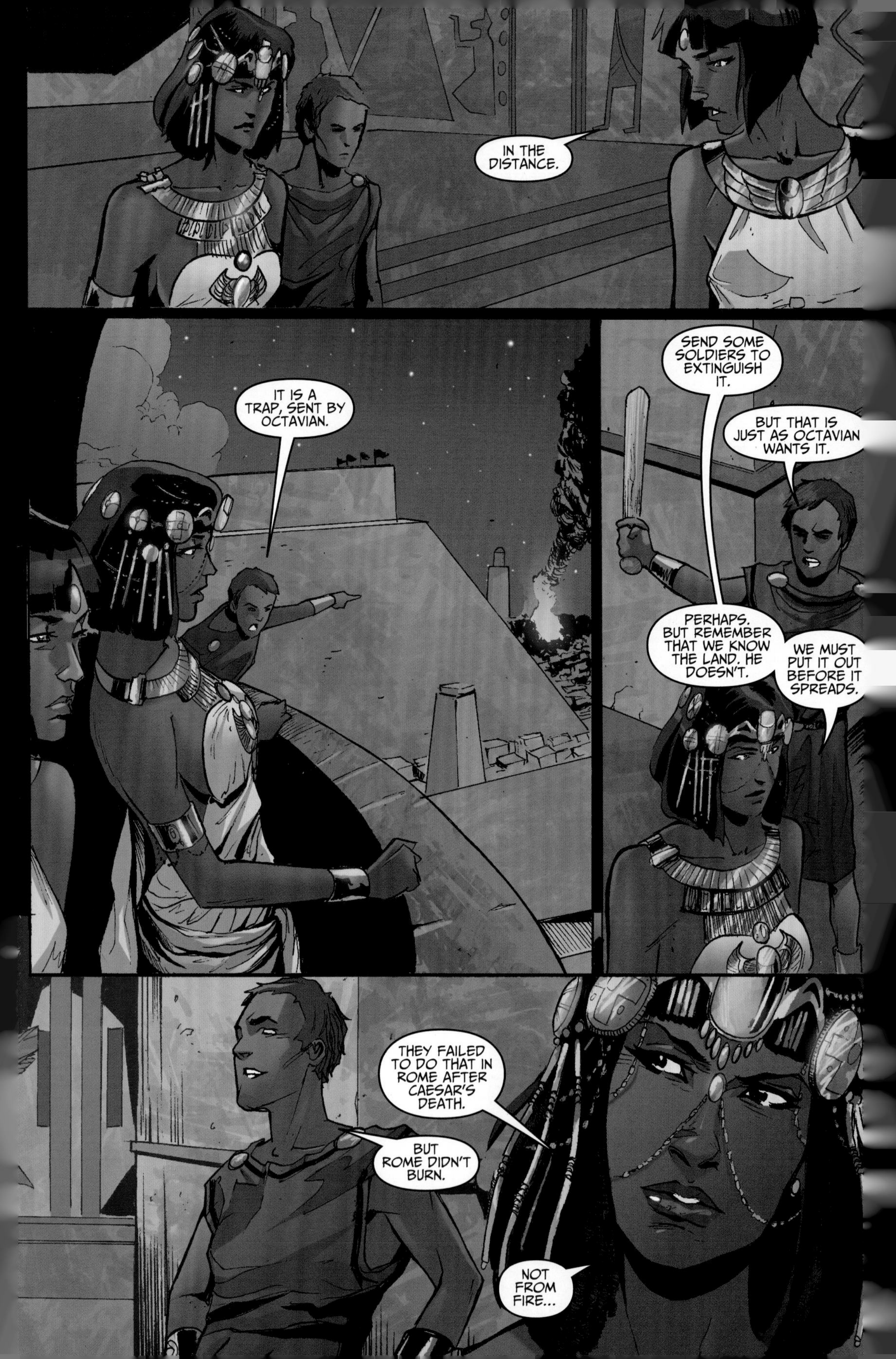
IN THE DISTANCE.
IT IS A TRAP, SENT BY OCTAVIAN.
SEND SOME SOLDIERS TO EXTINGUISH IT.
BUT THAT IS JUST AS OCTAVIAN WANTS IT.
PERHAPS. BUT REMEMBER THAT WE KNOW THE LAND. HE DOESN'T.
WE MUST PUT IT OUT BEFORE IT SPREADS.
THEY FAILED TO DO THAT IN ROME AFTER CAESAR'S DEATH.
BUT ROME DIDN'T BURN.
NOT FROM FIRE...

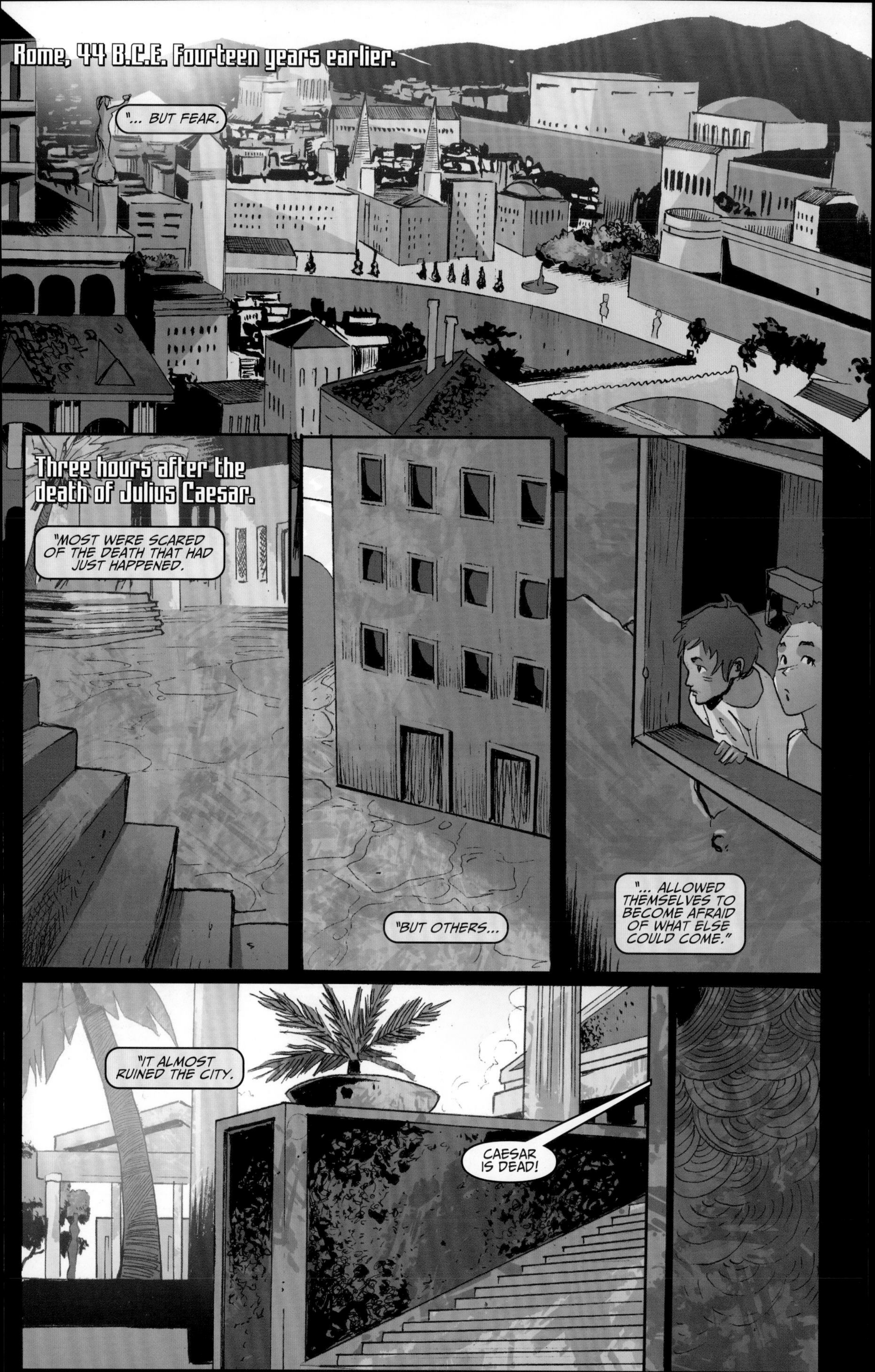
Rome, 44 B.C.E. Fourteen years earlier.
"... BUT FEAR.
Three hours after the death of Julius Caesar.
"MOST WERE SCARED OF THE DEATH THAT HAD JUST HAPPENED.
"BUT OTHERS...
"... ALLOWED THEMSELVES TO BECOME AFRAID OF WHAT ELSE COULD COME."
"IT ALMOST RUINED THE CITY.
CAESAR IS DEAD!

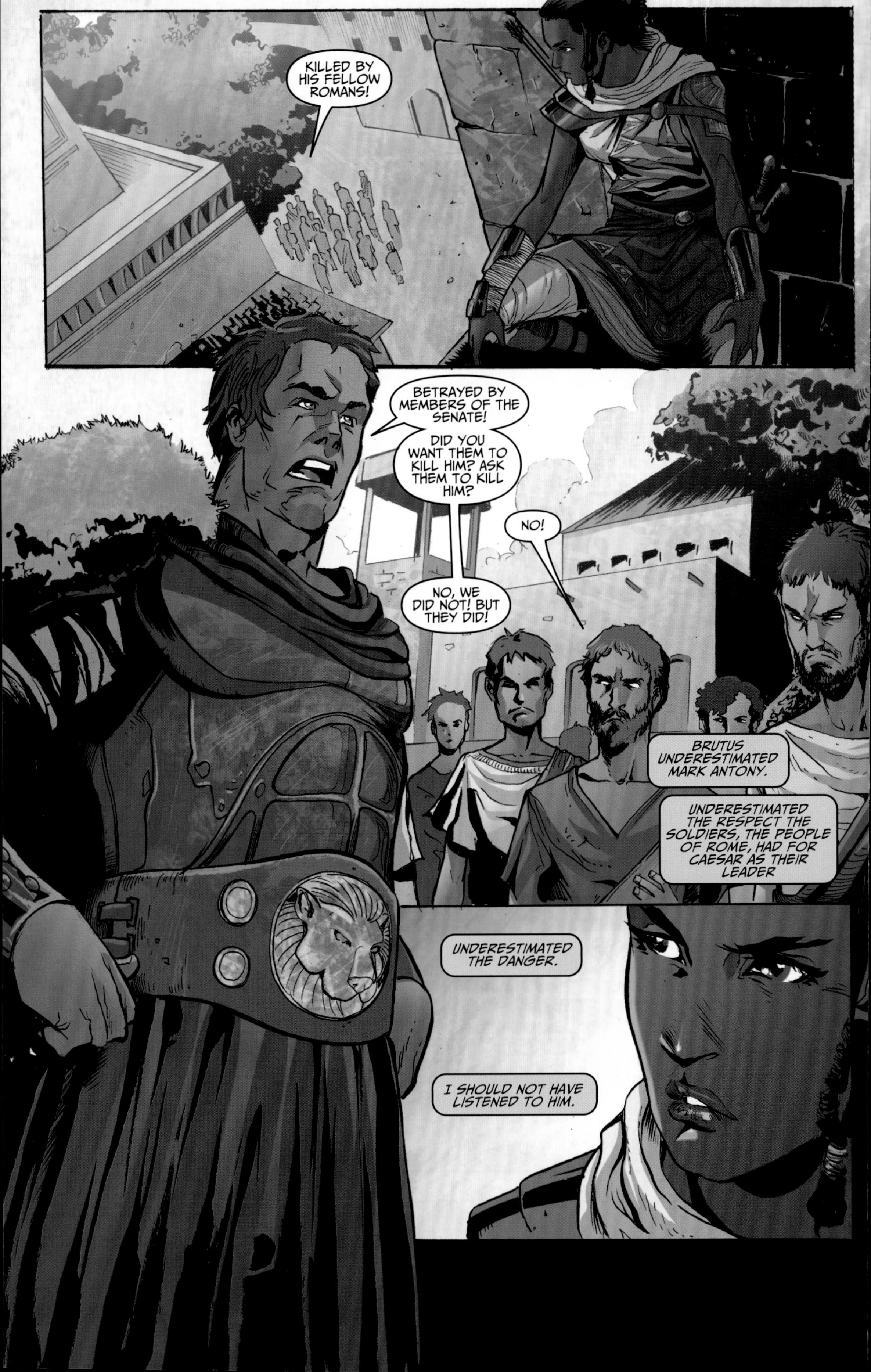
KILLED BY HIS FELLOW ROMANS!
BETRAYED BY MEMBERS OF THE SENATE!
DID YOU WANT THEM TO KILL HIM? ASK THEM TO KILL HIM?
NO!
NO, WE DID NOT! BUT THEY DID!
BRUTUS UNDERESTIMATED MARK ANTONY.
UNDERESTIMATED THE RESPECT THE SOLDIERS, THE PEOPLE OF ROME, HAD FOR CAESAR AS THEIR LEADER
UNDERESTIMATED THE DANGER.
I SHOULD NOT HAVE LISTENED TO HIM.

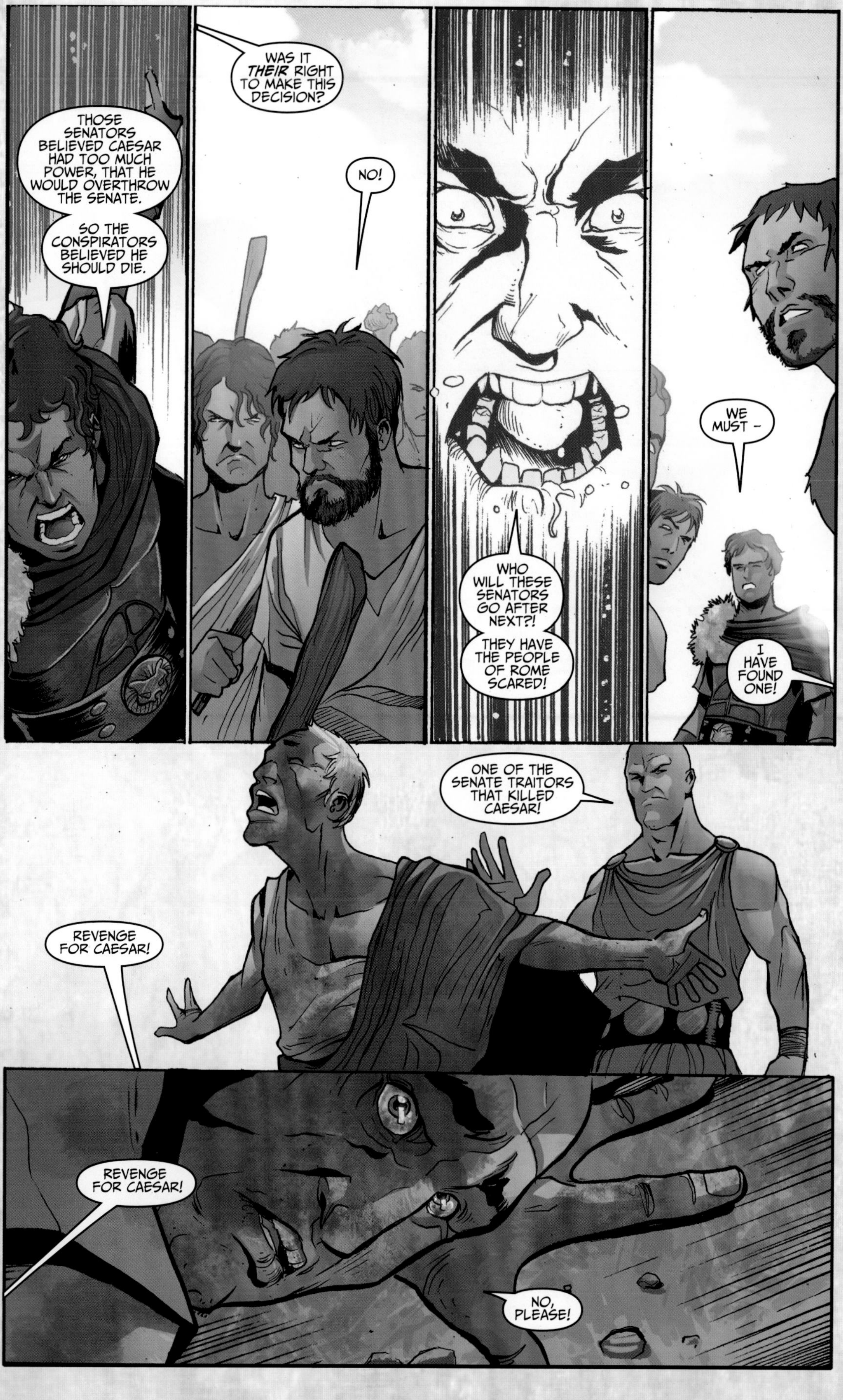
THOSE SENATORS BELIEVED CAESAR HAD TOO MUCH POWER, THAT HE WOULD OVERTHROW THE SENATE.
SO THE CONSPIRATORS BELIEVED HE SHOULD DIE.
WAS IT *THEIR* RIGHT TO MAKE THIS DECISION?
NO!
WHO WILL THESE SENATORS GO AFTER NEXT?!
THEY HAVE THE PEOPLE OF ROME SCARED!
WE MUST –
I HAVE FOUND ONE!
ONE OF THE SENATE TRAITORS THAT KILLED CAESAR!
REVENGE FOR CAESAR!
REVENGE FOR CAESAR!
NO, PLEASE!

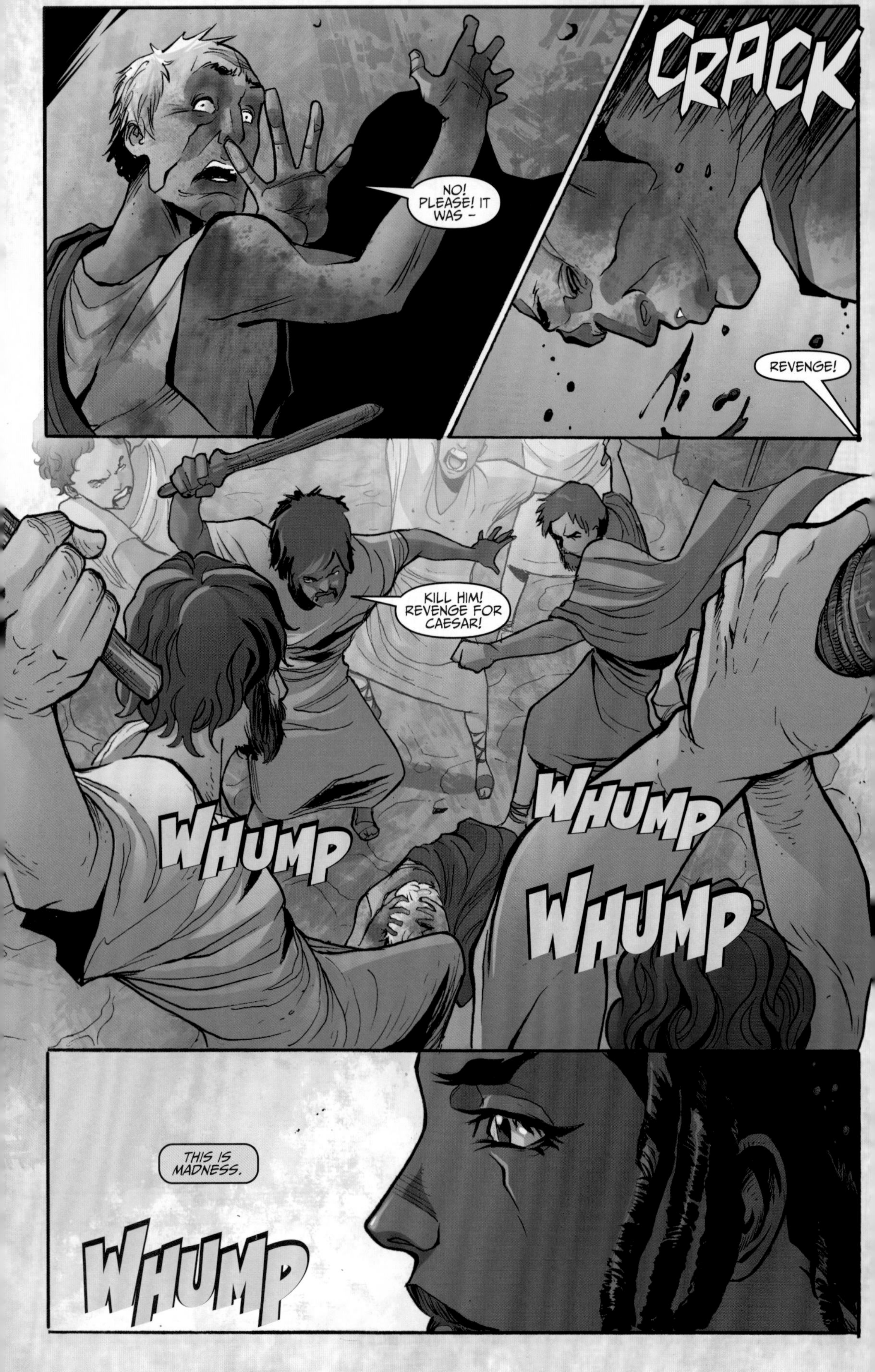
NO! PLEASE! IT WAS –
CRACK
REVENGE!
KILL HIM! REVENGE FOR CAESAR!
WHUMP
WHUMP
WHUMP
THIS IS MADNESS.
WHUMP

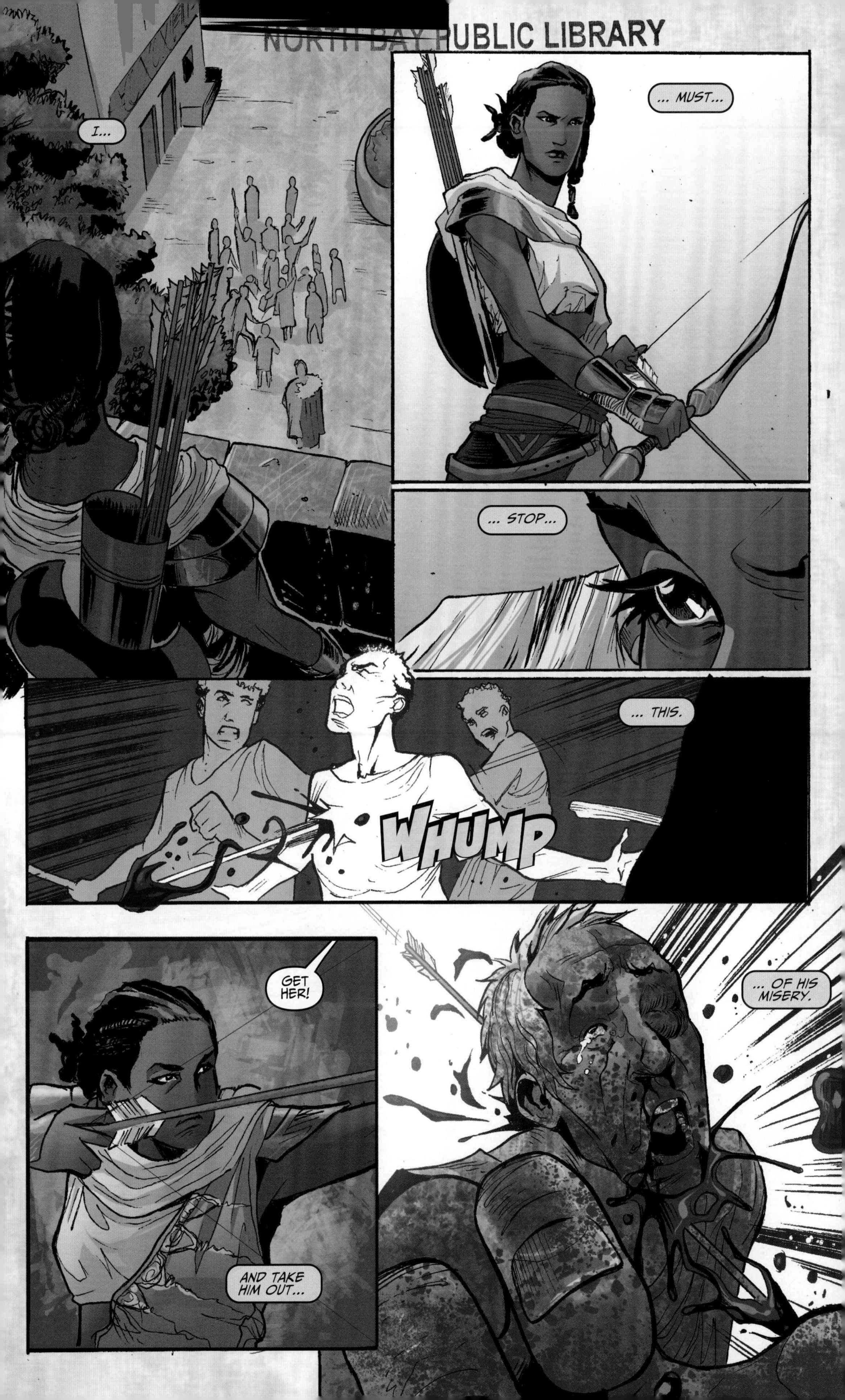
I...
... MUST...
... STOP...
... THIS.
WHUMP
GET HER!
AND TAKE HIM OUT...
... OF HIS MISERY.

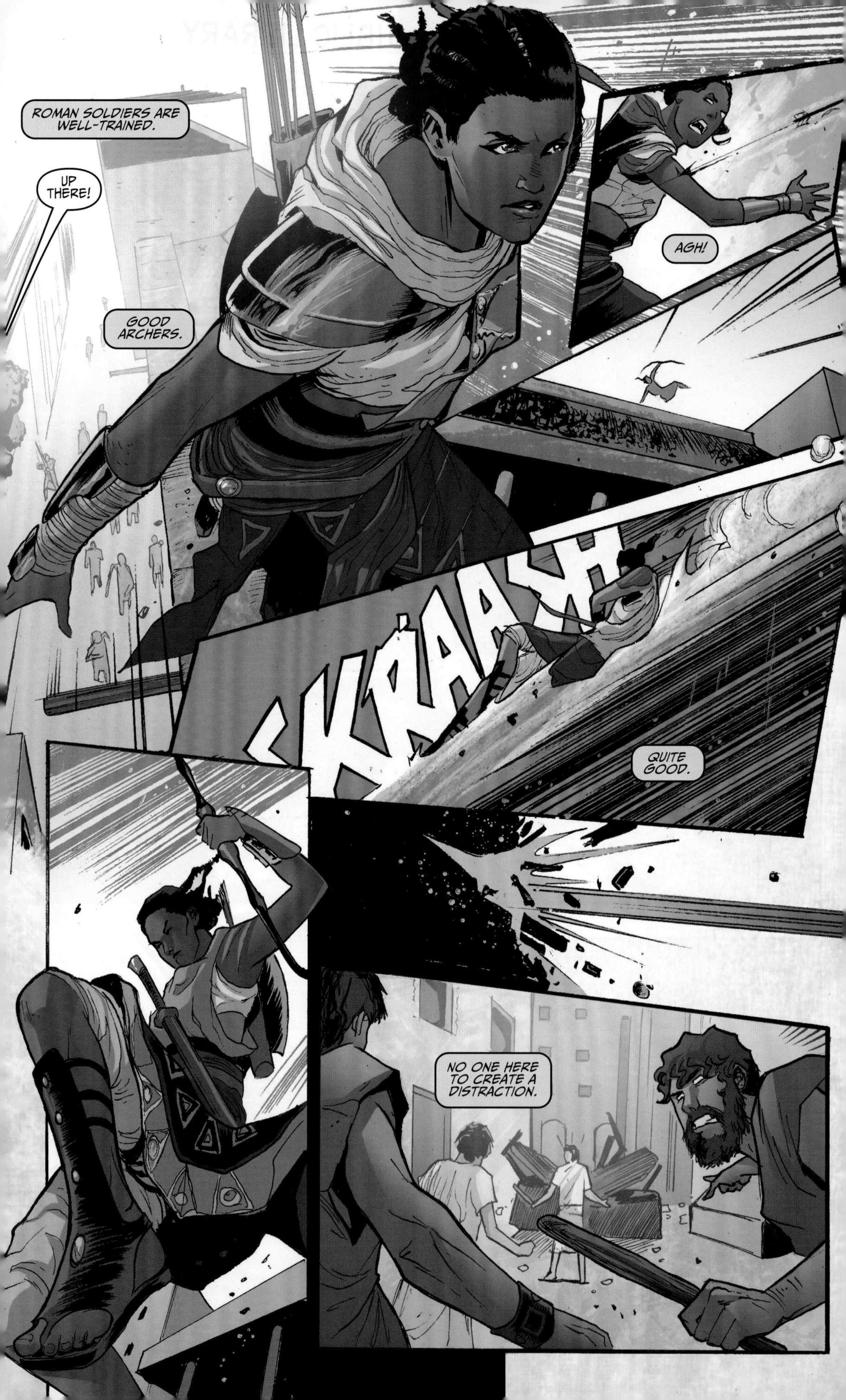
ROMAN SOLDIERS ARE WELL-TRAINED.
UP THERE!
GOOD ARCHERS.
AGH!
KRAASH
QUITE GOOD.
NO ONE HERE TO CREATE A DISTRACTION.

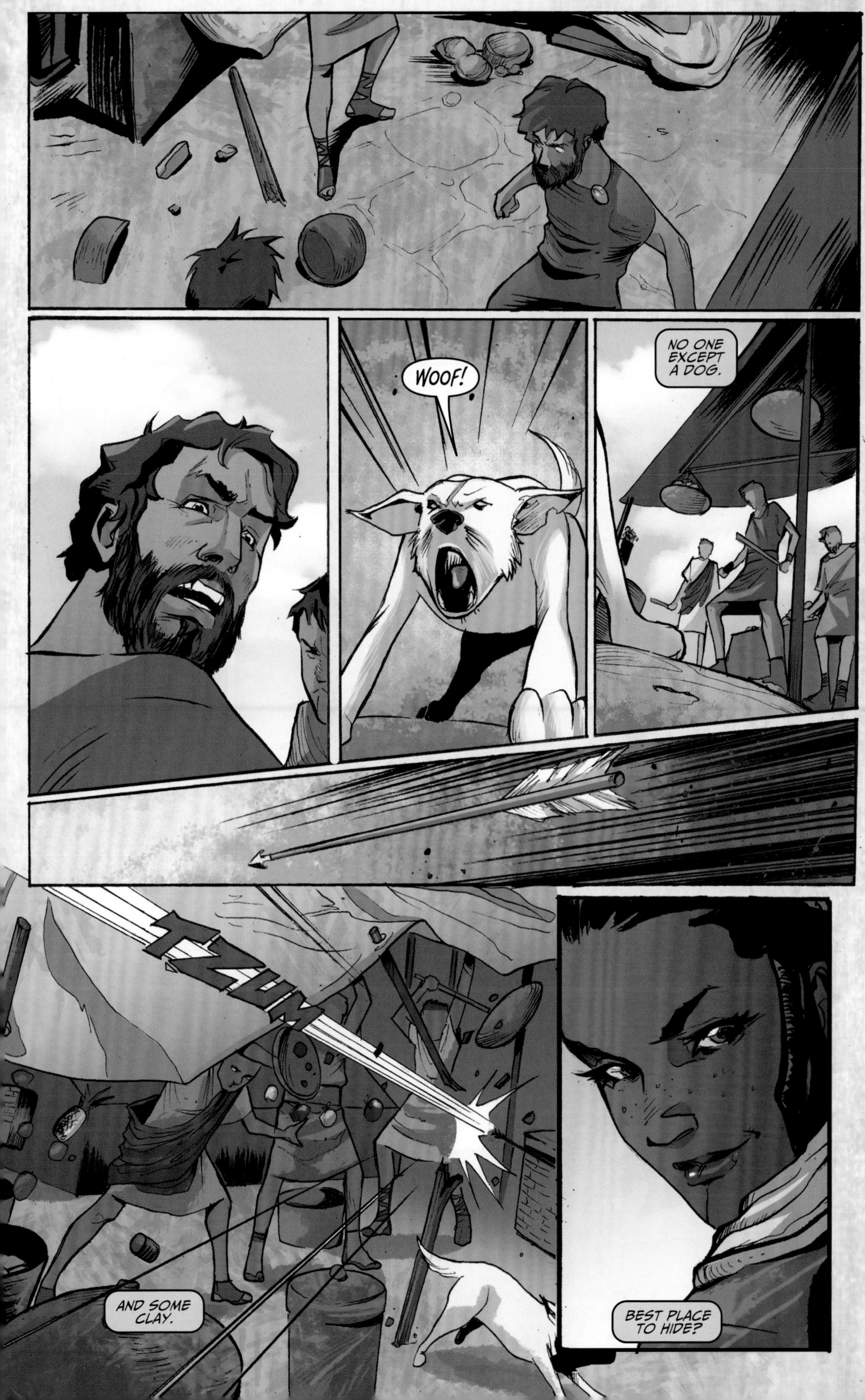
WOOF!
NO ONE EXCEPT A DOG.
TZUM
AND SOME CLAY.
BEST PLACE TO HIDE?

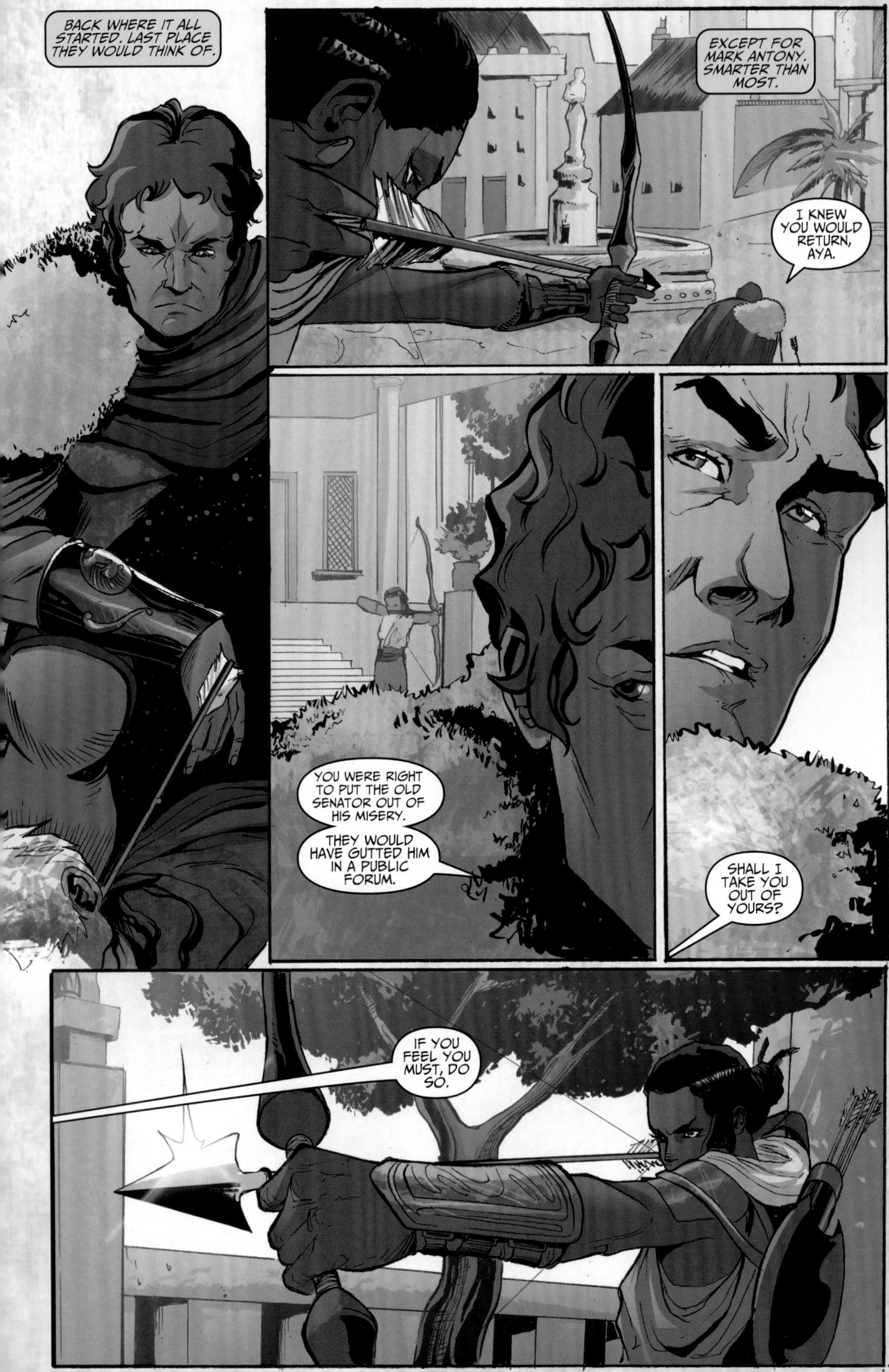
BACK WHERE IT ALL STARTED. LAST PLACE THEY WOULD THINK OF.
EXCEPT FOR MARK ANTONY. SMARTER THAN MOST.
I KNEW YOU WOULD RETURN, AYA.
YOU WERE RIGHT TO PUT THE OLD SENATOR OUT OF HIS MISERY.
THEY WOULD HAVE GUTTED HIM IN A PUBLIC FORUM.
SHALL I TAKE YOU OUT OF YOURS?
IF YOU FEEL YOU MUST, DO SO.

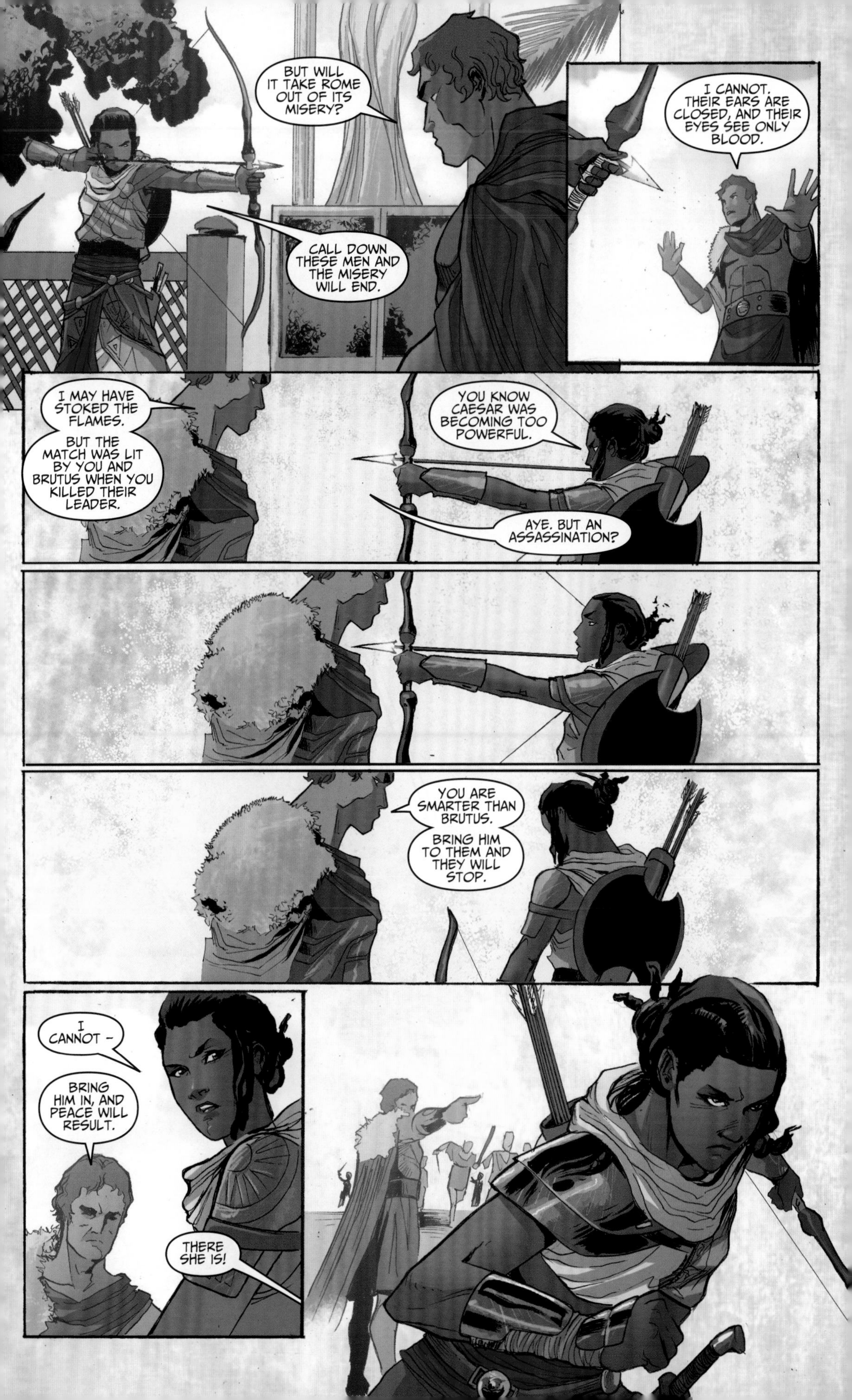
BUT WILL IT TAKE ROME OUT OF ITS MISERY?
CALL DOWN THESE MEN AND THE MISERY WILL END.
I CANNOT. THEIR EARS ARE CLOSED, AND THEIR EYES SEE ONLY BLOOD.
I MAY HAVE STOKED THE FLAMES.
BUT THE MATCH WAS LIT BY YOU AND BRUTUS WHEN YOU KILLED THEIR LEADER.
YOU KNOW CAESAR WAS BECOMING TOO POWERFUL.
AYE. BUT AN ASSASSINATION?
YOU ARE SMARTER THAN BRUTUS.
BRING HIM TO THEM AND THEY WILL STOP.
I CANNOT –
BRING HIM IN, AND PEACE WILL RESULT.
THERE SHE IS!

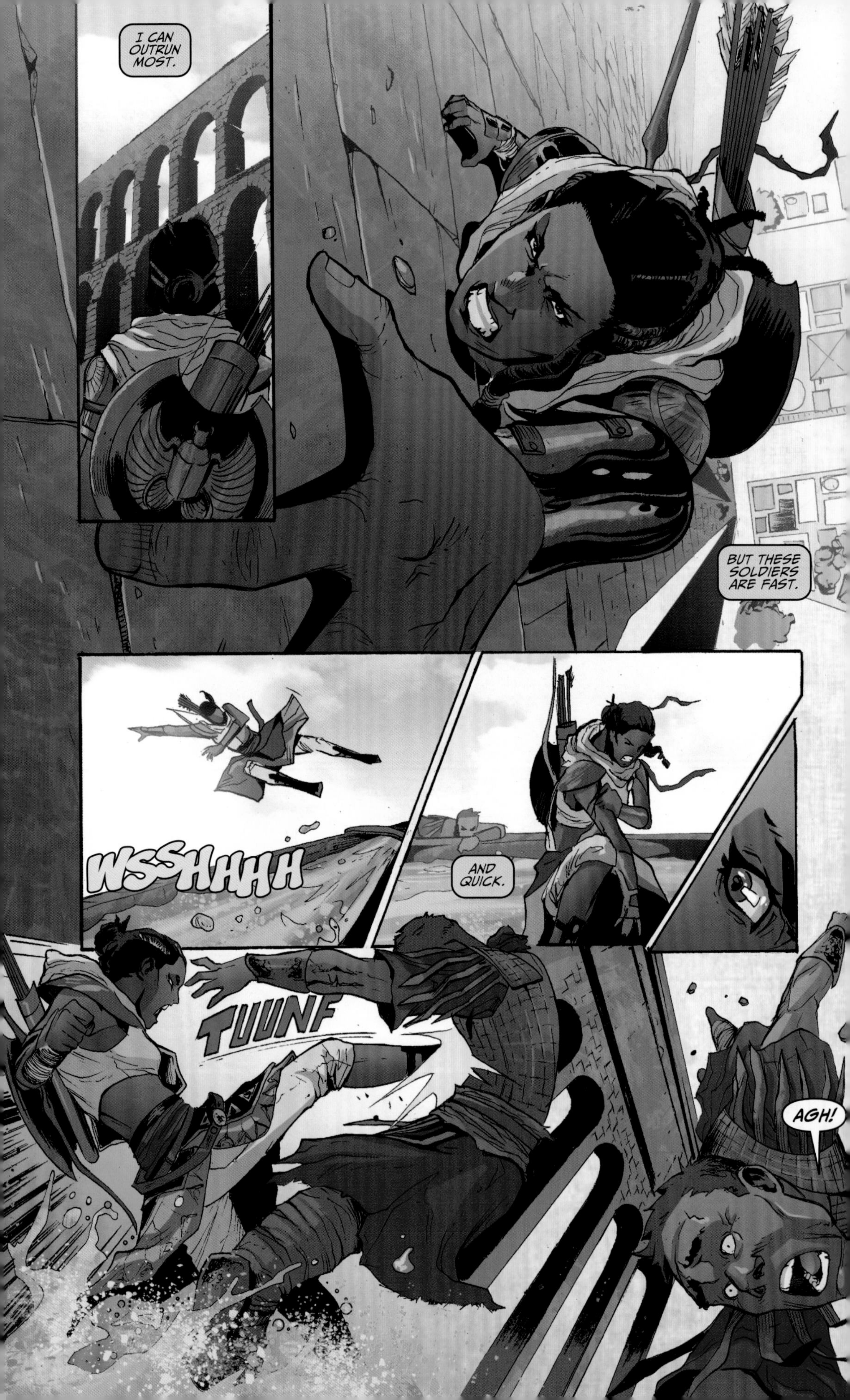
I CAN OUTRUN MOST.
BUT THESE SOLDIERS ARE FAST.
WSSHHHH
AND QUICK.
TUUNF
AGH!

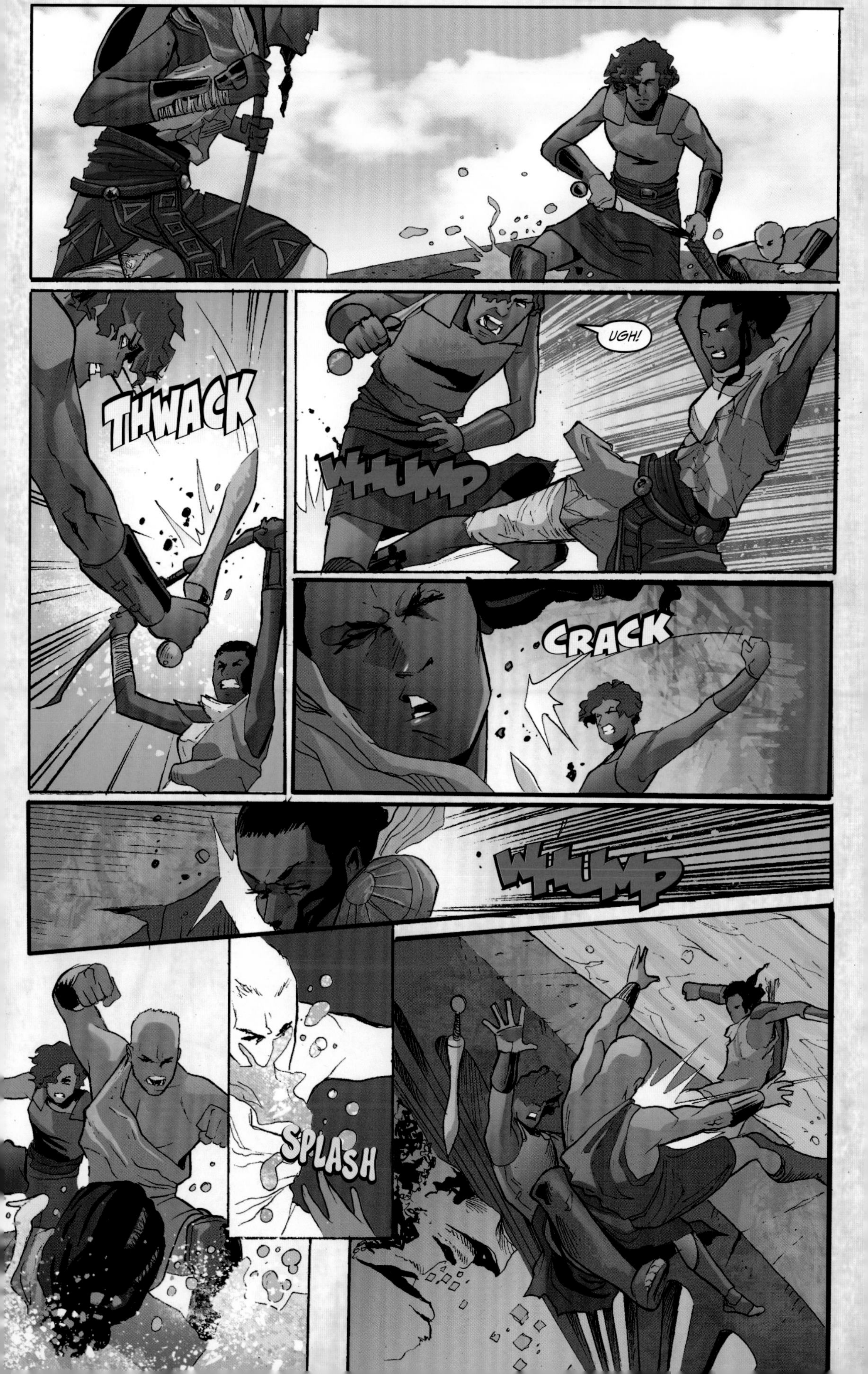
THWACK
UGH!
WHUMP
CRACK
WHUMP
SPLASH

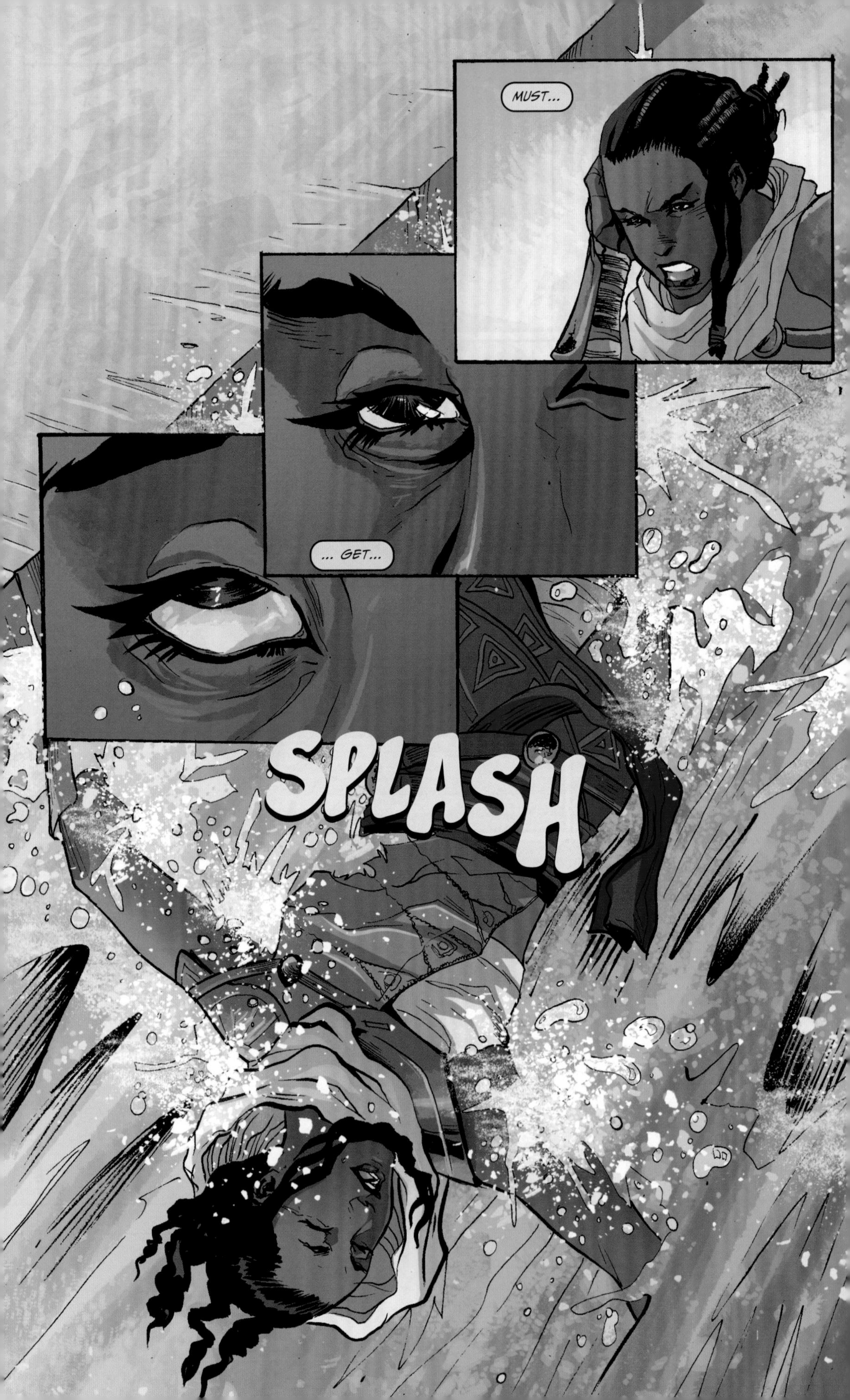
MUST...
... GET...
SPLASH

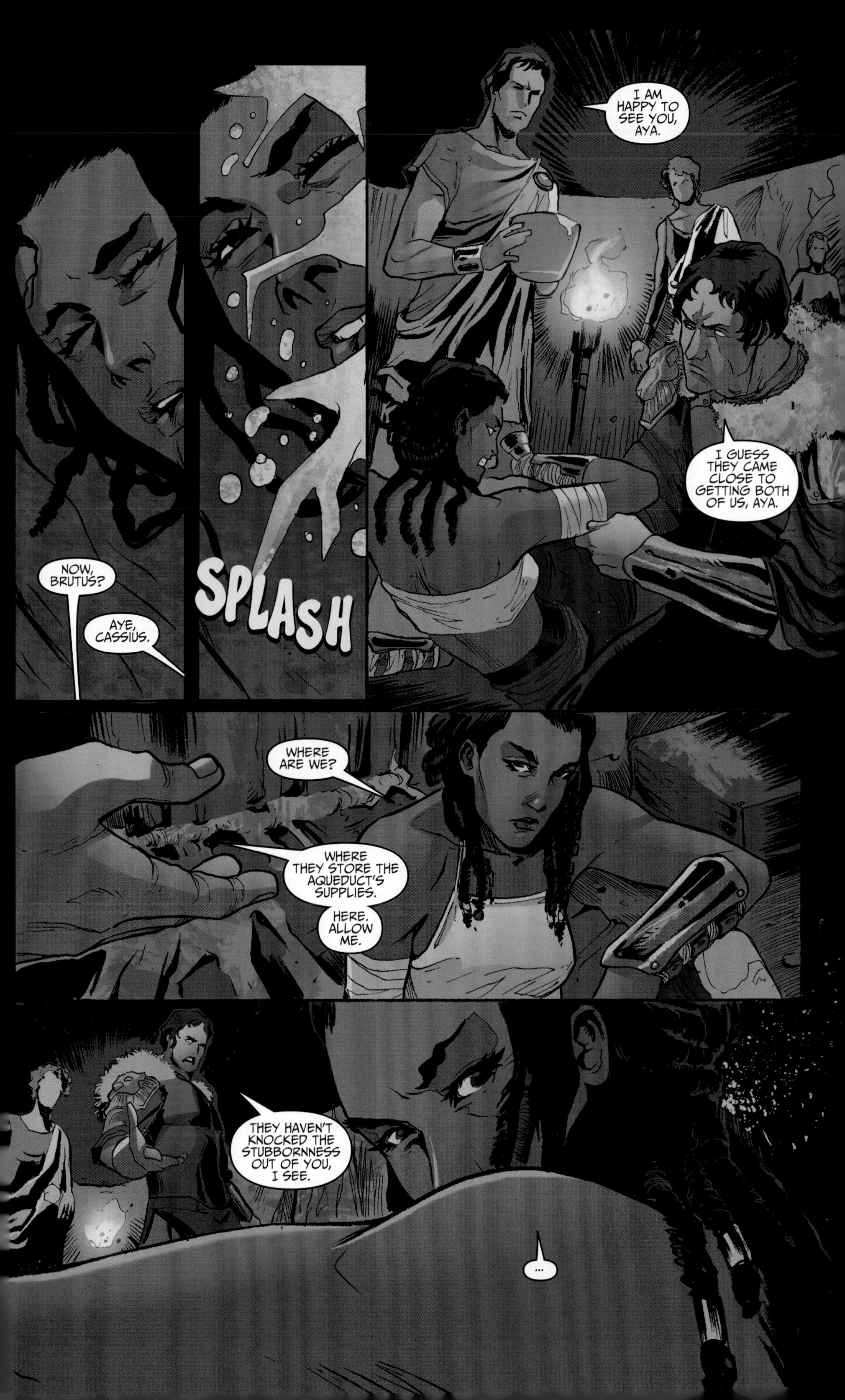
NOW, BRUTUS?
AYE, CASSIUS.
SPLASH
I AM HAPPY TO SEE YOU, AYA.
I GUESS THEY CAME CLOSE TO GETTING BOTH OF US, AYA.
WHERE ARE WE?
WHERE THEY STORE THE AQUEDUCT'S SUPPLIES.
HERE. ALLOW ME.
THEY HAVEN'T KNOCKED THE STUBBORNNESS OUT OF YOU, I SEE.
...

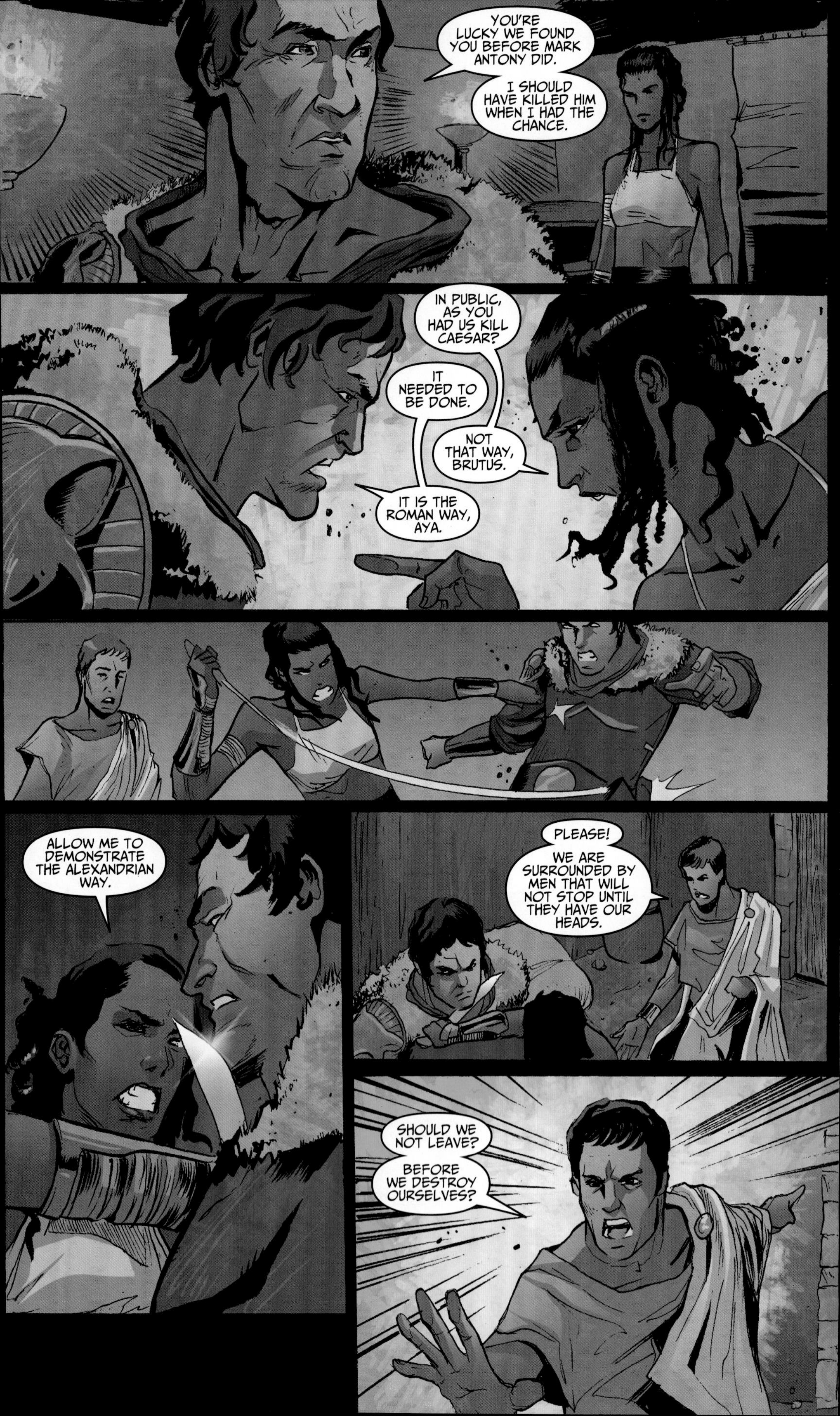
YOU'RE LUCKY WE FOUND YOU BEFORE MARK ANTONY DID.
I SHOULD HAVE KILLED HIM WHEN I HAD THE CHANCE.
IN PUBLIC, AS YOU HAD US KILL CAESAR?
IT NEEDED TO BE DONE.
NOT THAT WAY, BRUTUS.
IT IS THE ROMAN WAY, AYA.
ALLOW ME TO DEMONSTRATE THE ALEXANDRIAN WAY.
PLEASE!
WE ARE SURROUNDED BY MEN THAT WILL NOT STOP UNTIL THEY HAVE OUR HEADS.
SHOULD WE NOT LEAVE?
BEFORE WE DESTROY OURSELVES?

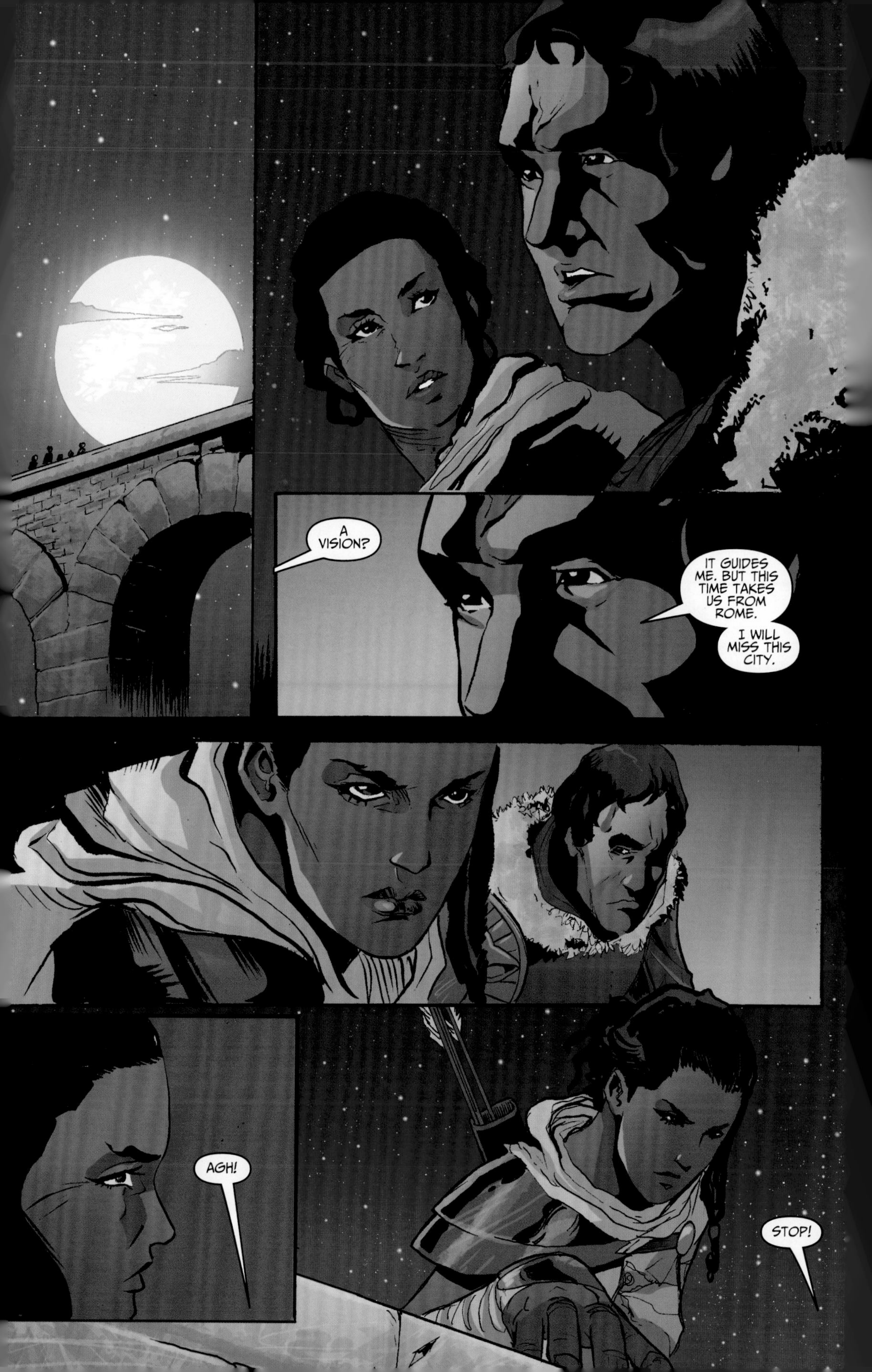
A VISION?
IT GUIDES ME. BUT THIS TIME TAKES US FROM ROME.
I WILL MISS THIS CITY.
AGH!
STOP!

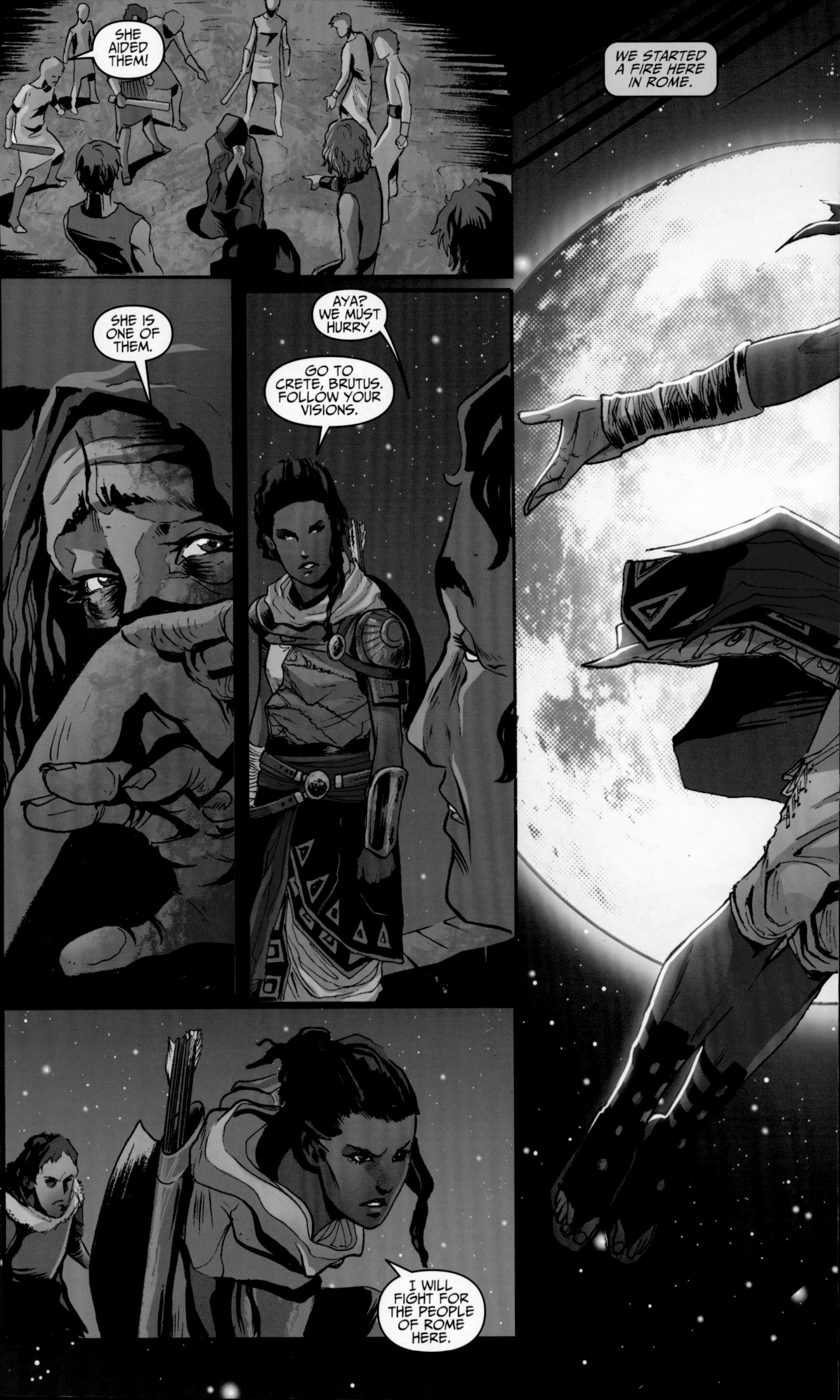
SHE AIDED THEM!
WE STARTED A FIRE HERE IN ROME.
SHE IS ONE OF THEM.
AYA? WE MUST HURRY.
GO TO CRETE, BRUTUS. FOLLOW YOUR VISIONS.
I WILL FIGHT FOR THE PEOPLE OF ROME HERE.

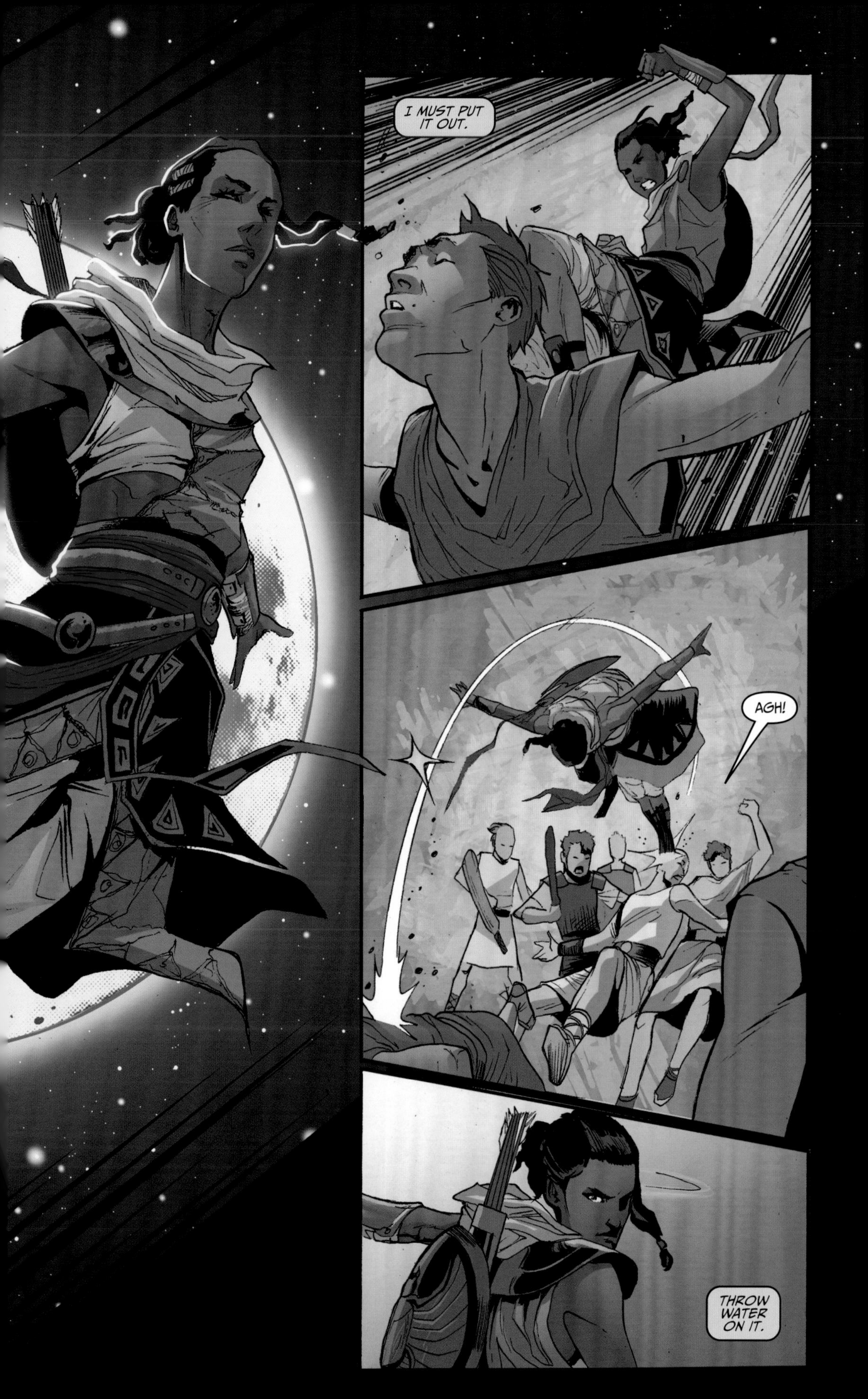
I MUST PUT IT OUT.
AGH!
THROW WATER ON IT.

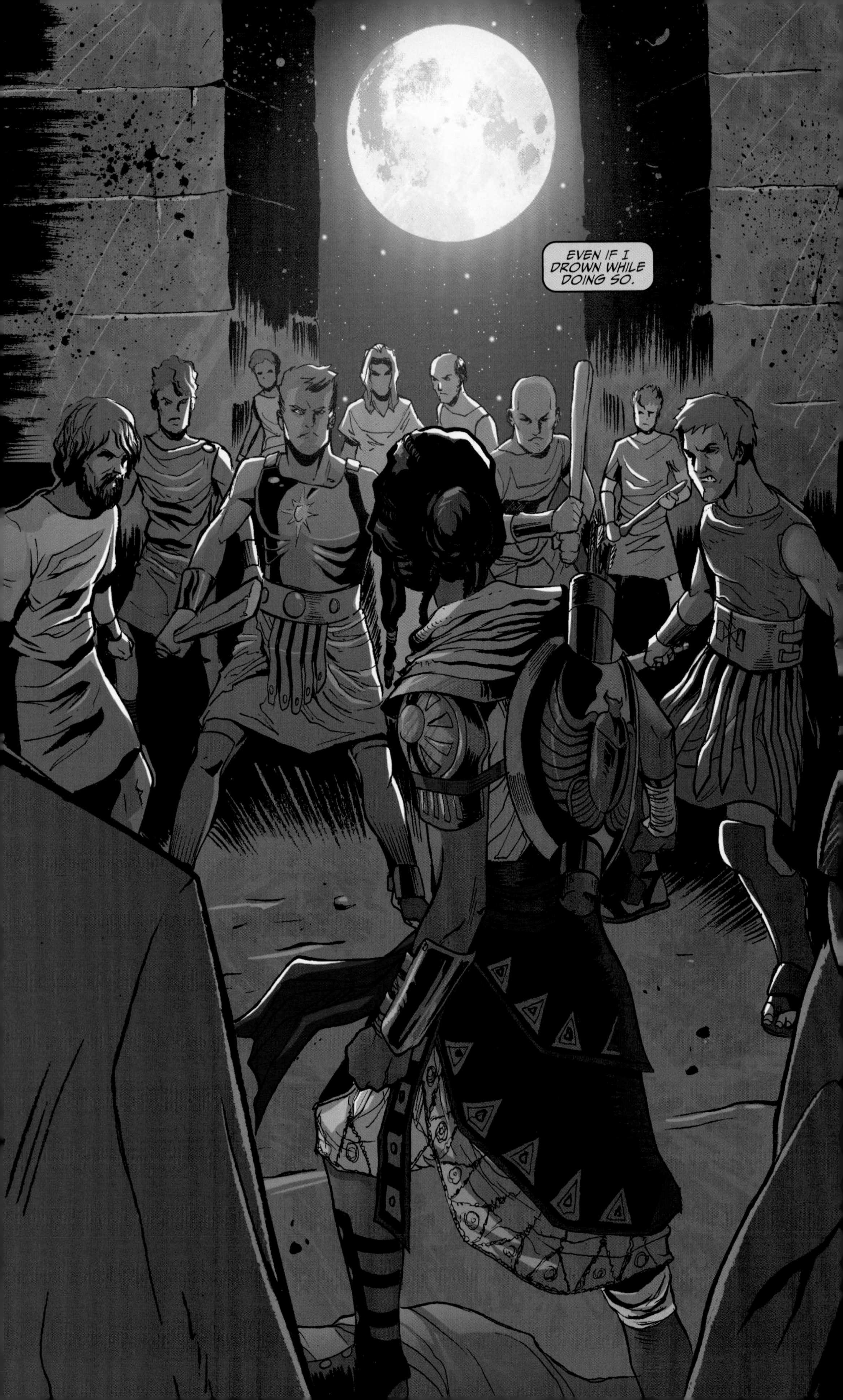
EVEN IF I DROWN WHILE DOING SO.

CHAPTER 3

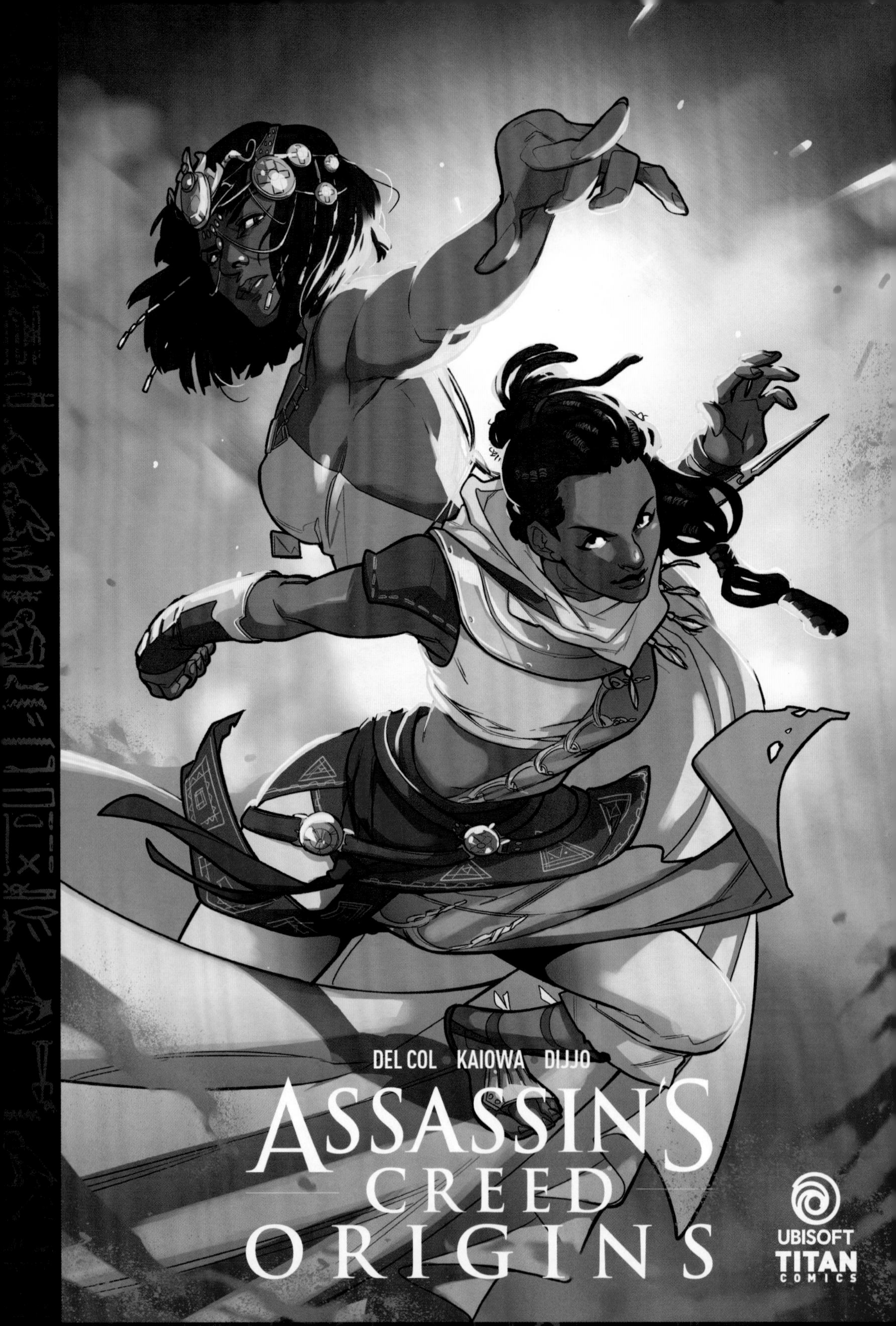
DEL COL • KAIOWA • DIJJO
ASSASSIN'S
CREED
ORIGINS
UBISOFT
TITAN
COMICS

> #3 COVER A / VALERIA FAVOCCIA

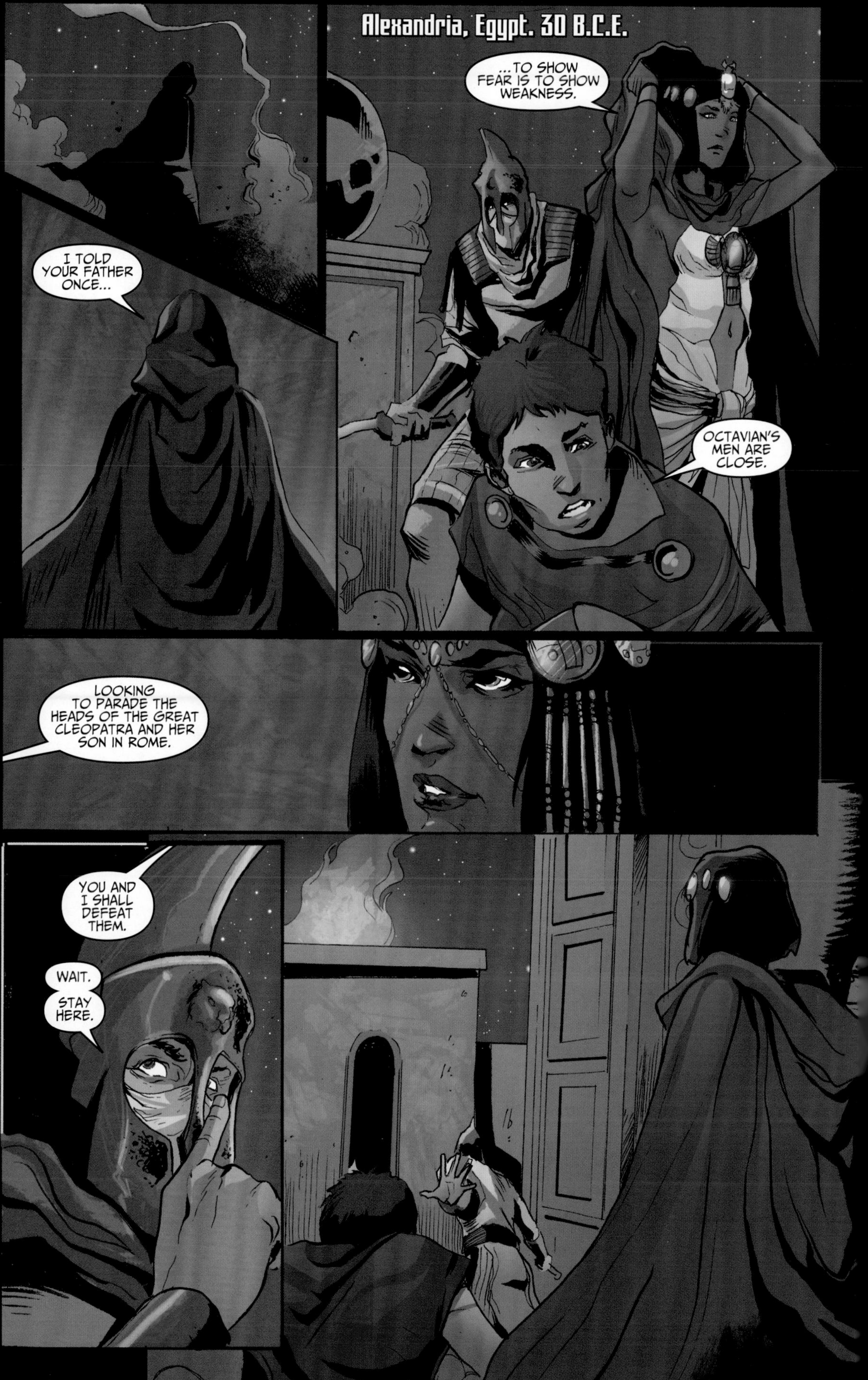
Alexandria, Egypt. 30 B.C.E.
I TOLD YOUR FATHER ONCE...
...TO SHOW FEAR IS TO SHOW WEAKNESS.
OCTAVIAN'S MEN ARE CLOSE.
LOOKING TO PARADE THE HEADS OF THE GREAT CLEOPATRA AND HER SON IN ROME.
YOU AND I SHALL DEFEAT THEM.
WAIT.
STAY HERE.

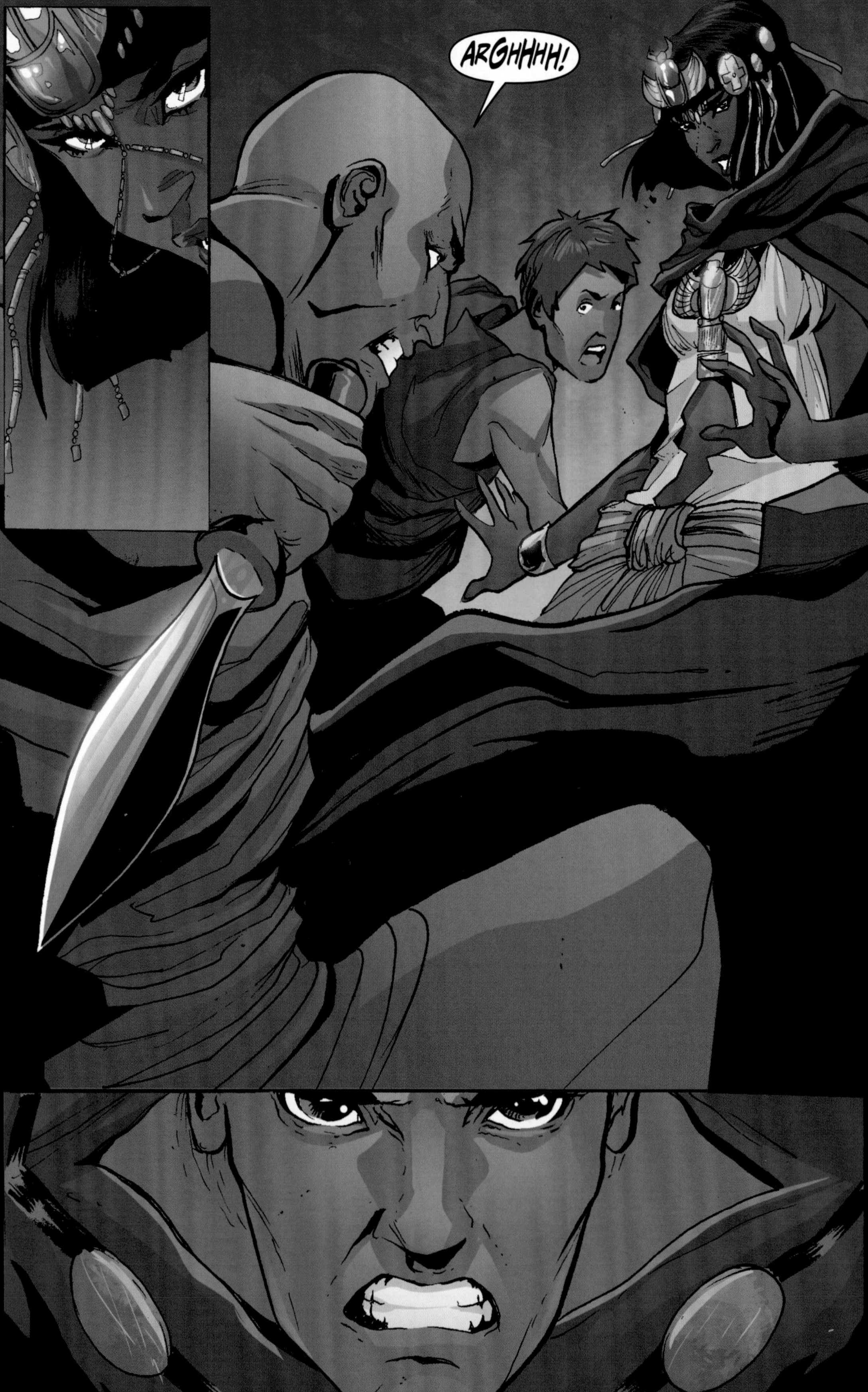
ARGHHHH!

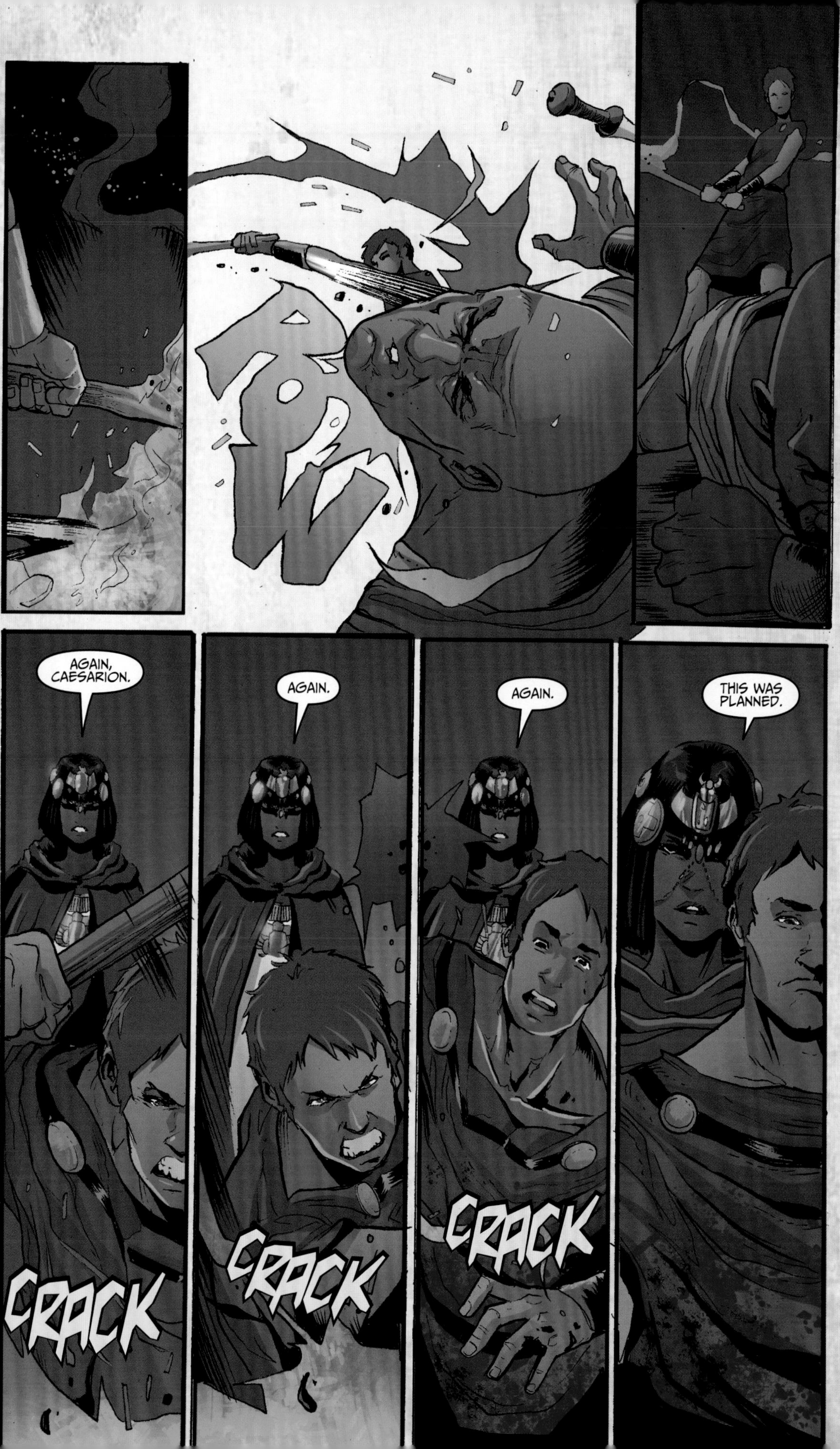
AGAIN, CAESARION.
CRACK
AGAIN.
CRACK
AGAIN.
CRACK
THIS WAS PLANNED.

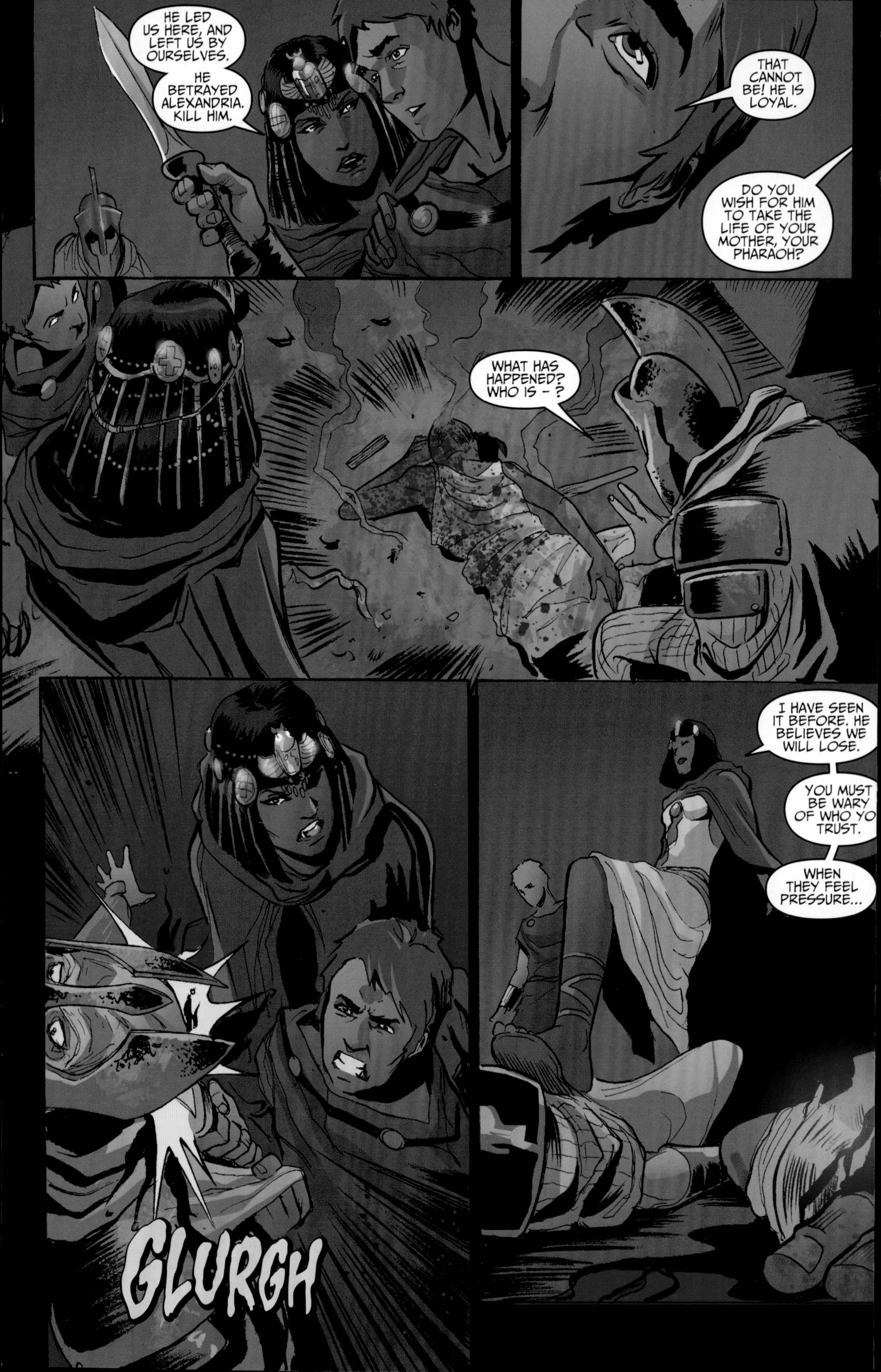
HE LED US HERE, AND LEFT US BY OURSELVES.
HE BETRAYED ALEXANDRIA. KILL HIM.
THAT CANNOT BE! HE IS LOYAL.
DO YOU WISH FOR HIM TO TAKE THE LIFE OF YOUR MOTHER, YOUR PHARAOH?
WHAT HAS HAPPENED? WHO IS - ?
GLURGH
I HAVE SEEN IT BEFORE. HE BELIEVES WE WILL LOSE.
YOU MUST BE WARY OF WHO YO TRUST.
WHEN THEY FEEL PRESSURE...

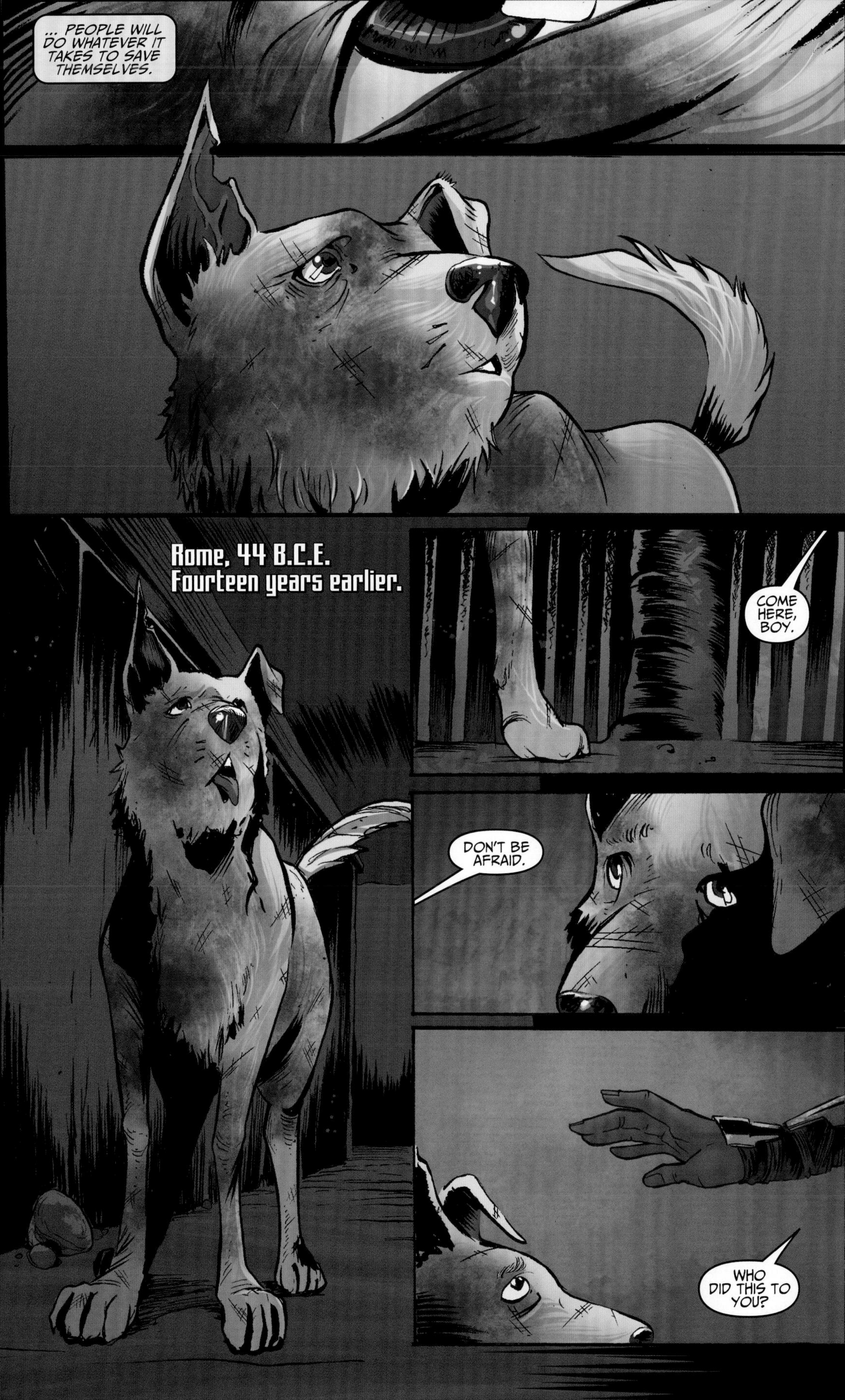
... PEOPLE WILL DO WHATEVER IT TAKES TO SAVE THEMSELVES.
Rome, 44 B.C.E.
Fourteen years earlier.
COME HERE, BOY.
DON'T BE AFRAID.
WHO DID THIS TO YOU?

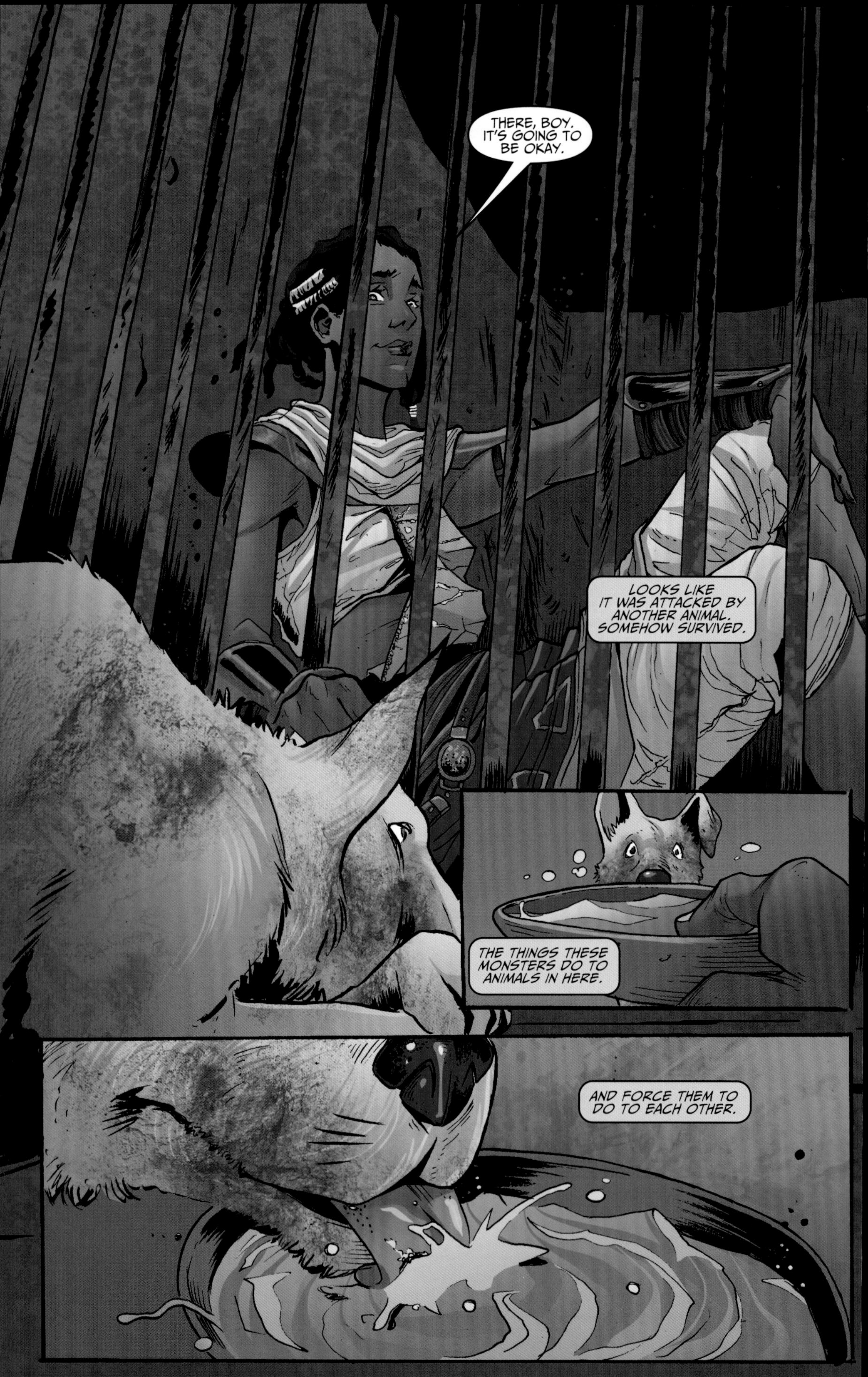
THERE, BOY. IT'S GOING TO BE OKAY.
LOOKS LIKE IT WAS ATTACKED BY ANOTHER ANIMAL. SOMEHOW SURVIVED.
THE THINGS THESE MONSTERS DO TO ANIMALS IN HERE.
AND FORCE THEM TO DO TO EACH OTHER.

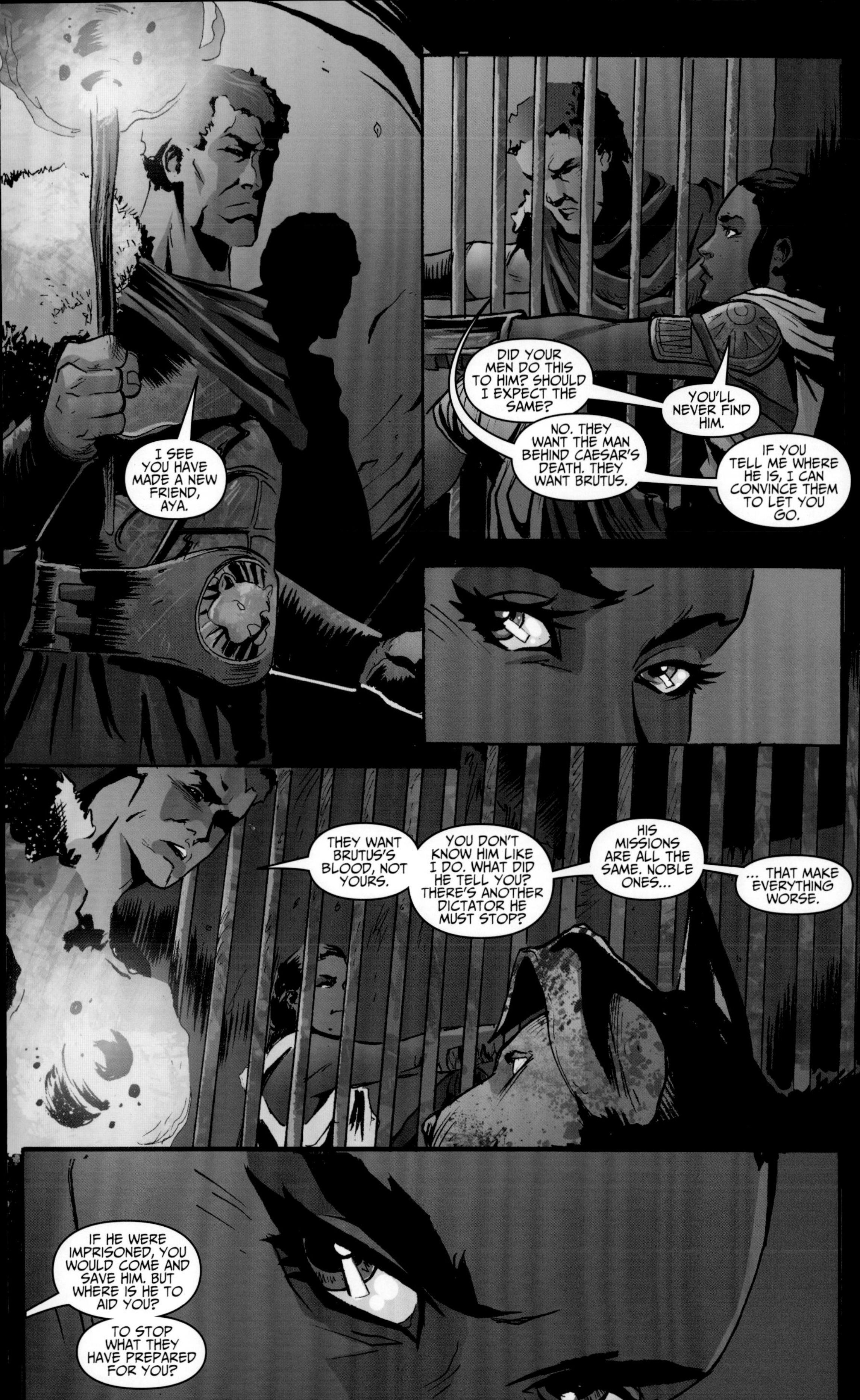
I SEE YOU HAVE MADE A NEW FRIEND, AYA.
DID YOUR MEN DO THIS TO HIM? SHOULD I EXPECT THE SAME?
NO. THEY WANT THE MAN BEHIND CAESAR'S DEATH. THEY WANT BRUTUS.
YOU'LL NEVER FIND HIM.
IF YOU TELL ME WHERE HE IS, I CAN CONVINCE THEM TO LET YOU GO.
THEY WANT BRUTUS'S BLOOD, NOT YOURS.
YOU DON'T KNOW HIM LIKE I DO. WHAT DID HE TELL YOU? THERE'S ANOTHER DICTATOR HE MUST STOP?
HIS MISSIONS ARE ALL THE SAME. NOBLE ONES...
... THAT MAKE EVERYTHING WORSE.
IF HE WERE IMPRISONED, YOU WOULD COME AND SAVE HIM. BUT WHERE IS HE TO AID YOU?
TO STOP WHAT THEY HAVE PREPARED FOR YOU?

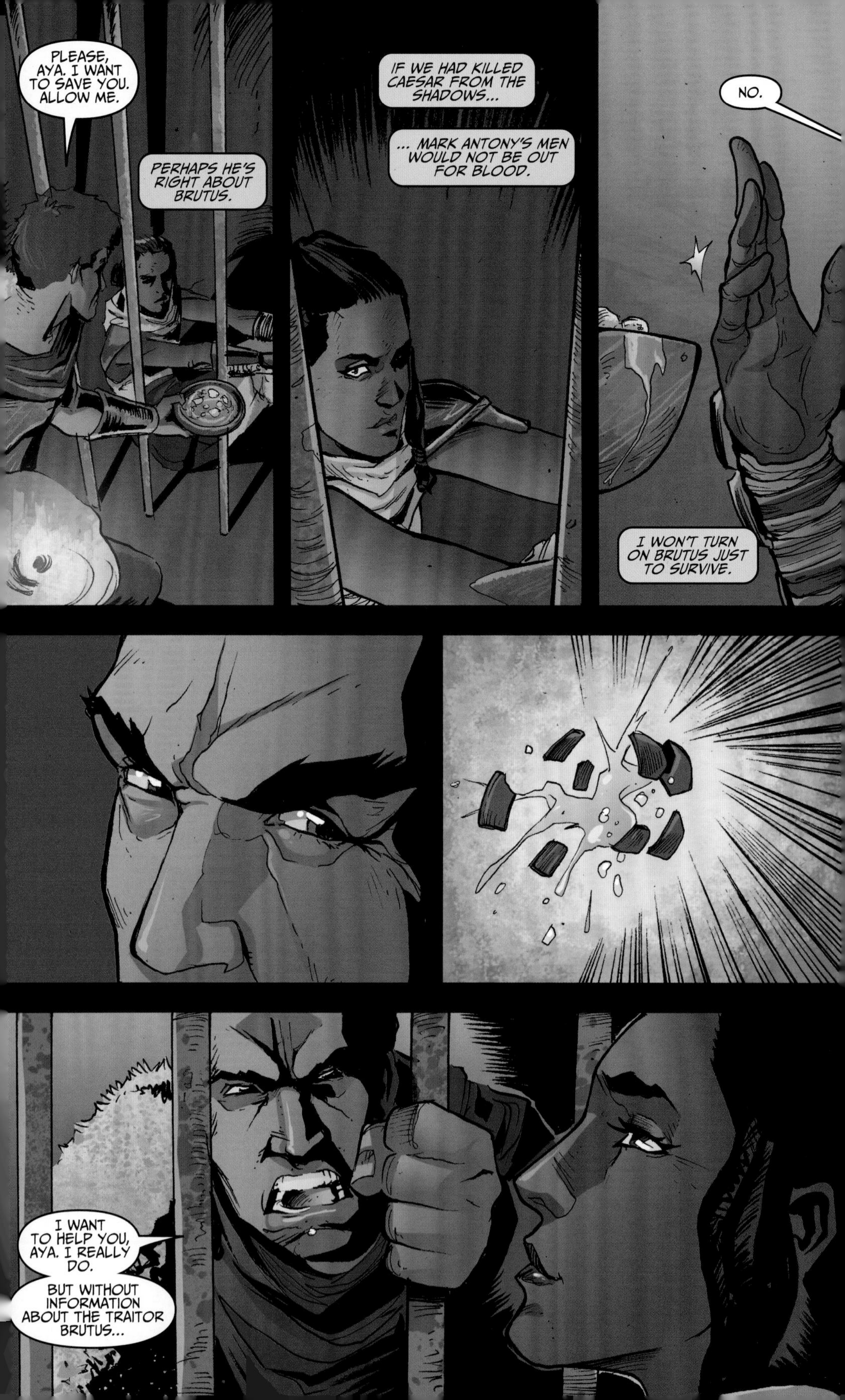
PLEASE, AYA. I WANT TO SAVE YOU. ALLOW ME.
PERHAPS HE'S RIGHT ABOUT BRUTUS.
IF WE HAD KILLED CAESAR FROM THE SHADOWS...
... MARK ANTONY'S MEN WOULD NOT BE OUT FOR BLOOD.
NO.
I WON'T TURN ON BRUTUS JUST TO SURVIVE.
I WANT TO HELP YOU, AYA. I REALLY DO.
BUT WITHOUT INFORMATION ABOUT THE TRAITOR BRUTUS...

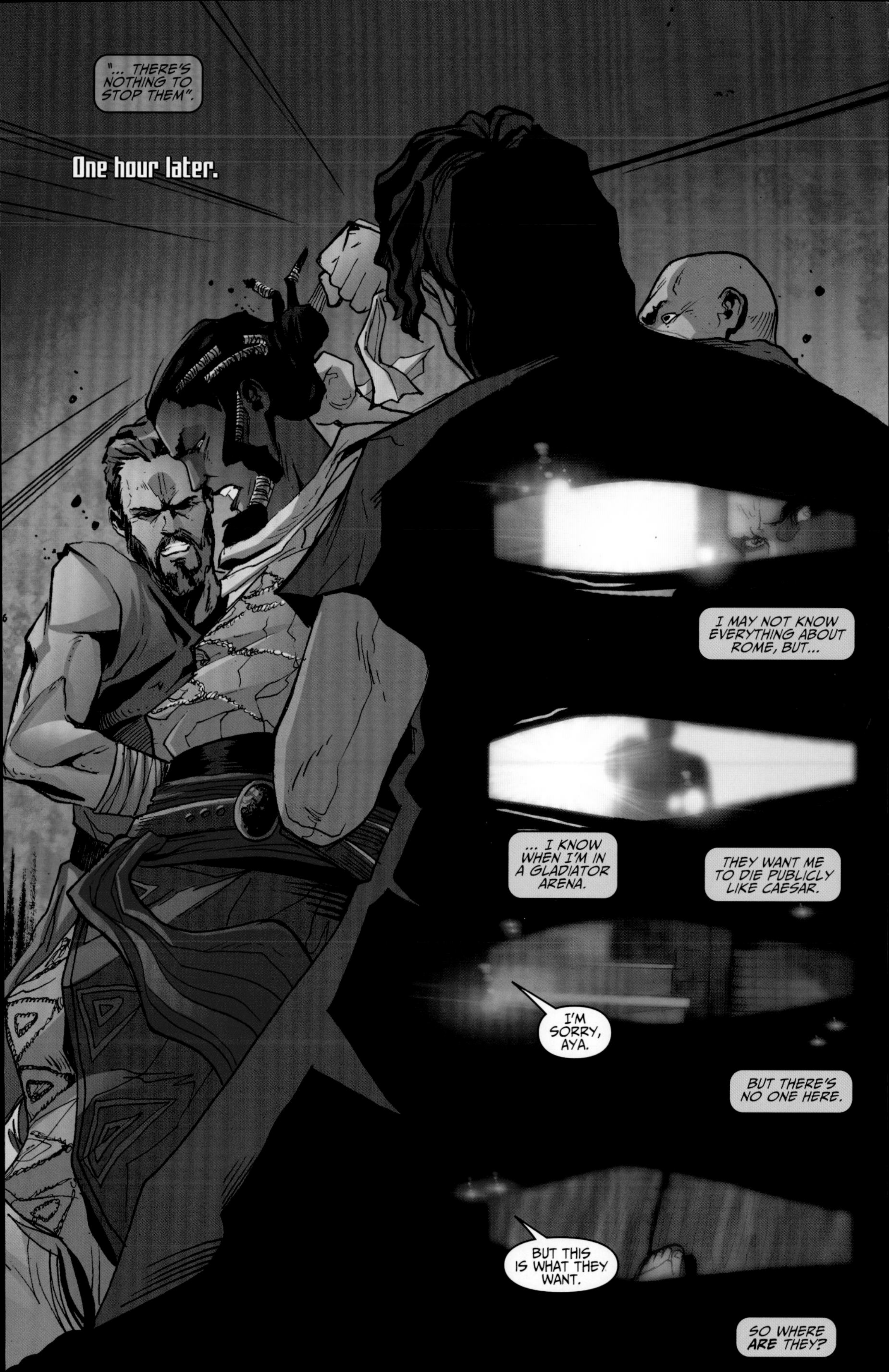
"... THERE'S NOTHING TO STOP THEM".
One hour later.
I MAY NOT KNOW EVERYTHING ABOUT ROME, BUT...
... I KNOW WHEN I'M IN A GLADIATOR ARENA.
THEY WANT ME TO DIE PUBLICLY LIKE CAESAR.
I'M SORRY, AYA.
BUT THERE'S NO ONE HERE.
BUT THIS IS WHAT THEY WANT.
SO WHERE **ARE** THEY?

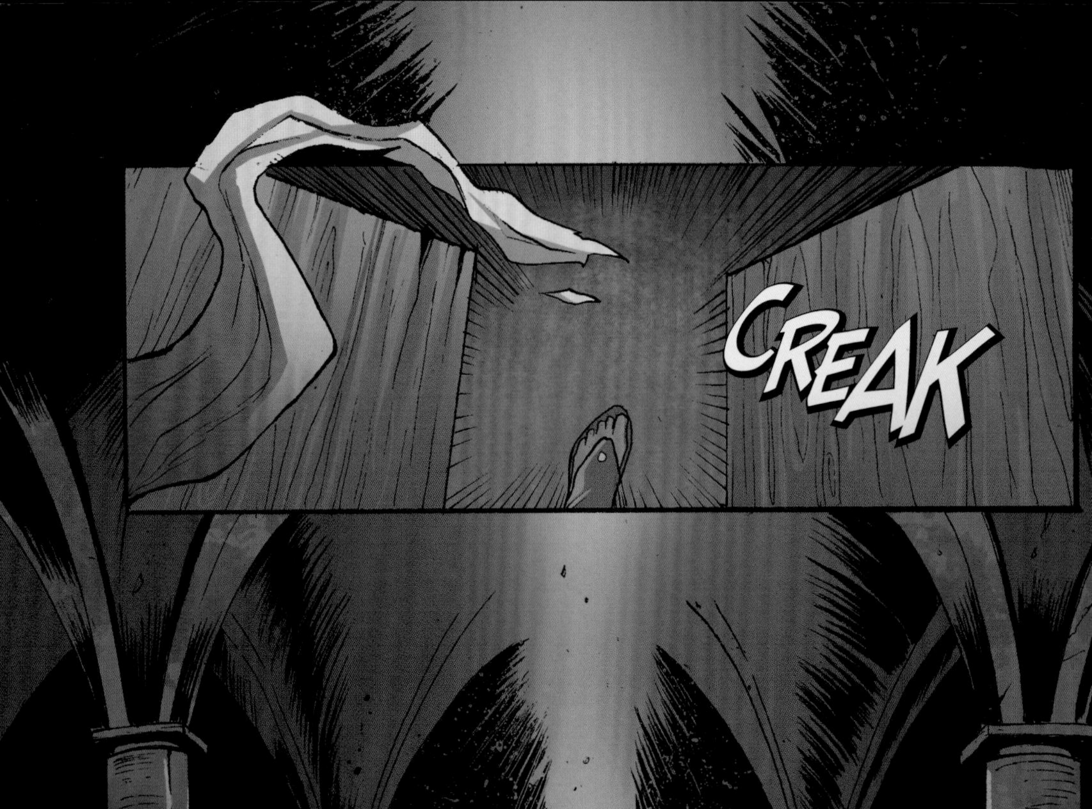
CREAK

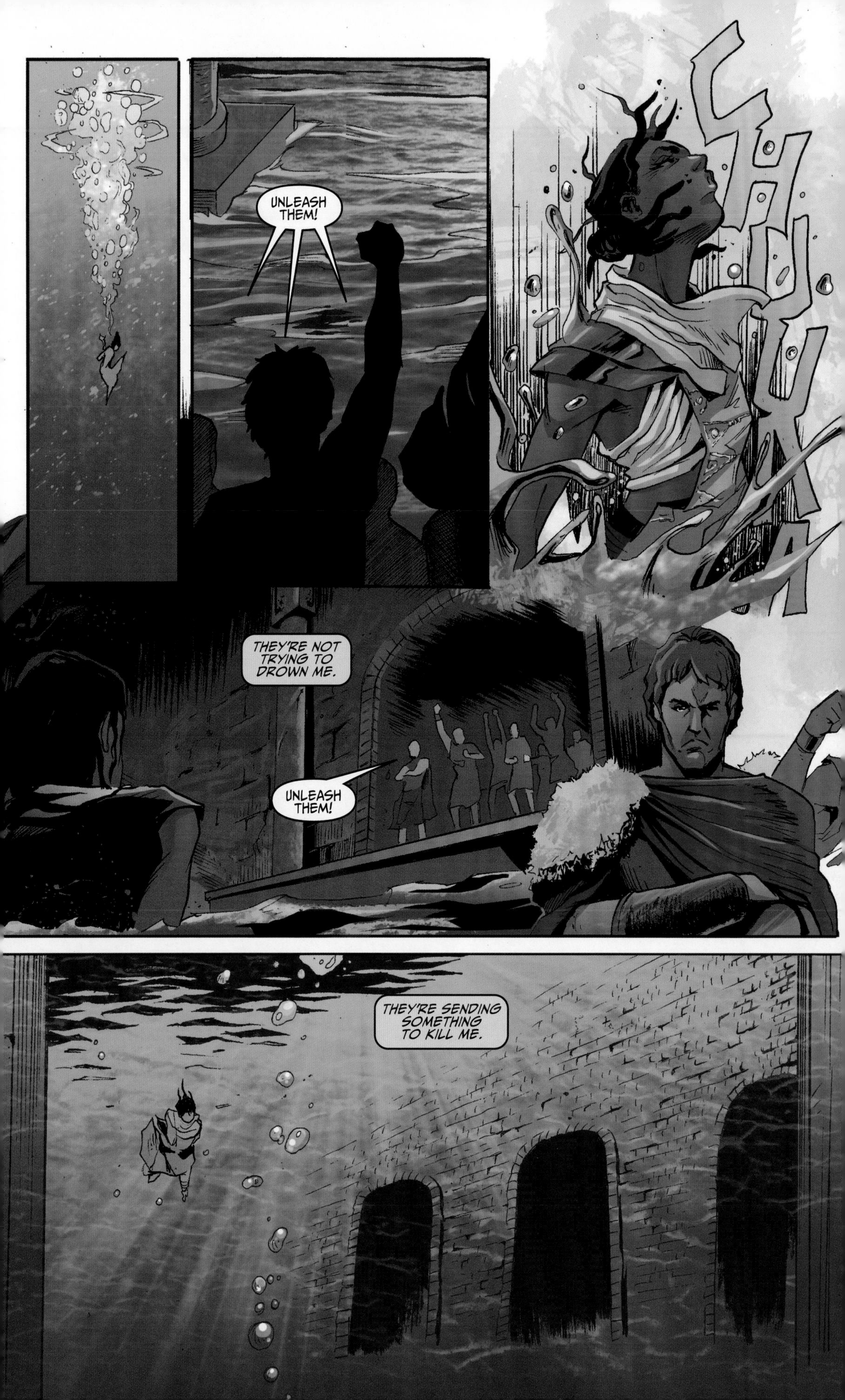
UNLEASH THEM!
THEY'RE NOT TRYING TO DROWN ME.
UNLEASH THEM!
THEY'RE SENDING SOMETHING TO KILL ME.

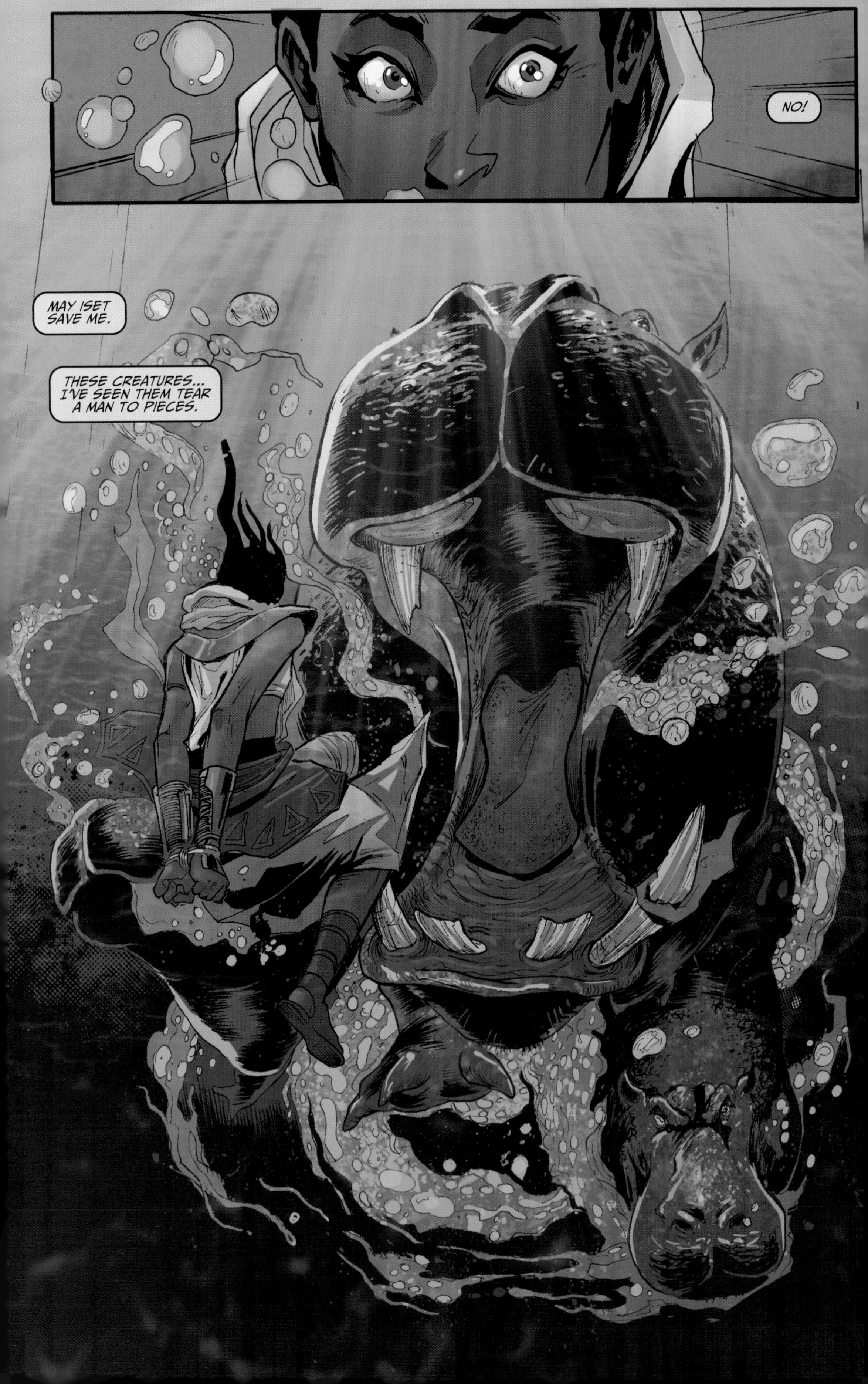
NO!
MAY ISET SAVE ME.
THESE CREATURES... I'VE SEEN THEM TEAR A MAN TO PIECES.

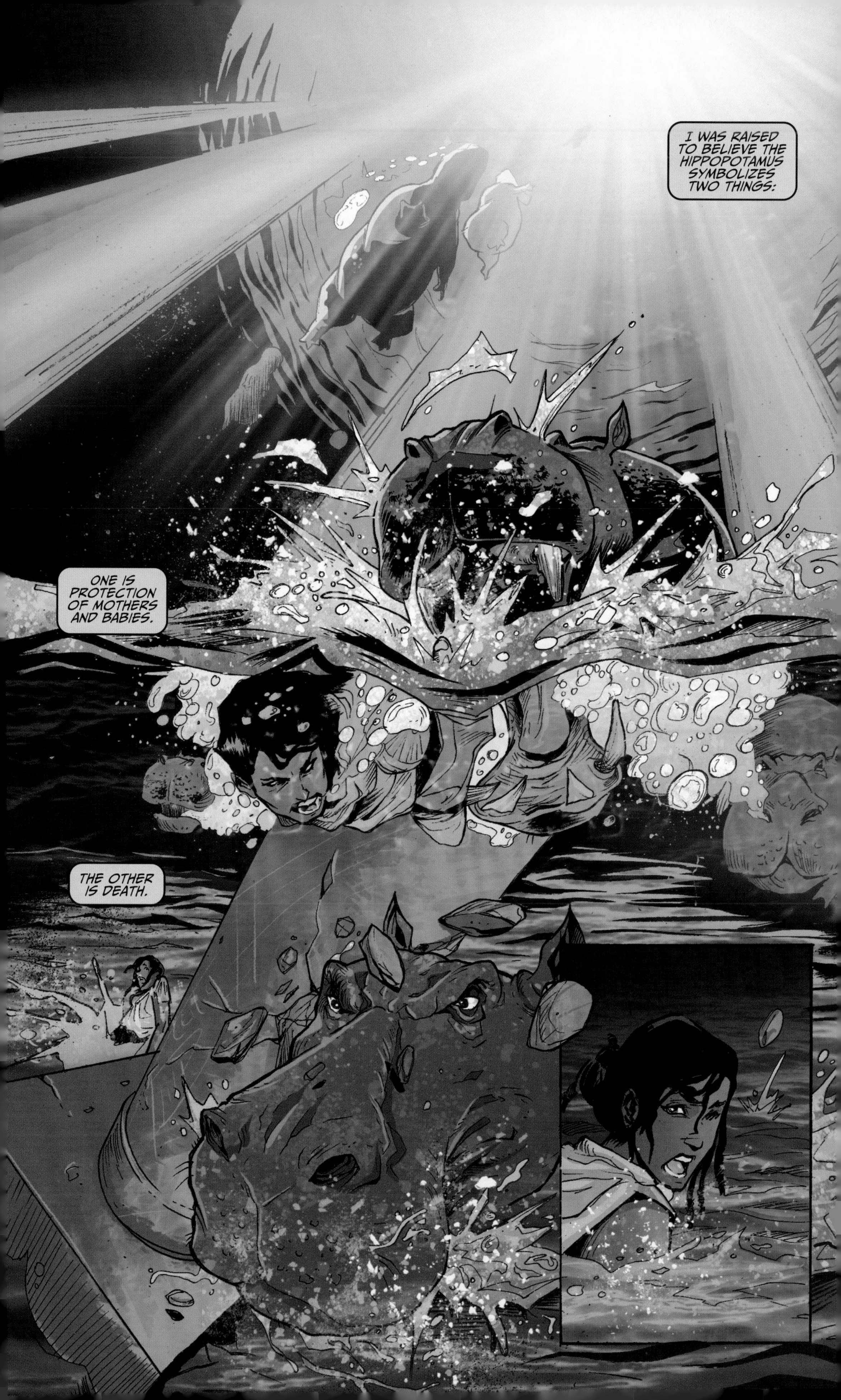
I WAS RAISED TO BELIEVE THE HIPPOPOTAMUS SYMBOLIZES TWO THINGS:
ONE IS PROTECTION OF MOTHERS AND BABIES.
THE OTHER IS DEATH.

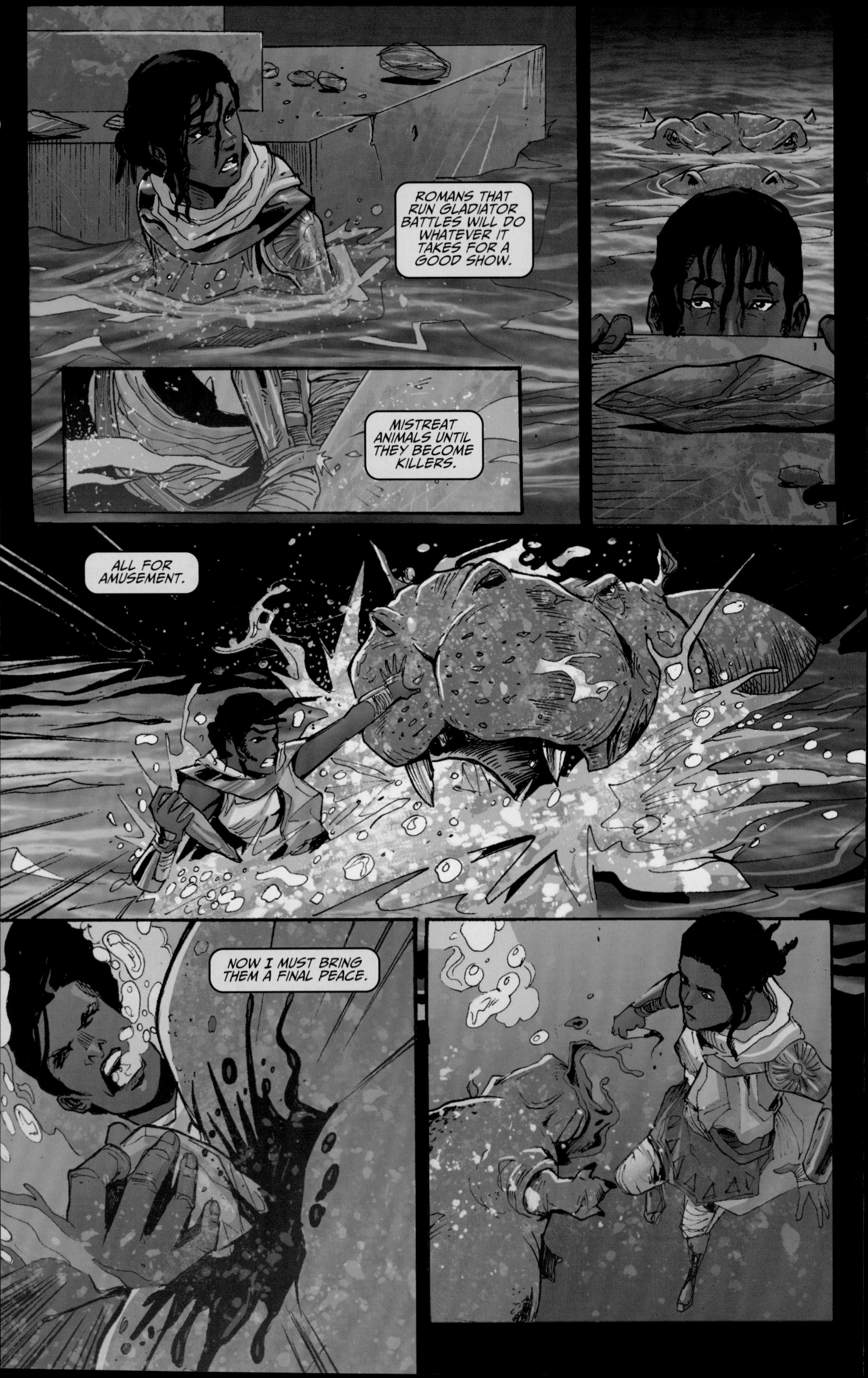
ROMANS THAT RUN GLADIATOR BATTLES WILL DO WHATEVER IT TAKES FOR A GOOD SHOW.
MISTREAT ANIMALS UNTIL THEY BECOME KILLERS.
ALL FOR AMUSEMENT.
NOW I MUST BRING THEM A FINAL PEACE.

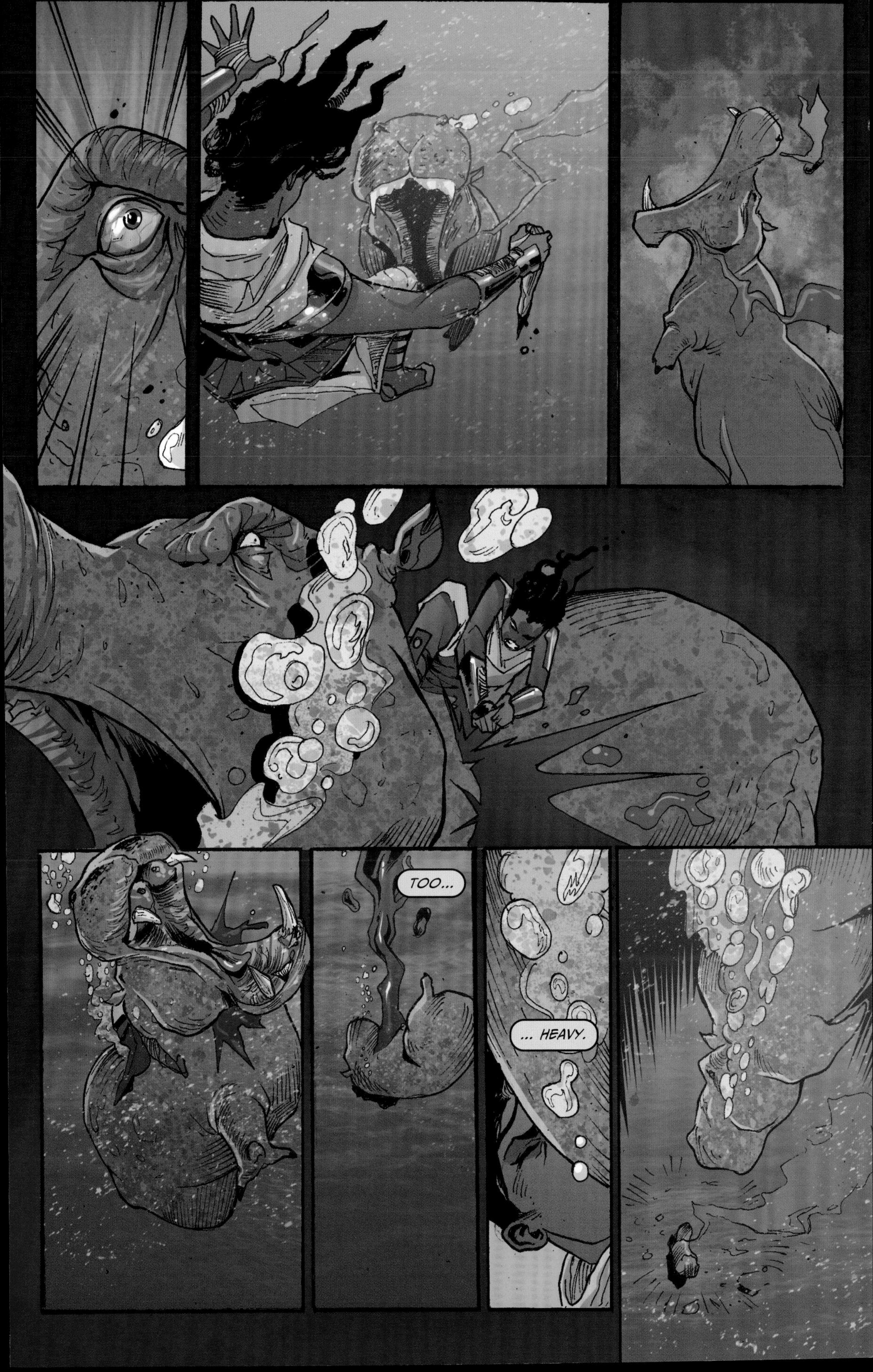
TOO...
... HEAVY.

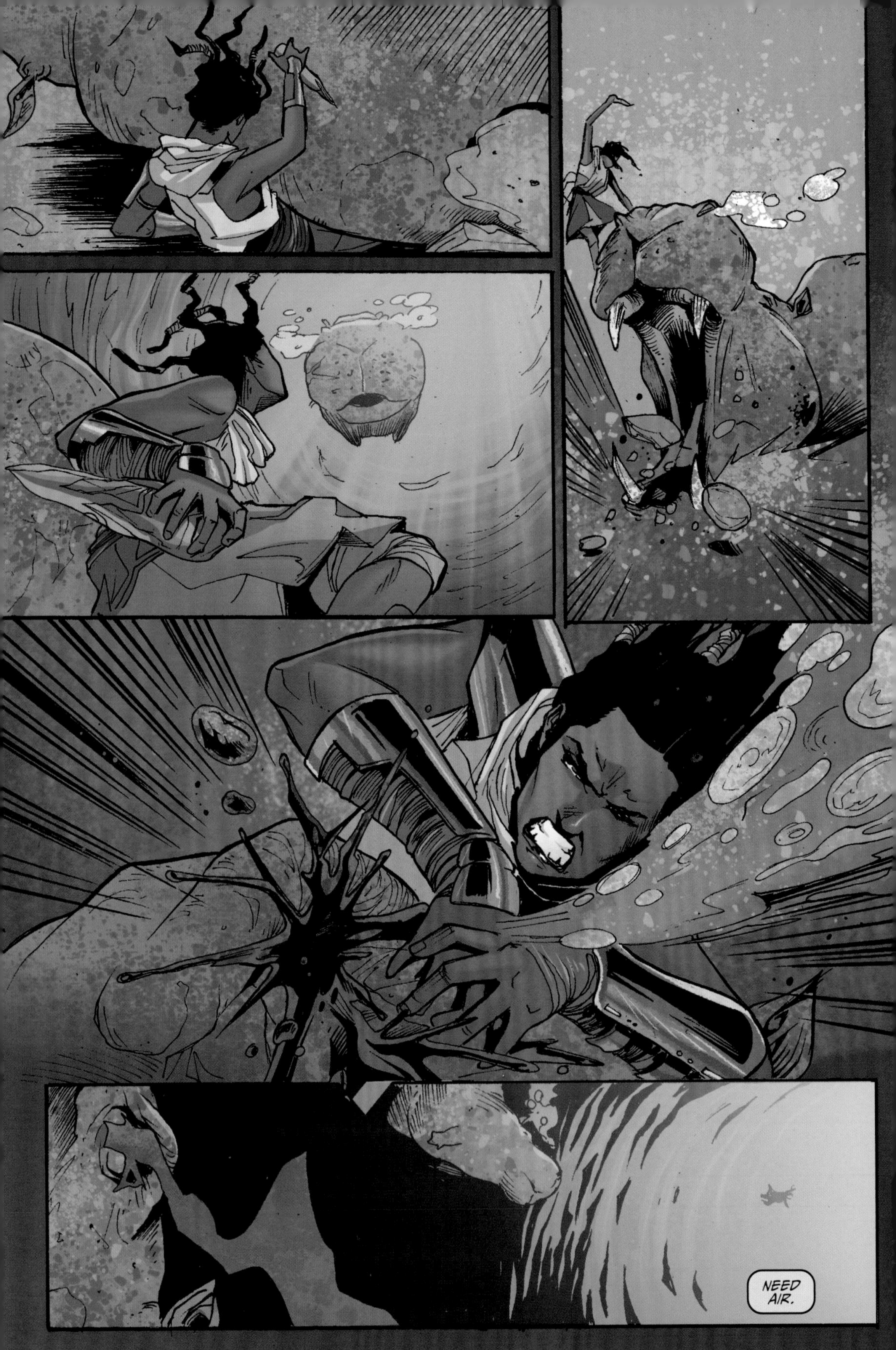
NEED AIR.

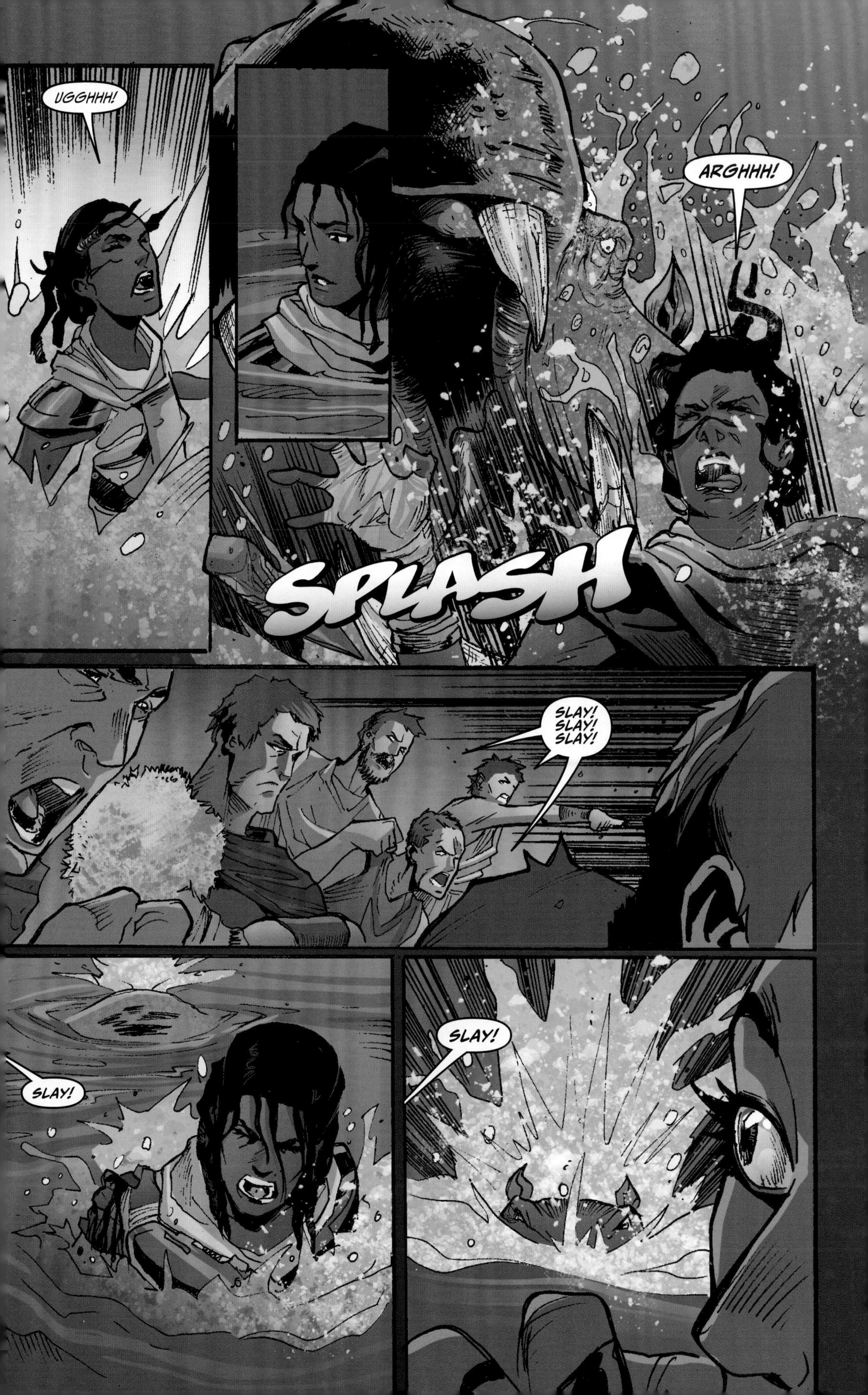
UGGHHH!
ARGHHH!
SPLASH
SLAY! SLAY! SLAY!
SLAY!
SLAY!

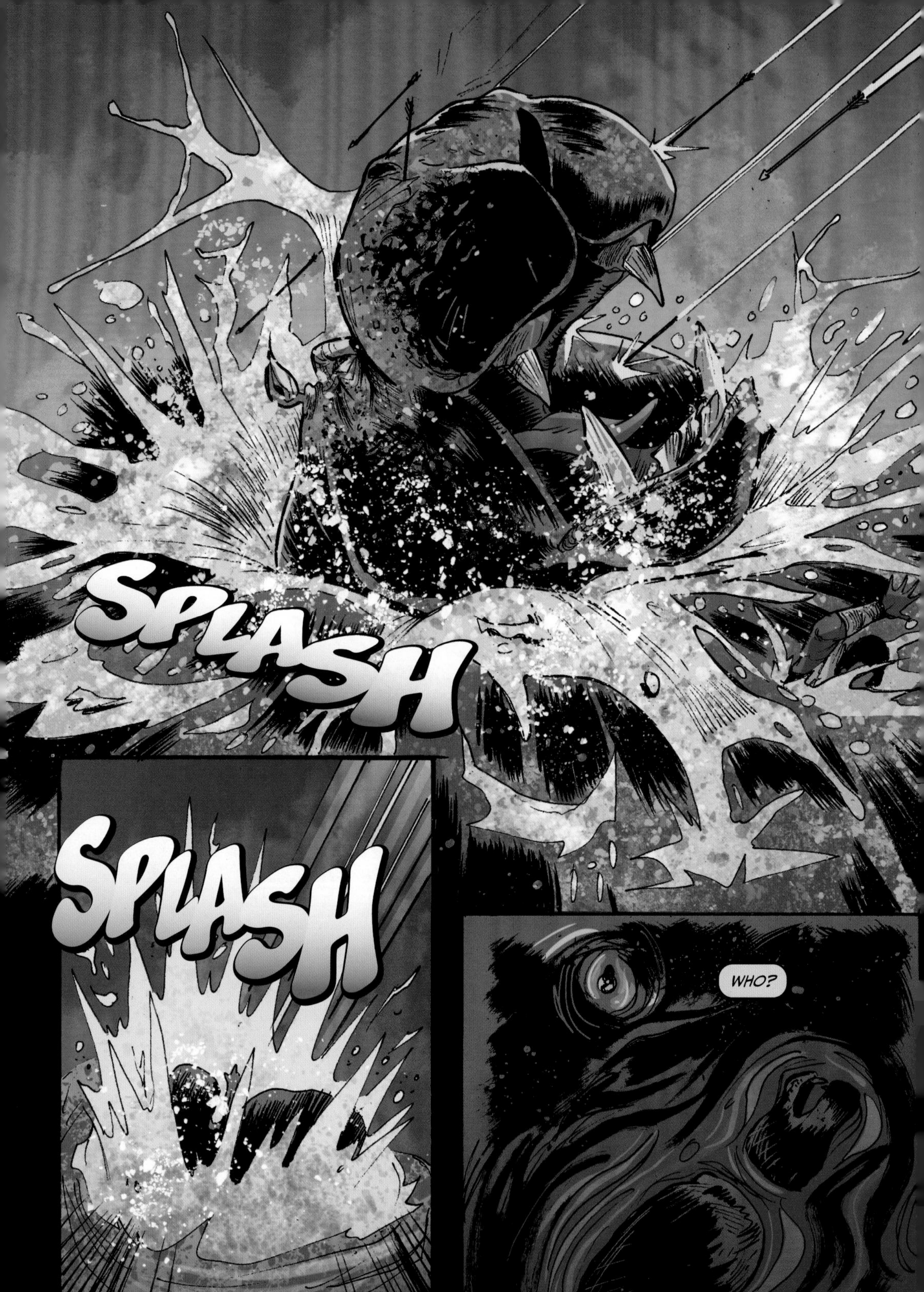
SPLASH
SPLASH
WHO?

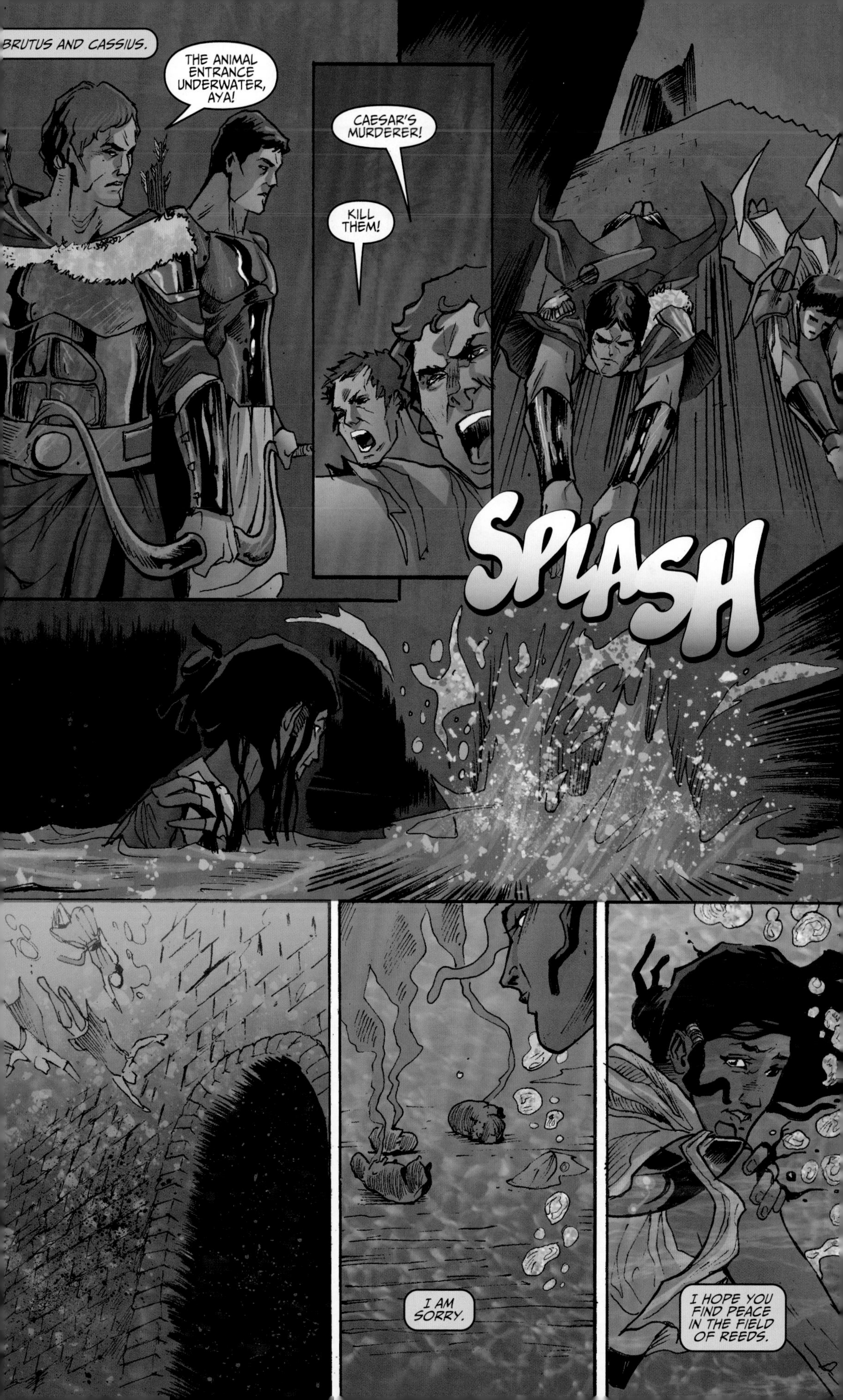
BRUTUS AND CASSIUS.
THE ANIMAL ENTRANCE UNDERWATER, AYA!
CAESAR'S MURDERER!
KILL THEM!
SPLASH
I AM SORRY.
I HOPE YOU FIND PEACE IN THE FIELD OF REEDS.

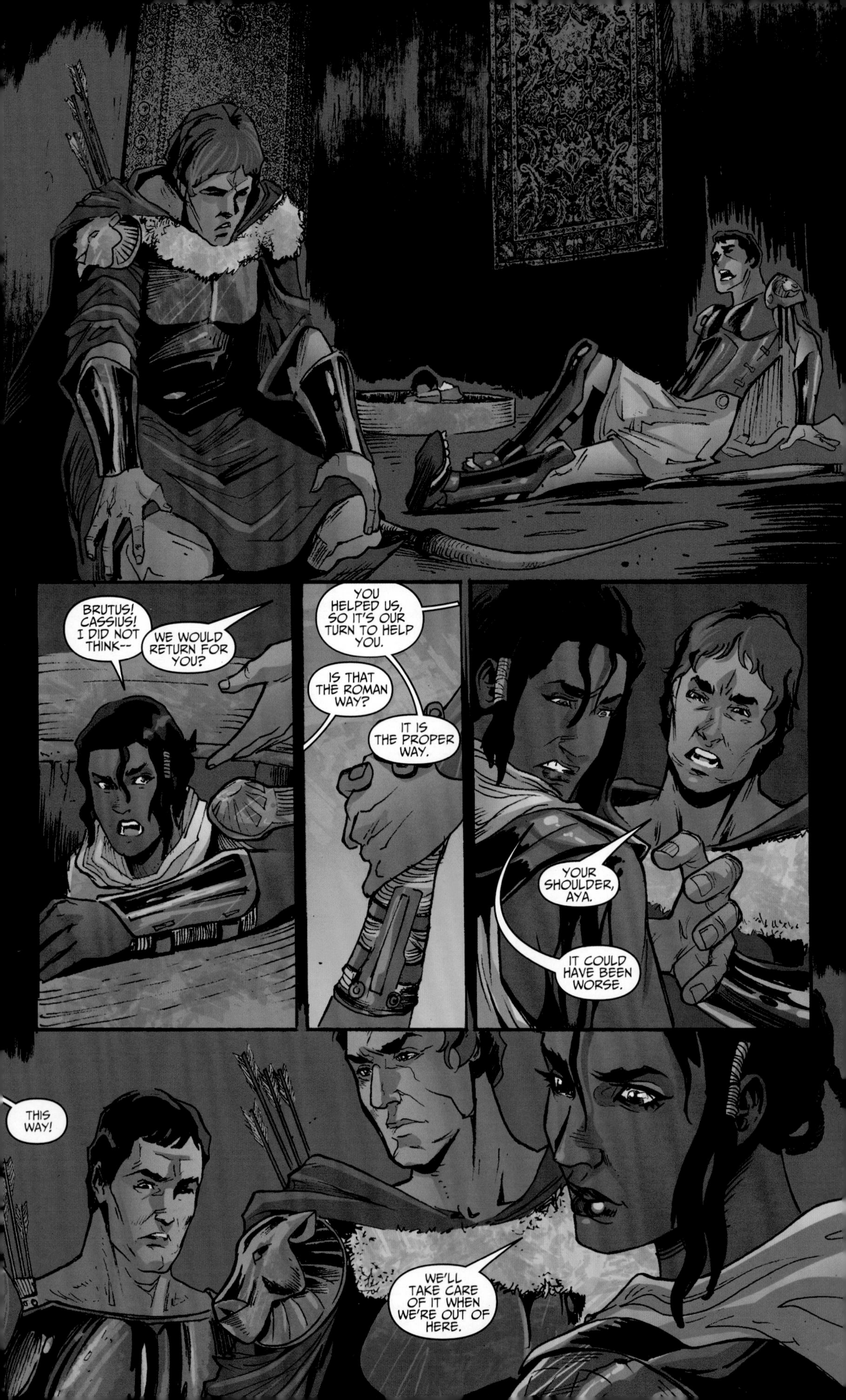
BRUTUS! CASSIUS! I DID NOT THINK--
WE WOULD RETURN FOR YOU?
YOU HELPED US, SO IT'S OUR TURN TO HELP YOU.
IS THAT THE ROMAN WAY?
IT IS THE PROPER WAY.
YOUR SHOULDER, AYA.
IT COULD HAVE BEEN WORSE.
THIS WAY!
WE'LL TAKE CARE OF IT WHEN WE'RE OUT OF HERE.

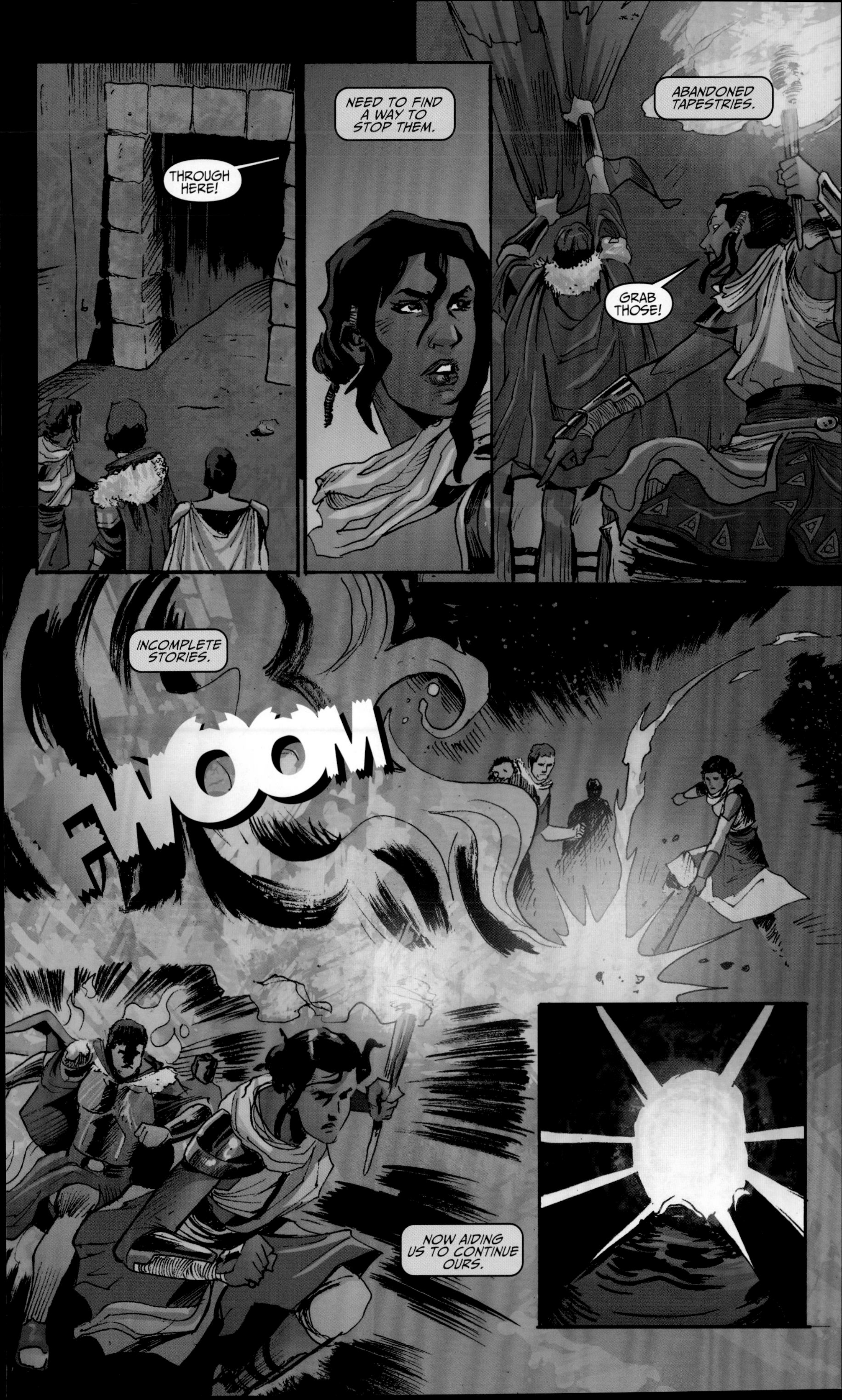
THROUGH HERE!
NEED TO FIND A WAY TO STOP THEM.
ABANDONED TAPESTRIES.
GRAB THOSE!
INCOMPLETE STORIES.
FWOOM
NOW AIDING US TO CONTINUE OURS.

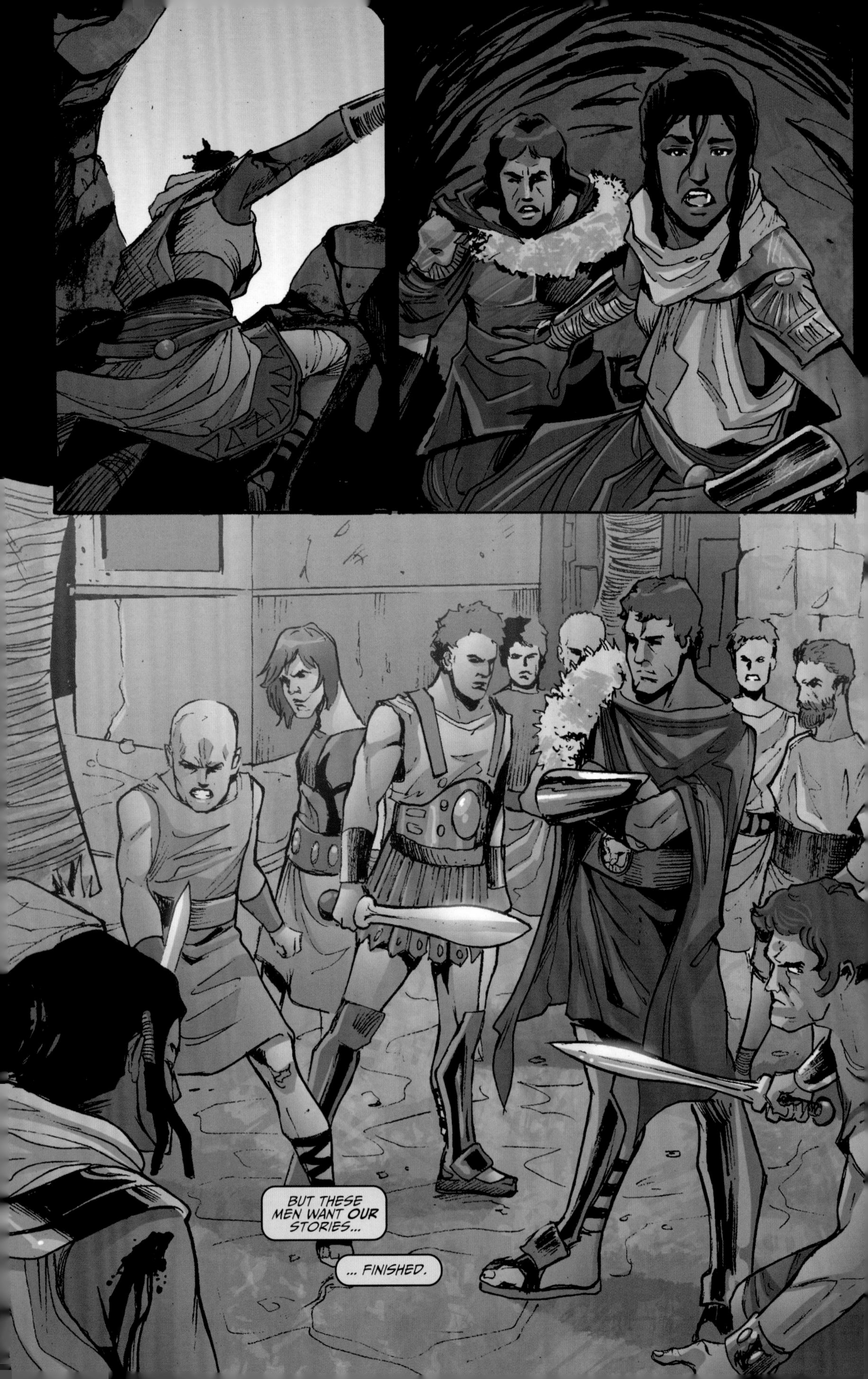
BUT THESE MEN WANT OUR STORIES...
... FINISHED.

CHAPTER 4

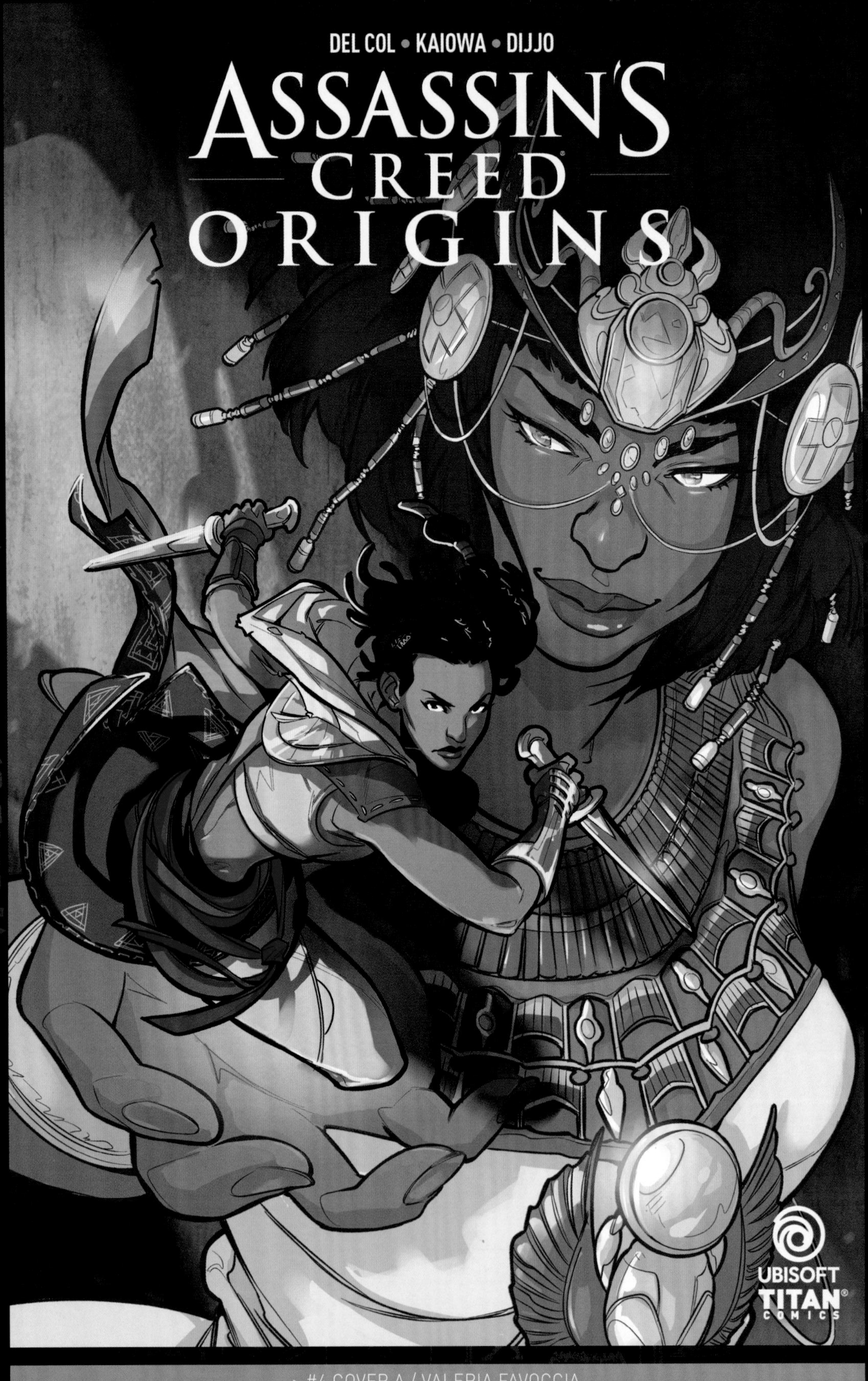
DEL COL • KAIOWA • DIJJO
ASSASSIN'S CREED ORIGINS
UBISOFT
TITAN COMICS

> #4 COVER A / VALERIA FAVOCCIA

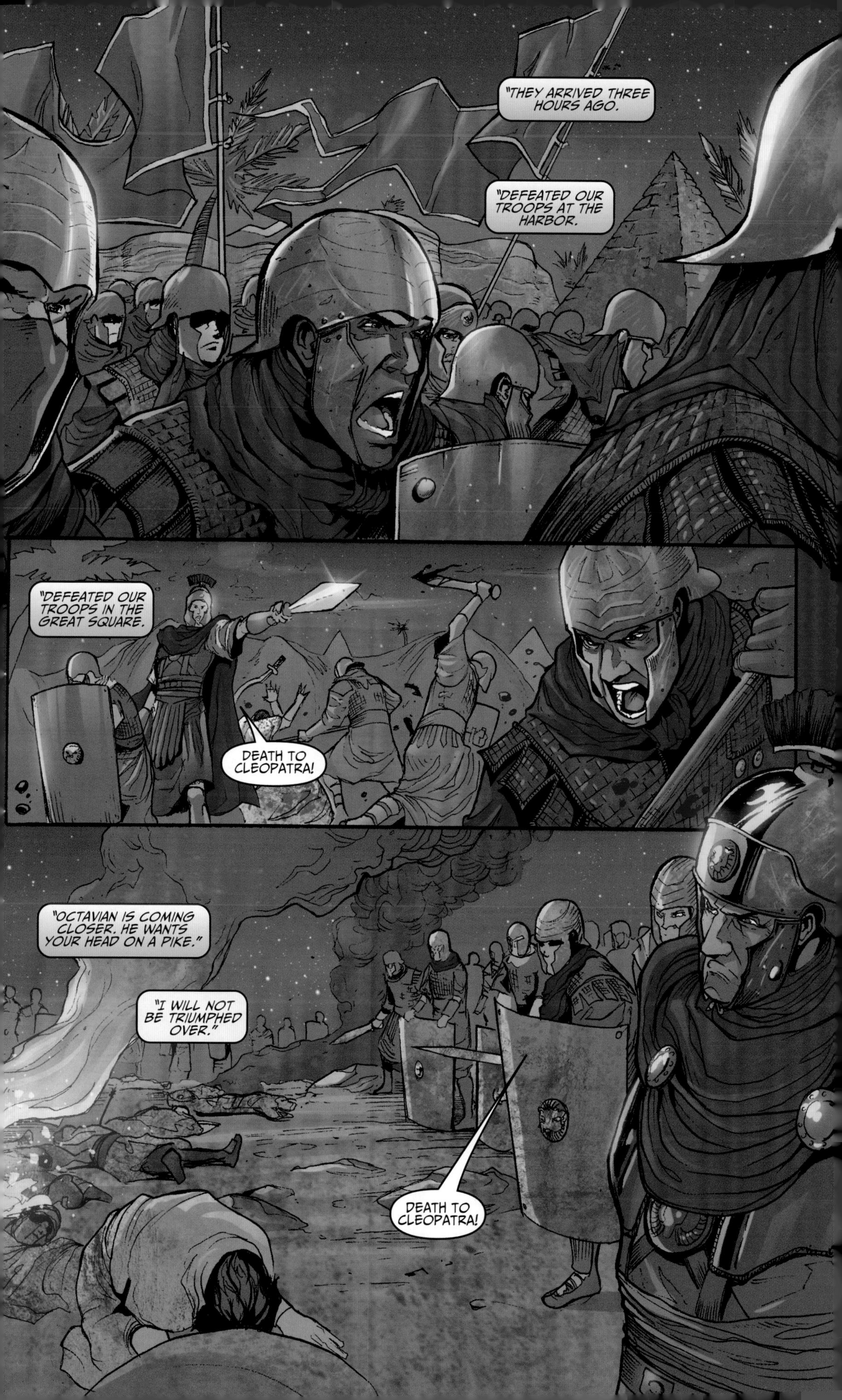
"THEY ARRIVED THREE HOURS AGO.
"DEFEATED OUR TROOPS AT THE HARBOR.
"DEFEATED OUR TROOPS IN THE GREAT SQUARE.
DEATH TO CLEOPATRA!
"OCTAVIAN IS COMING CLOSER. HE WANTS YOUR HEAD ON A PIKE."
"I WILL NOT BE TRIUMPHED OVER."
DEATH TO CLEOPATRA!

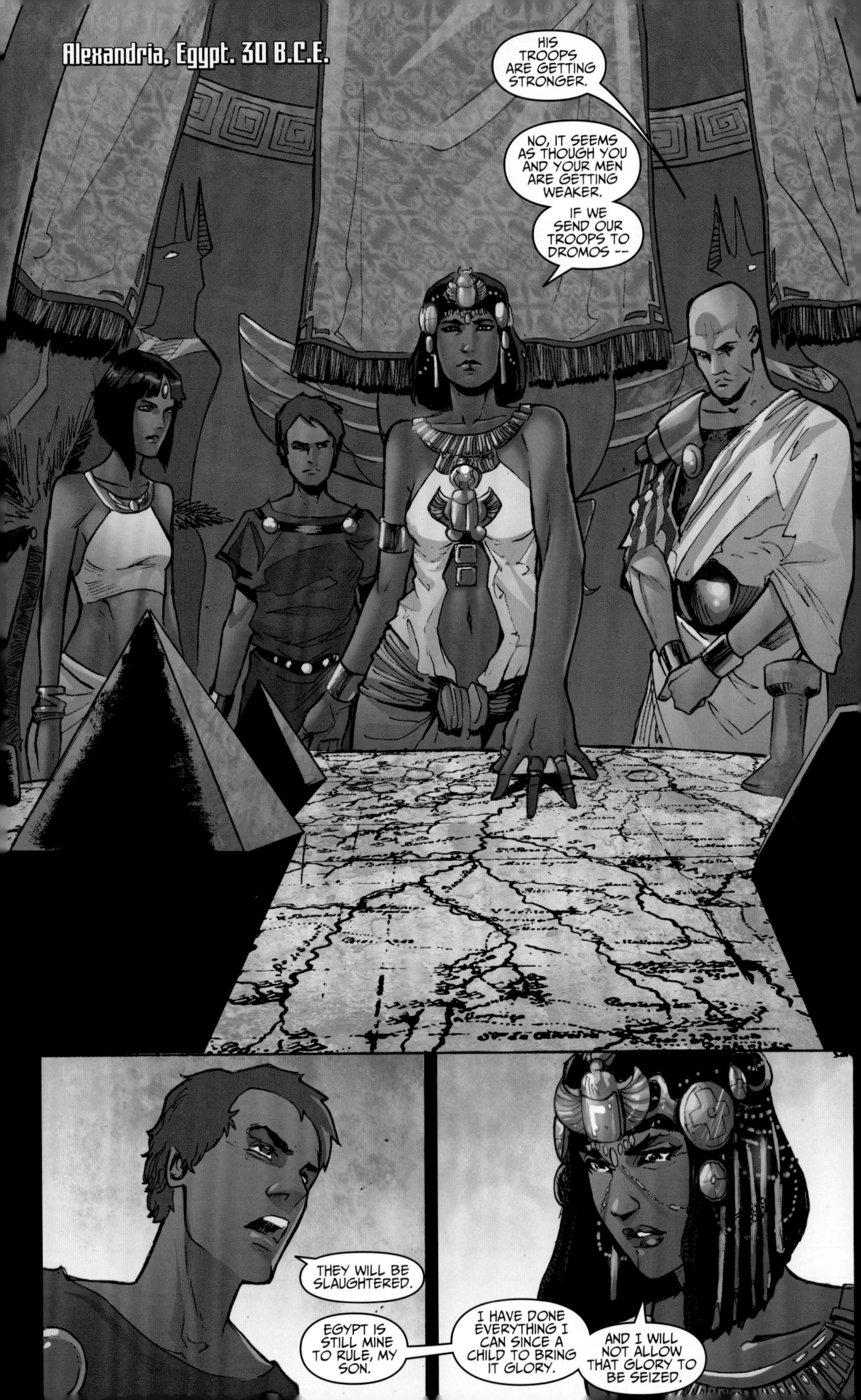
Alexandria, Egypt. 30 B.C.E.
HIS TROOPS ARE GETTING STRONGER.
NO, IT SEEMS AS THOUGH YOU AND YOUR MEN ARE GETTING WEAKER.
IF WE SEND OUR TROOPS TO DROMOS --
THEY WILL BE SLAUGHTERED.
EGYPT IS STILL MINE TO RULE, MY SON.
I HAVE DONE EVERYTHING I CAN SINCE A CHILD TO BRING IT GLORY.
AND I WILL NOT ALLOW THAT GLORY TO BE SEIZED.

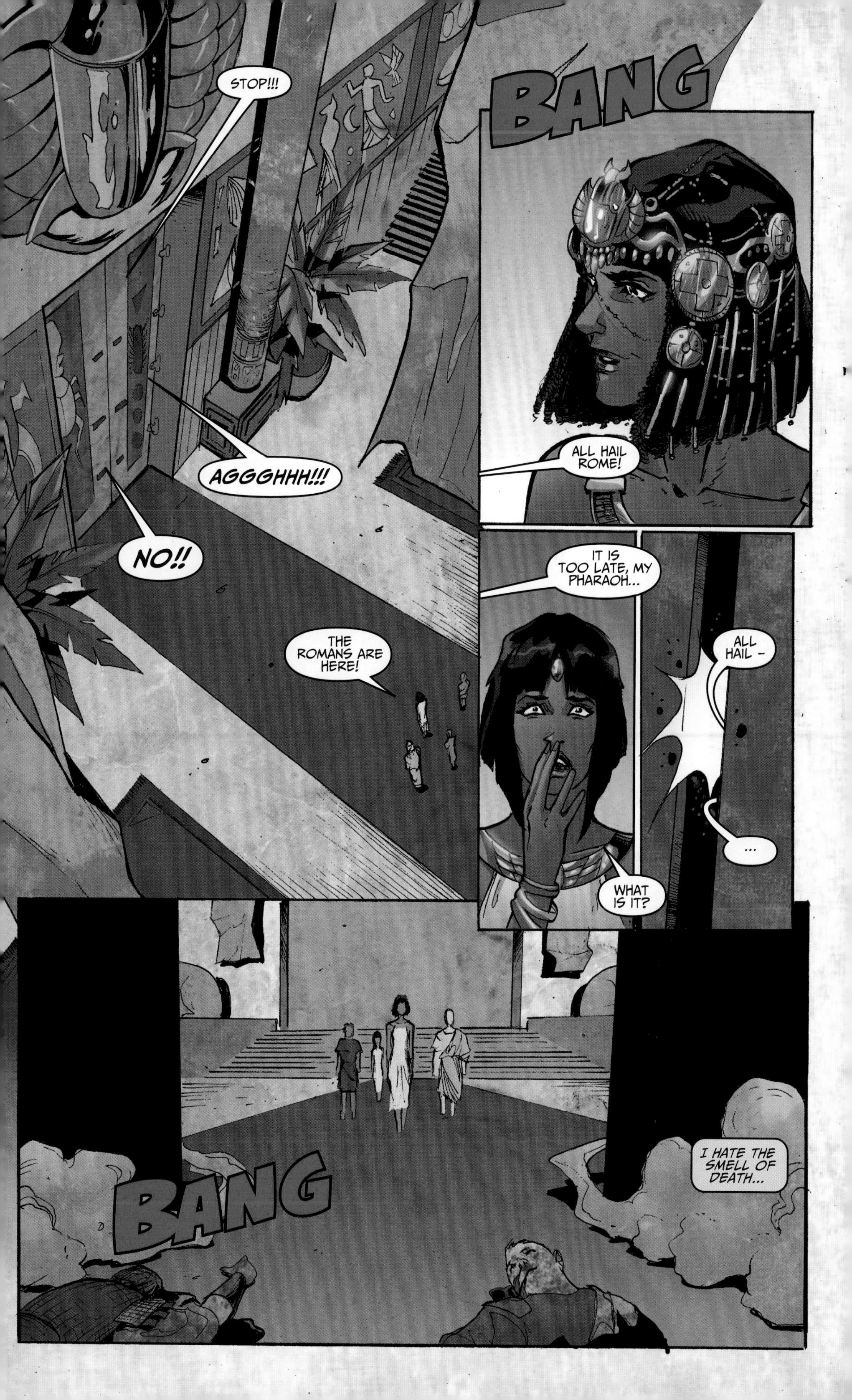
STOP!!!
AGGGHHH!!!
NO!!
THE ROMANS ARE HERE!
BANG
ALL HAIL ROME!
IT IS TOO LATE, MY PHARAOH...
ALL HAIL -
...
WHAT IS IT?
BANG
I HATE THE SMELL OF DEATH...

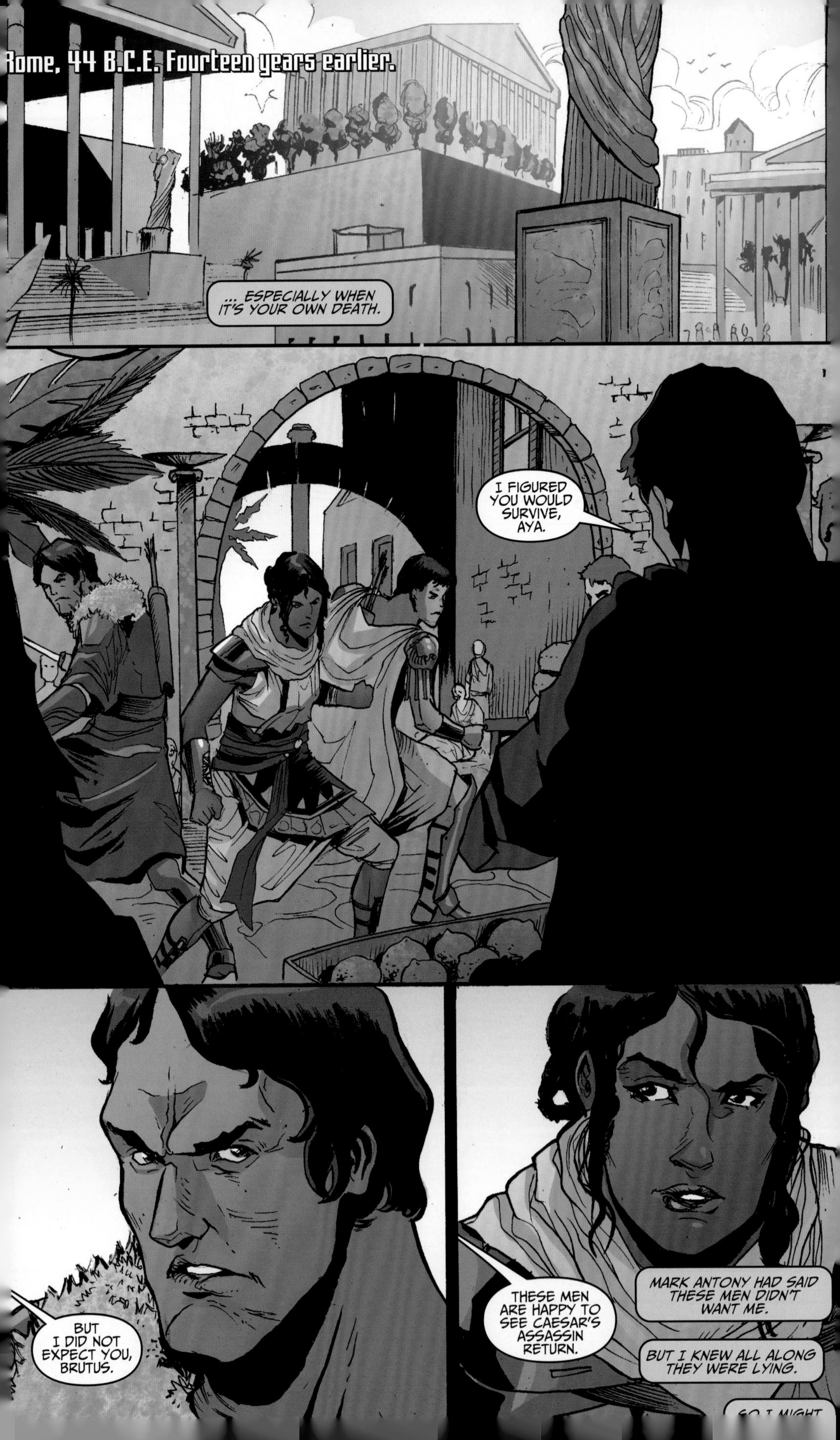
Rome, 44 B.C.E. Fourteen years earlier.
... ESPECIALLY WHEN IT'S YOUR OWN DEATH.
I FIGURED YOU WOULD SURVIVE, AYA.
BUT I DID NOT EXPECT YOU, BRUTUS.
THESE MEN ARE HAPPY TO SEE CAESAR'S ASSASSIN RETURN.
MARK ANTONY HAD SAID THESE MEN DIDN'T WANT ME.
BUT I KNEW ALL ALONG THEY WERE LYING.

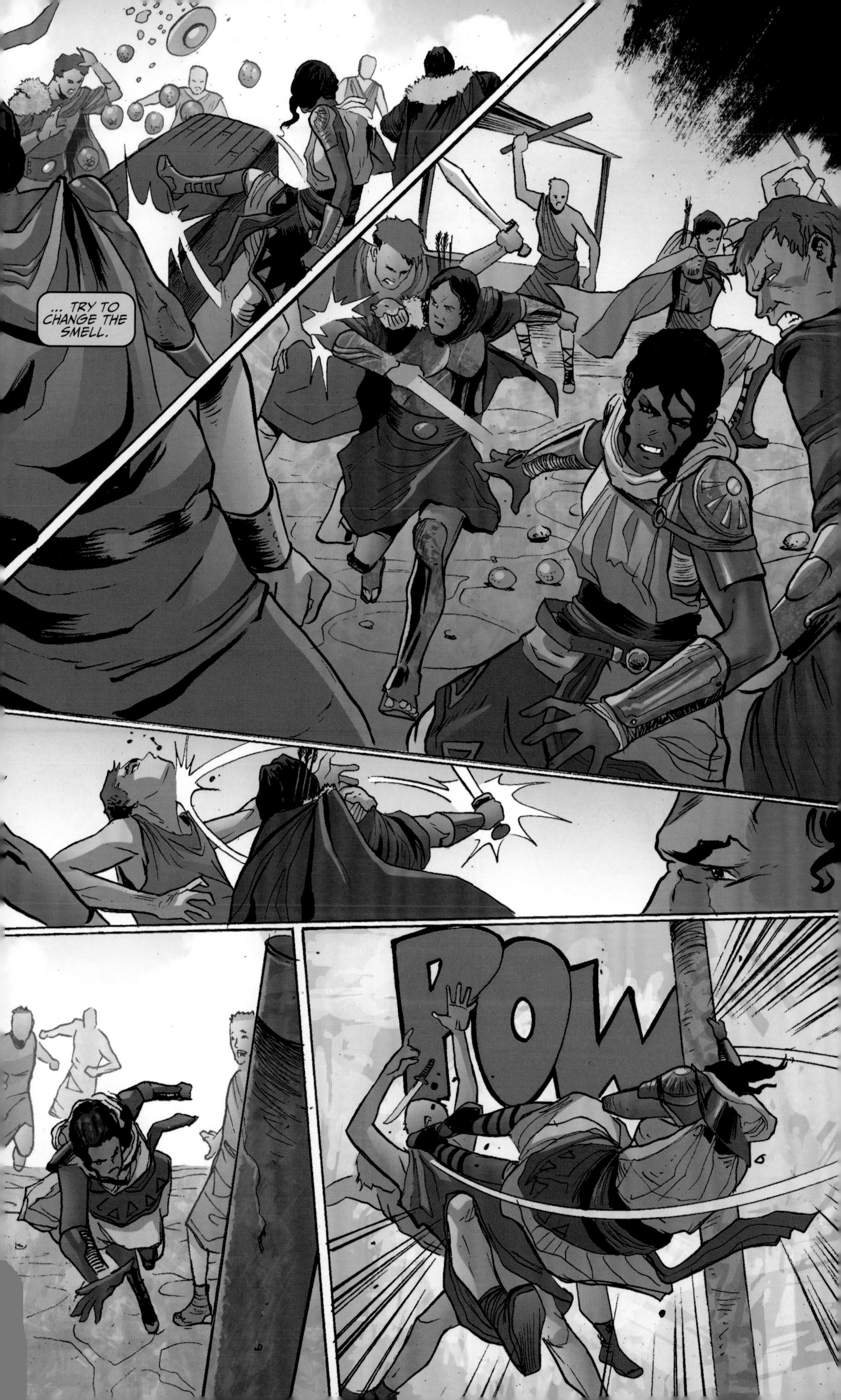
... TRY TO CHANGE THE SMELL.
POW

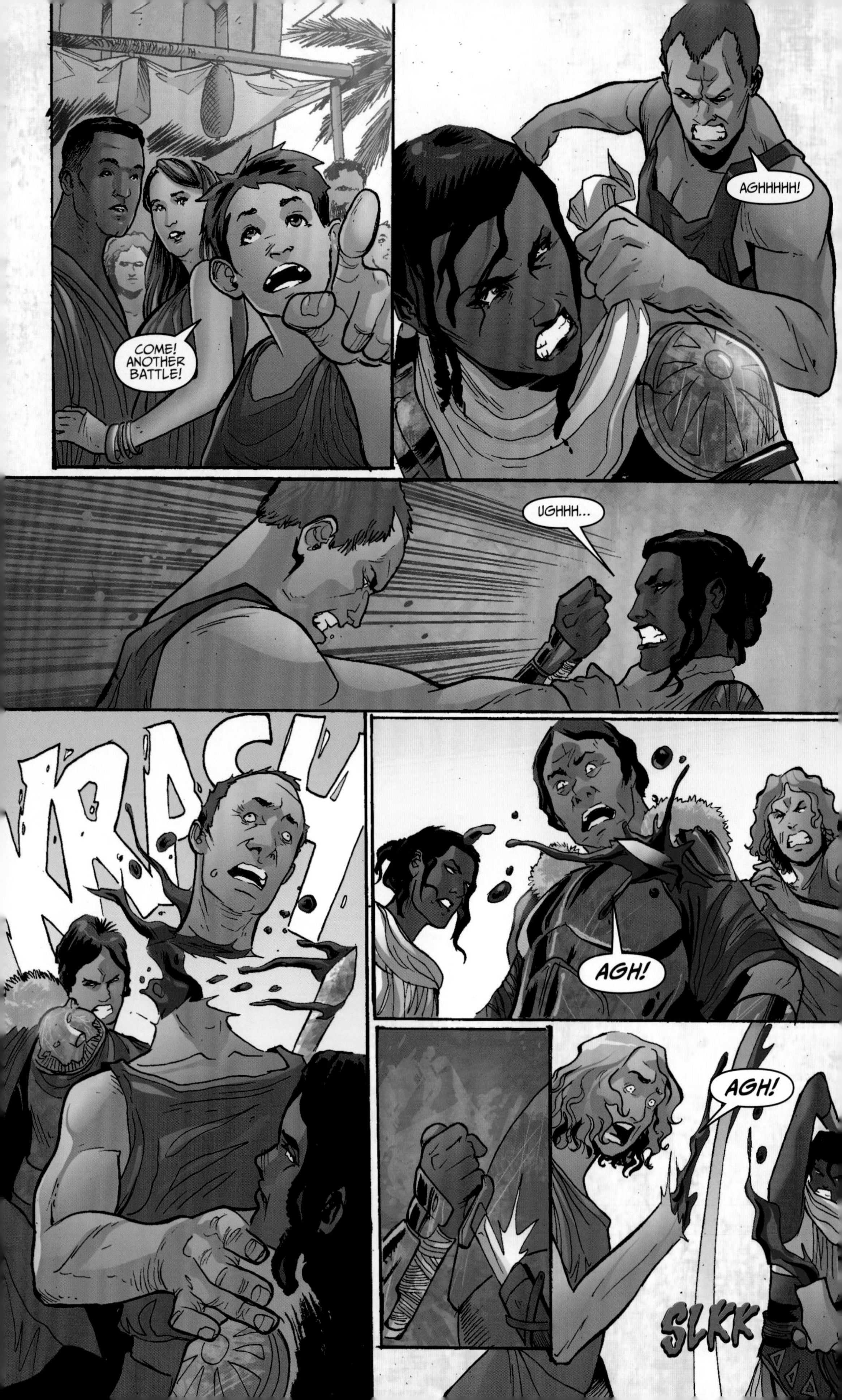
COME! ANOTHER BATTLE!
AGHHHHH!
UGHHH...
KRASH
AGH!
AGH!
SLKK

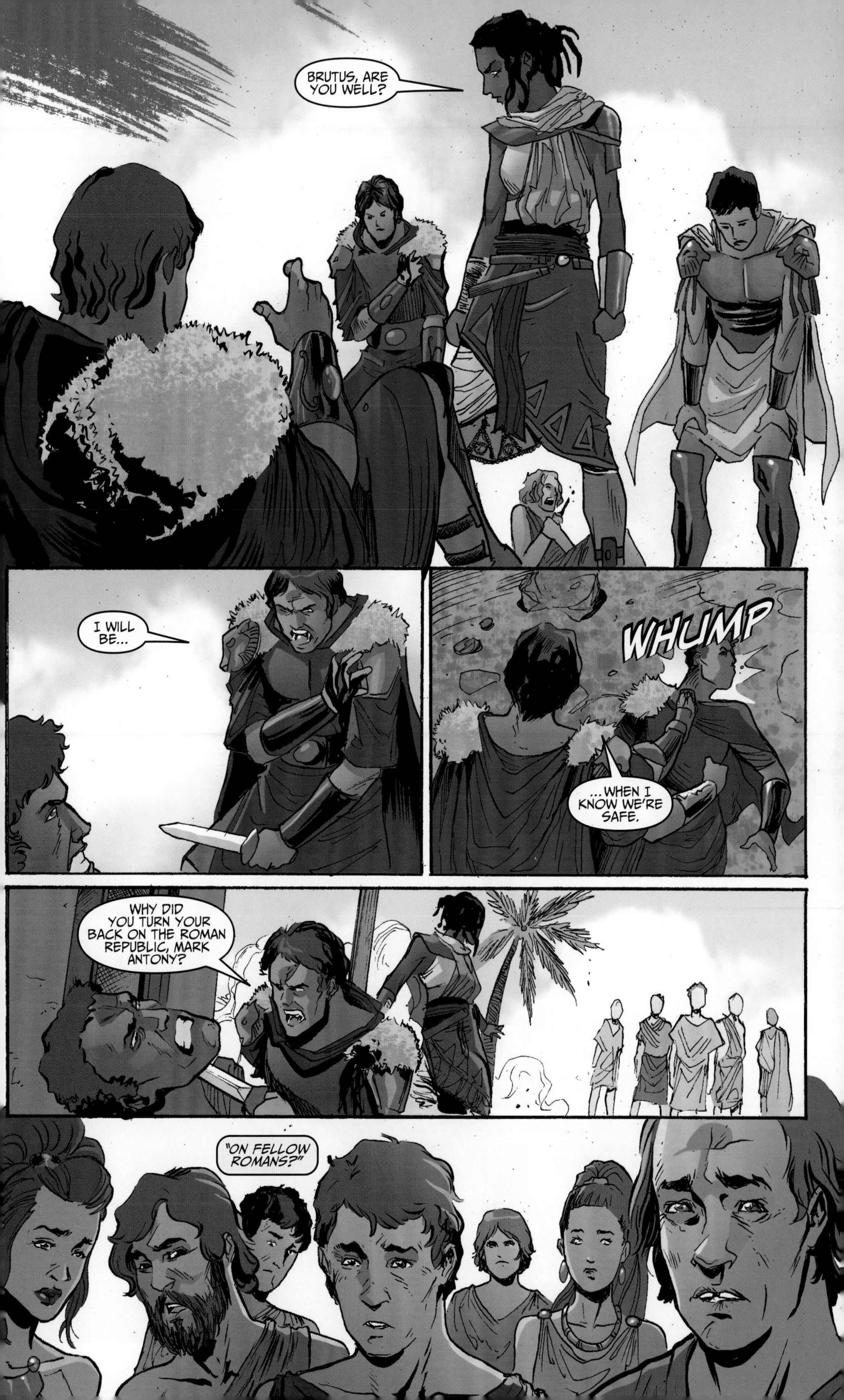
BRUTUS, ARE YOU WELL?
I WILL BE...
WHUMP
...WHEN I KNOW WE'RE SAFE.
WHY DID YOU TURN YOUR BACK ON THE ROMAN REPUBLIC, MARK ANTONY?
"ON FELLOW ROMANS?"

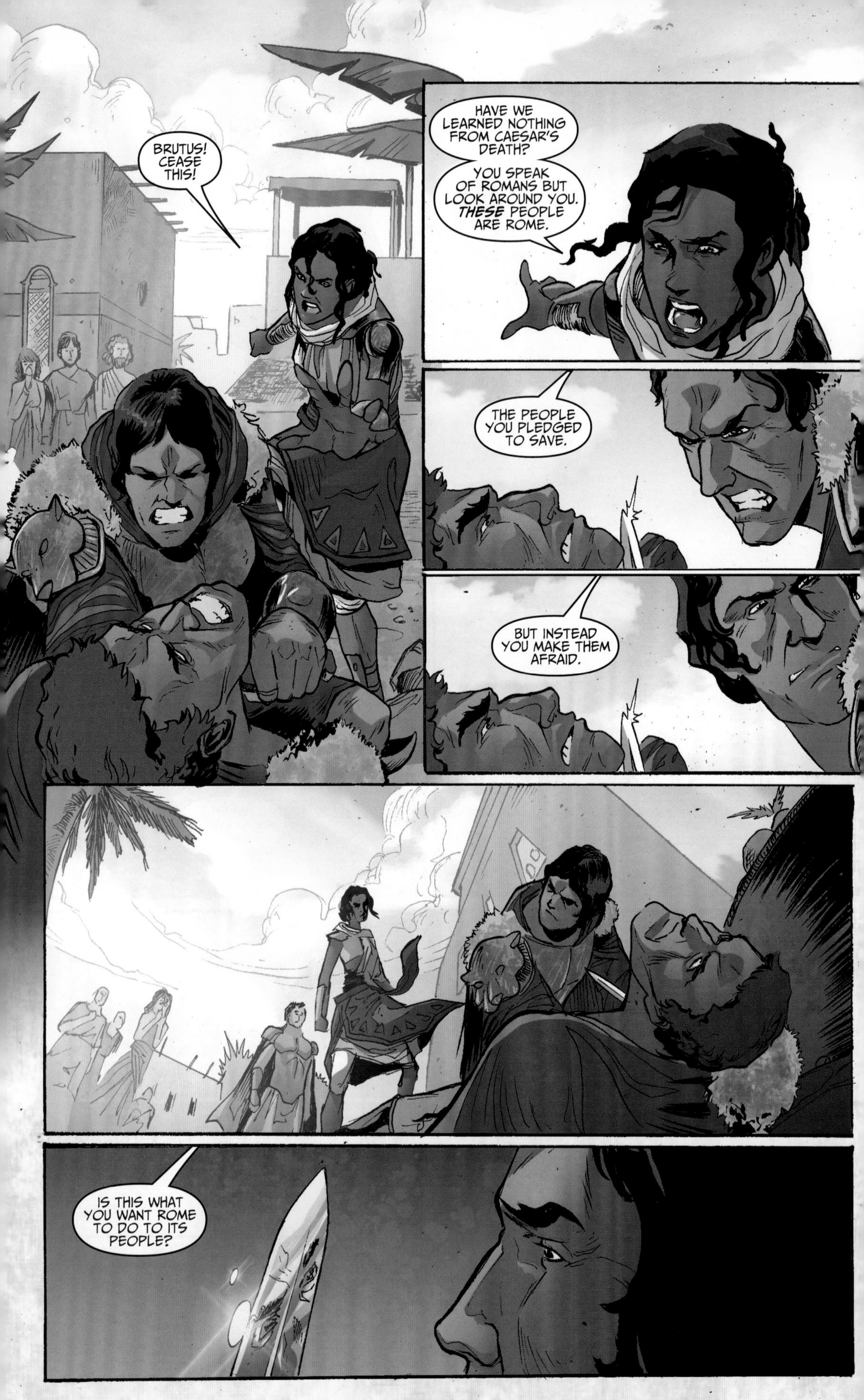
BRUTUS! CEASE THIS!
HAVE WE LEARNED NOTHING FROM CAESAR'S DEATH?
YOU SPEAK OF ROMANS BUT LOOK AROUND YOU. *THESE* PEOPLE ARE ROME.
THE PEOPLE YOU PLEDGED TO SAVE.
BUT INSTEAD YOU MAKE THEM AFRAID.
IS THIS WHAT YOU WANT ROME TO DO TO ITS PEOPLE?

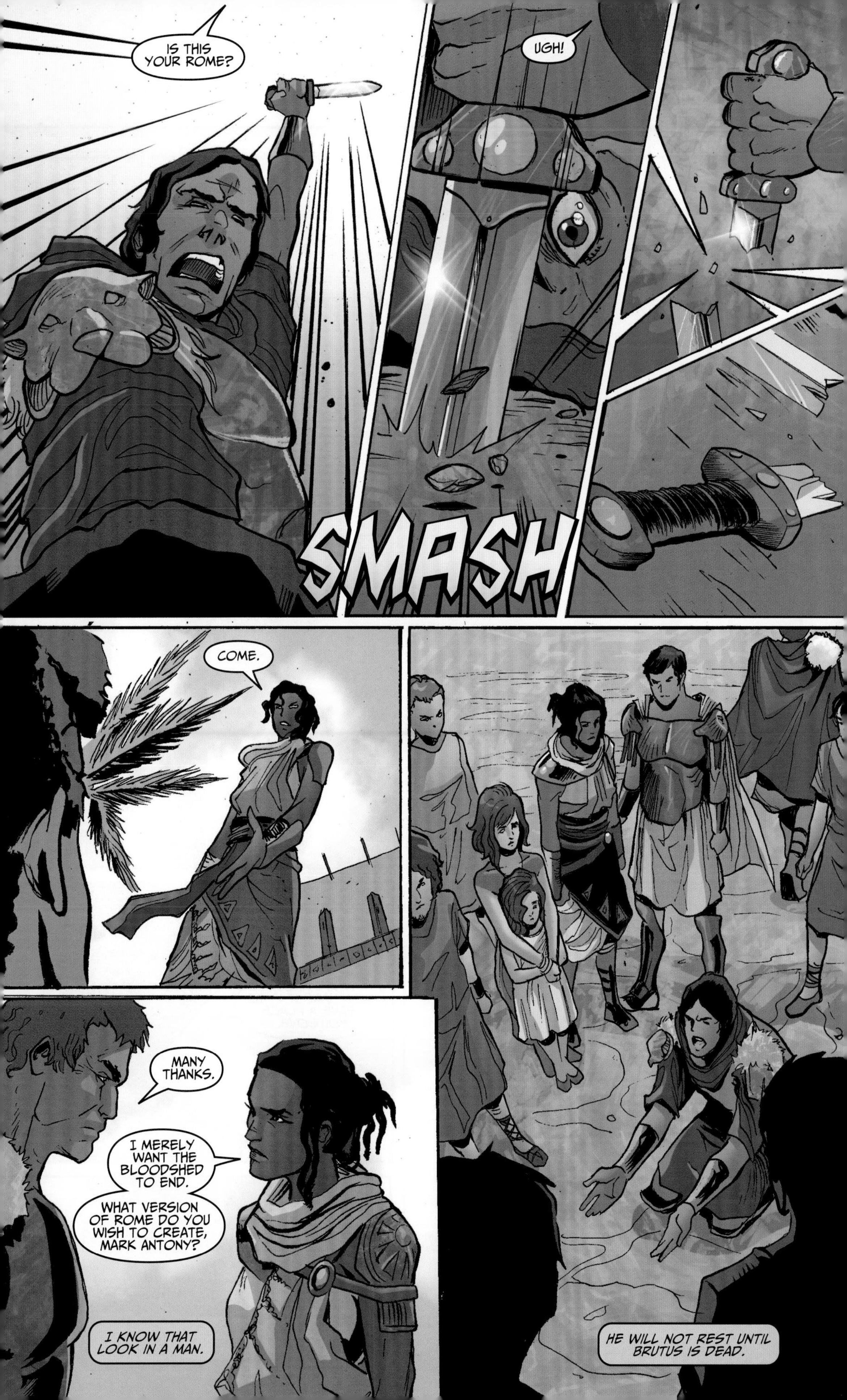
IS THIS YOUR ROME?
UGH!
SMASH
COME.
MANY THANKS.
I MERELY WANT THE BLOODSHED TO END.
WHAT VERSION OF ROME DO YOU WISH TO CREATE, MARK ANTONY?
I KNOW THAT LOOK IN A MAN.
HE WILL NOT REST UNTIL BRUTUS IS DEAD.

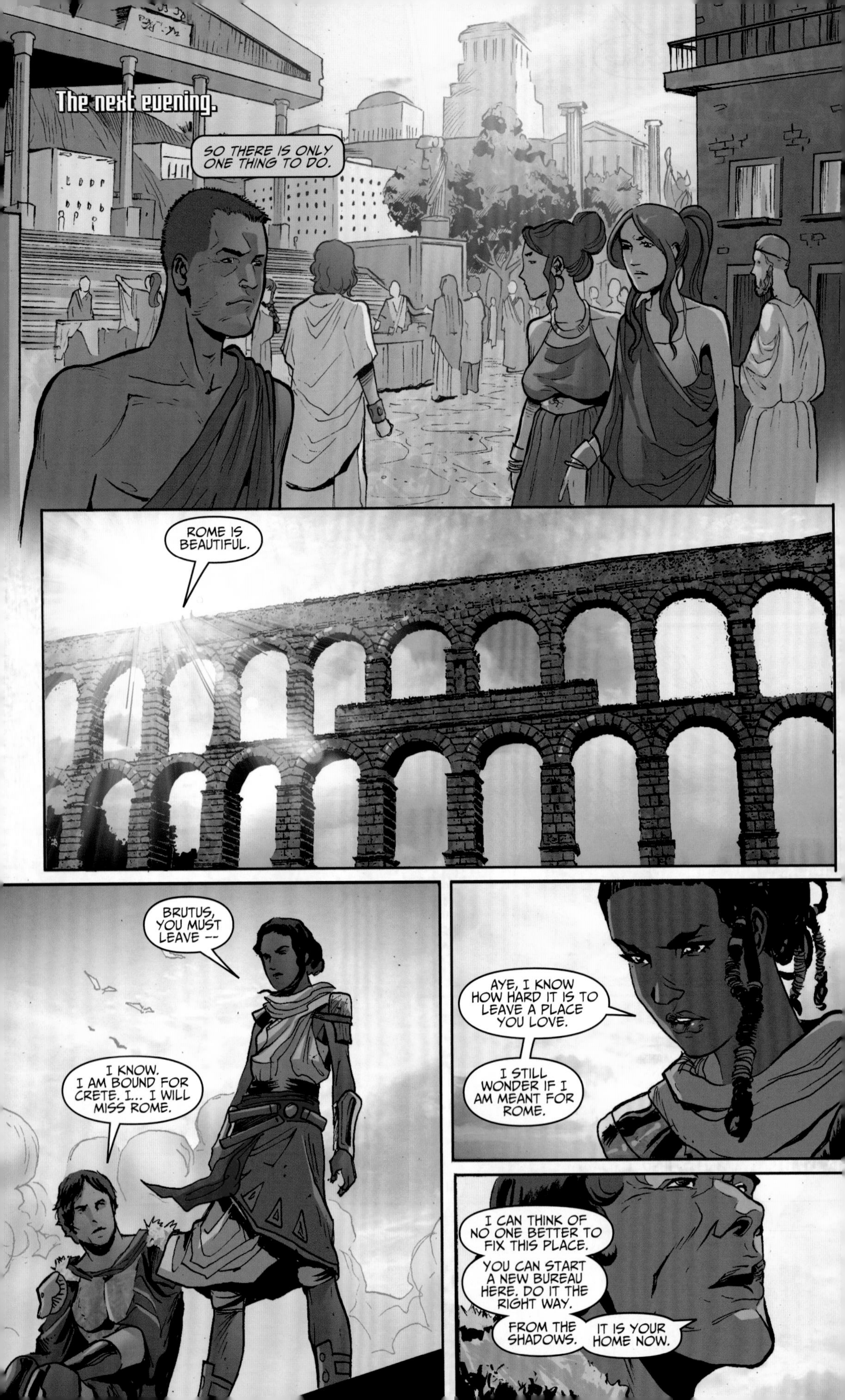
The next evening.
SO THERE IS ONLY ONE THING TO DO.
ROME IS BEAUTIFUL.
BRUTUS, YOU MUST LEAVE --
I KNOW. I AM BOUND FOR CRETE. I... I WILL MISS ROME.
AYE, I KNOW HOW HARD IT IS TO LEAVE A PLACE YOU LOVE.
I STILL WONDER IF I AM MEANT FOR ROME.
I CAN THINK OF NO ONE BETTER TO FIX THIS PLACE.
YOU CAN START A NEW BUREAU HERE. DO IT THE RIGHT WAY.
FROM THE SHADOWS.
IT IS YOUR HOME NOW.

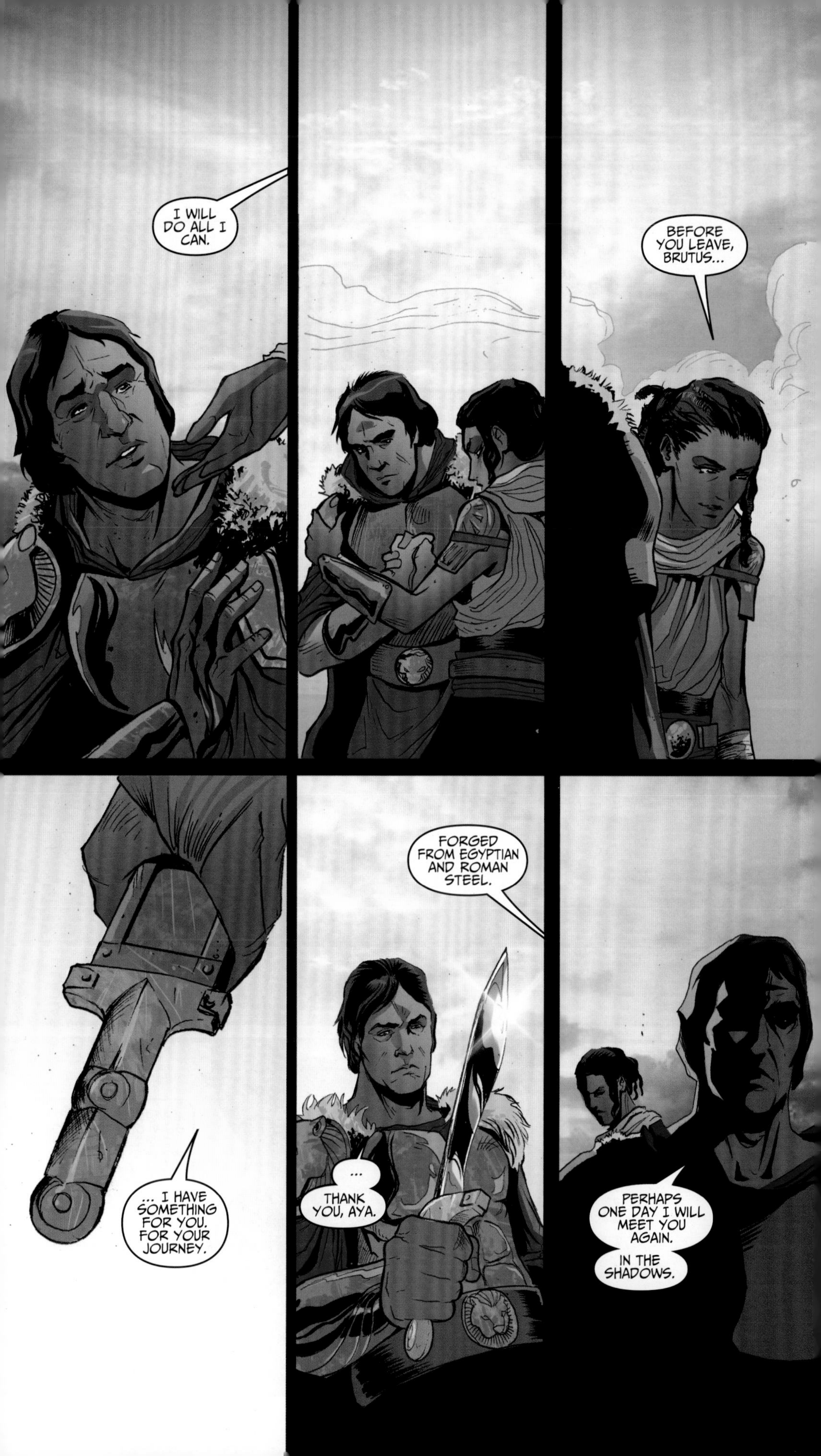
I WILL DO ALL I CAN.
BEFORE YOU LEAVE, BRUTUS...
... I HAVE SOMETHING FOR YOU. FOR YOUR JOURNEY.
FORGED FROM EGYPTIAN AND ROMAN STEEL.
...
THANK YOU, AYA.
PERHAPS ONE DAY I WILL MEET YOU AGAIN.
IN THE SHADOWS.

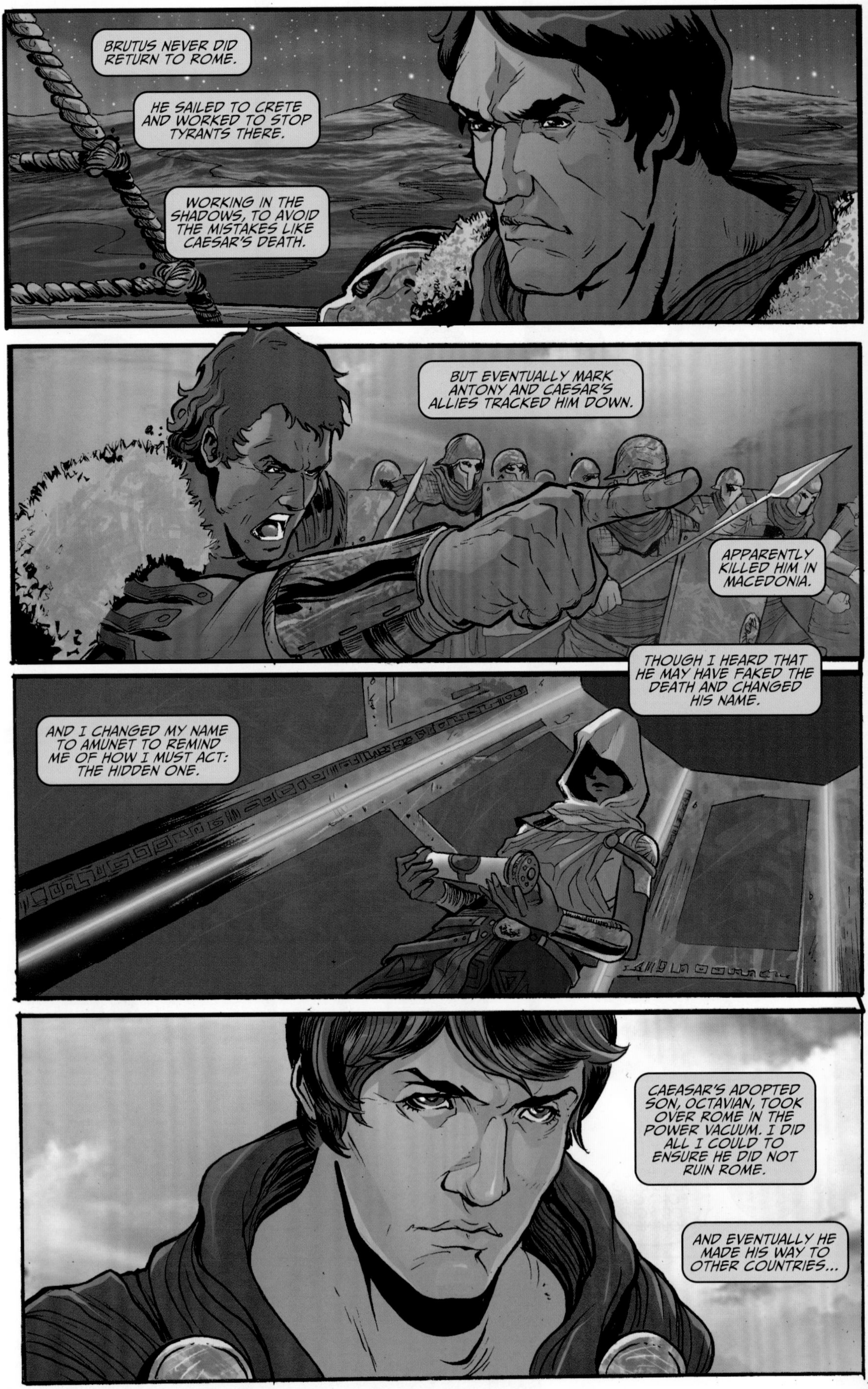
BRUTUS NEVER DID RETURN TO ROME.
HE SAILED TO CRETE AND WORKED TO STOP TYRANTS THERE.
WORKING IN THE SHADOWS, TO AVOID THE MISTAKES LIKE CAESAR'S DEATH.
BUT EVENTUALLY MARK ANTONY AND CAESAR'S ALLIES TRACKED HIM DOWN.
APPARENTLY KILLED HIM IN MACEDONIA.
THOUGH I HEARD THAT HE MAY HAVE FAKED THE DEATH AND CHANGED HIS NAME.
AND I CHANGED MY NAME TO AMUNET TO REMIND ME OF HOW I MUST ACT: THE HIDDEN ONE.
CAEASAR'S ADOPTED SON, OCTAVIAN, TOOK OVER ROME IN THE POWER VACUUM. I DID ALL I COULD TO ENSURE HE DID NOT RUIN ROME.
AND EVENTUALLY HE MADE HIS WAY TO OTHER COUNTRIES...

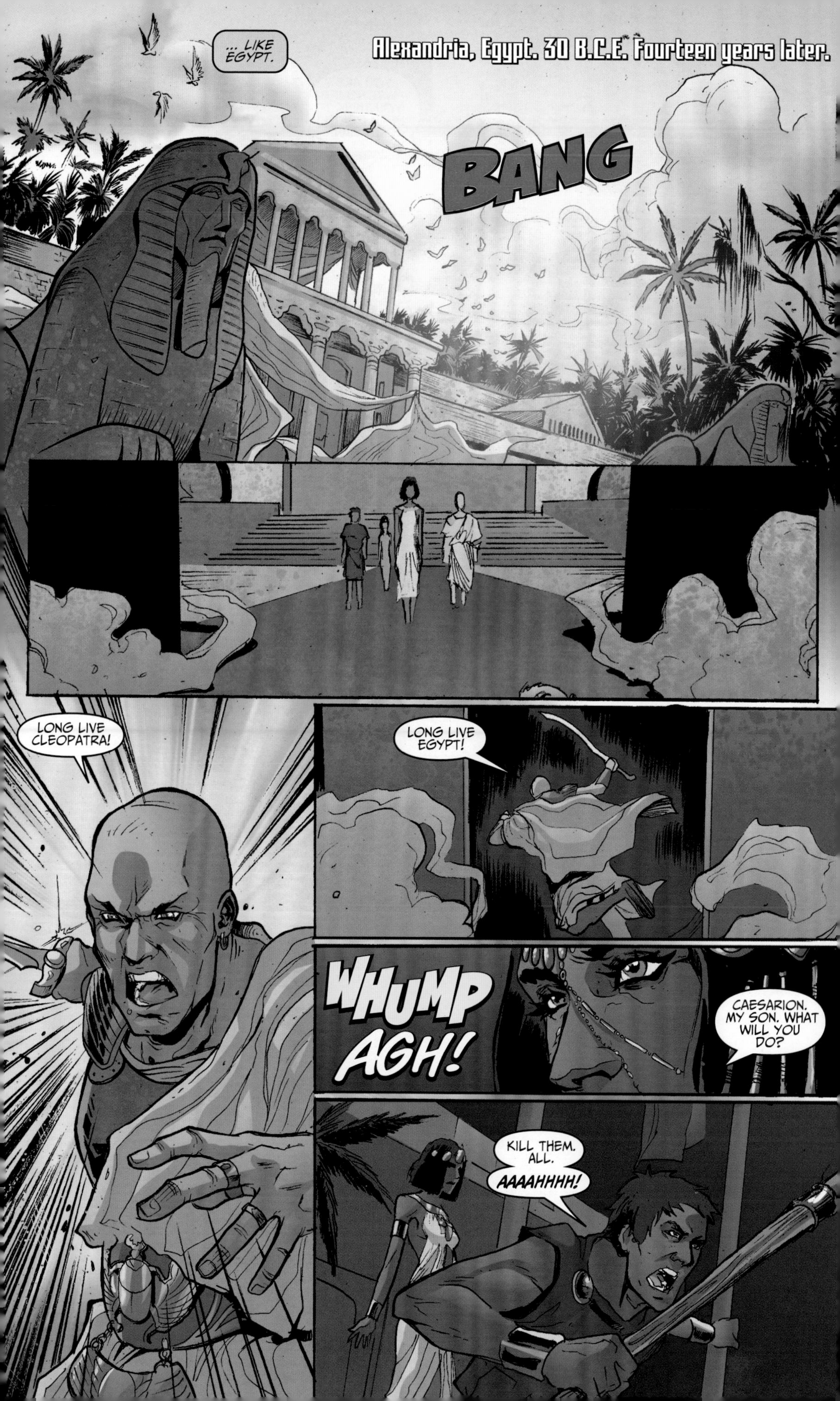

... LIKE EGYPT.
Alexandria, Egypt. 30 B.C.E. Fourteen years later.
BANG
LONG LIVE CLEOPATRA!
LONG LIVE EGYPT!
WHUMP
AGH!
CAESARION. MY SON. WHAT WILL YOU DO?
KILL THEM. ALL.
AAAAHHHH!

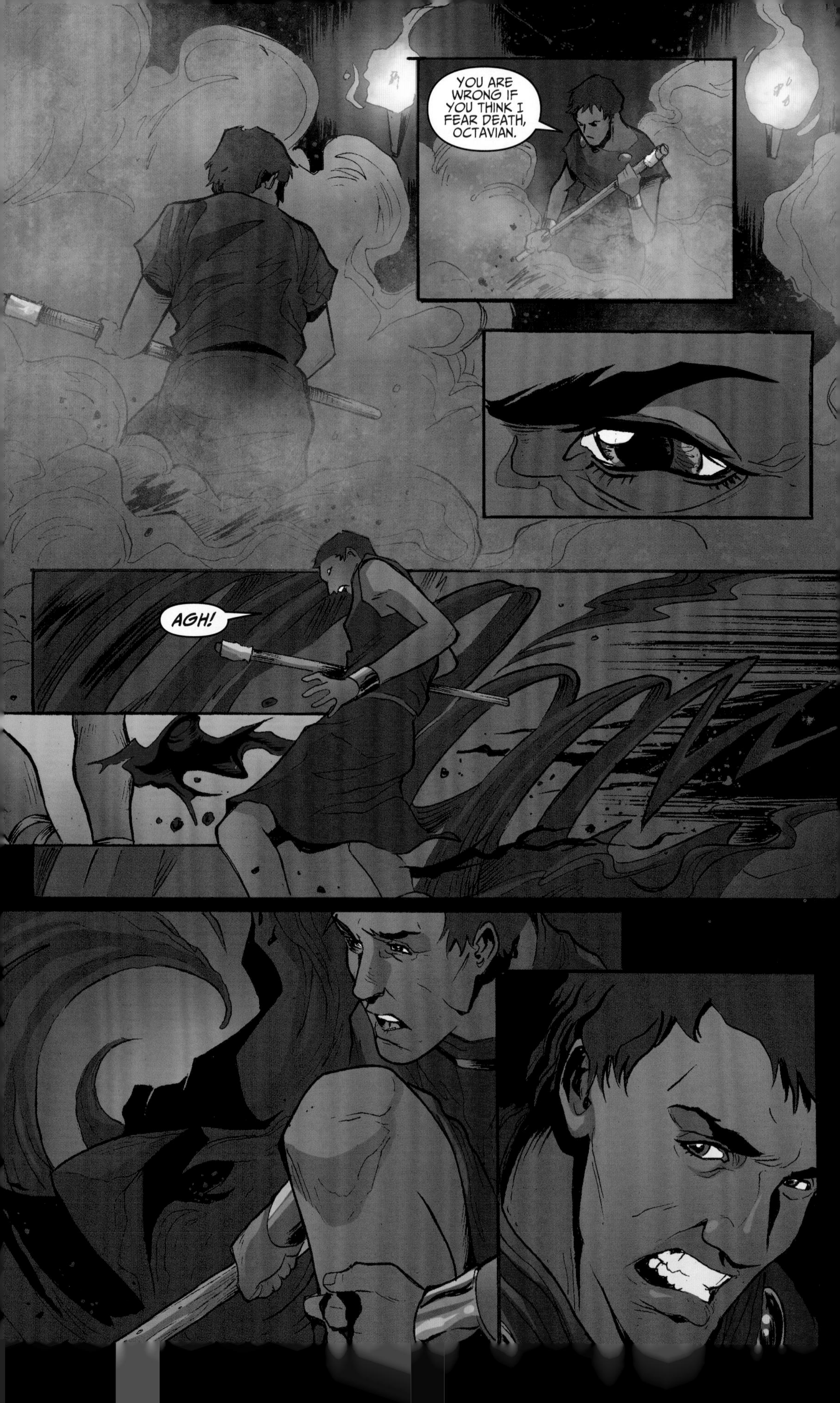
YOU ARE WRONG IF YOU THINK I FEAR DEATH, OCTAVIAN.
AGH!

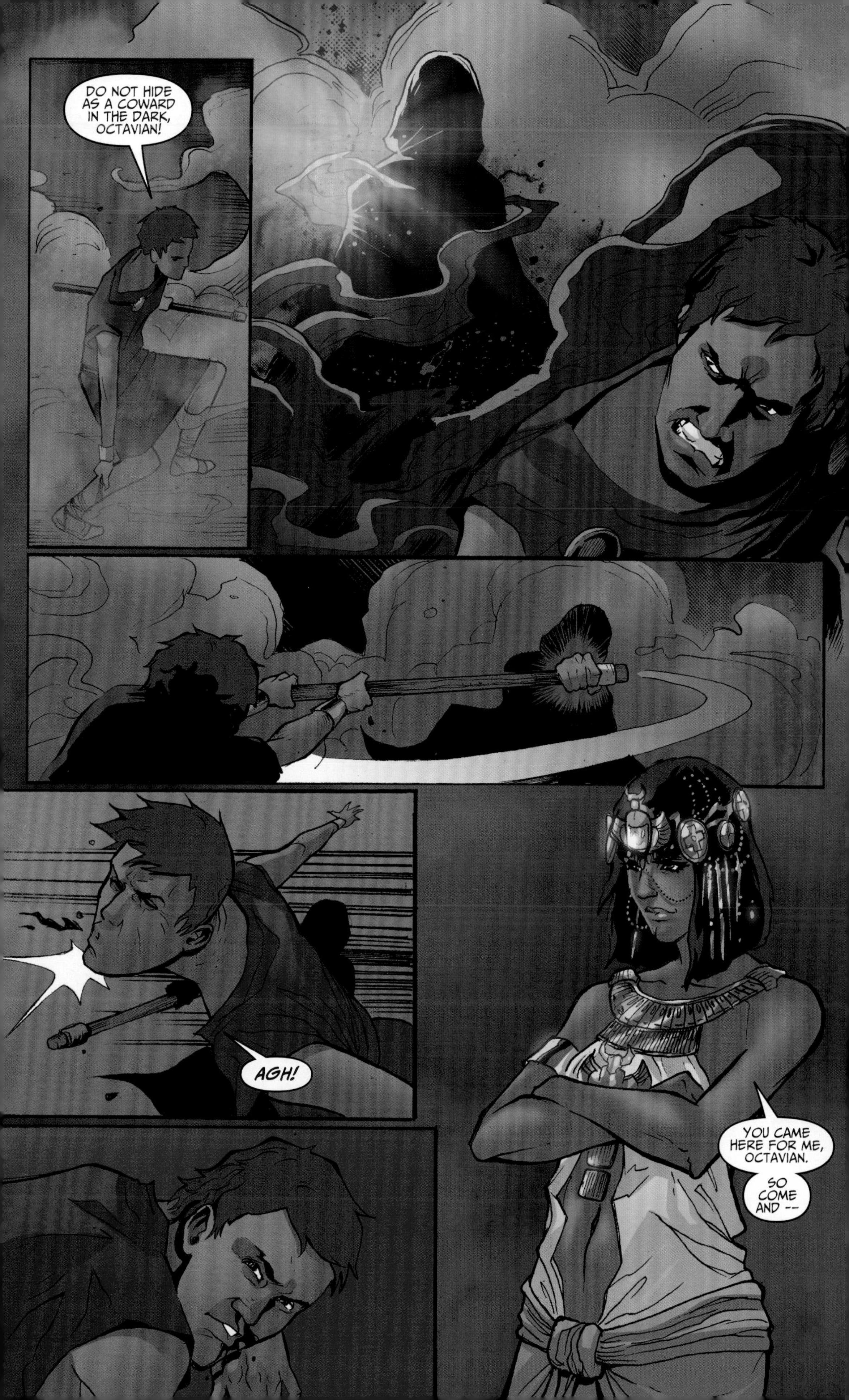
DO NOT HIDE AS A COWARD IN THE DARK, OCTAVIAN!
AGH!
YOU CAME HERE FOR ME, OCTAVIAN.
SO COME AND --

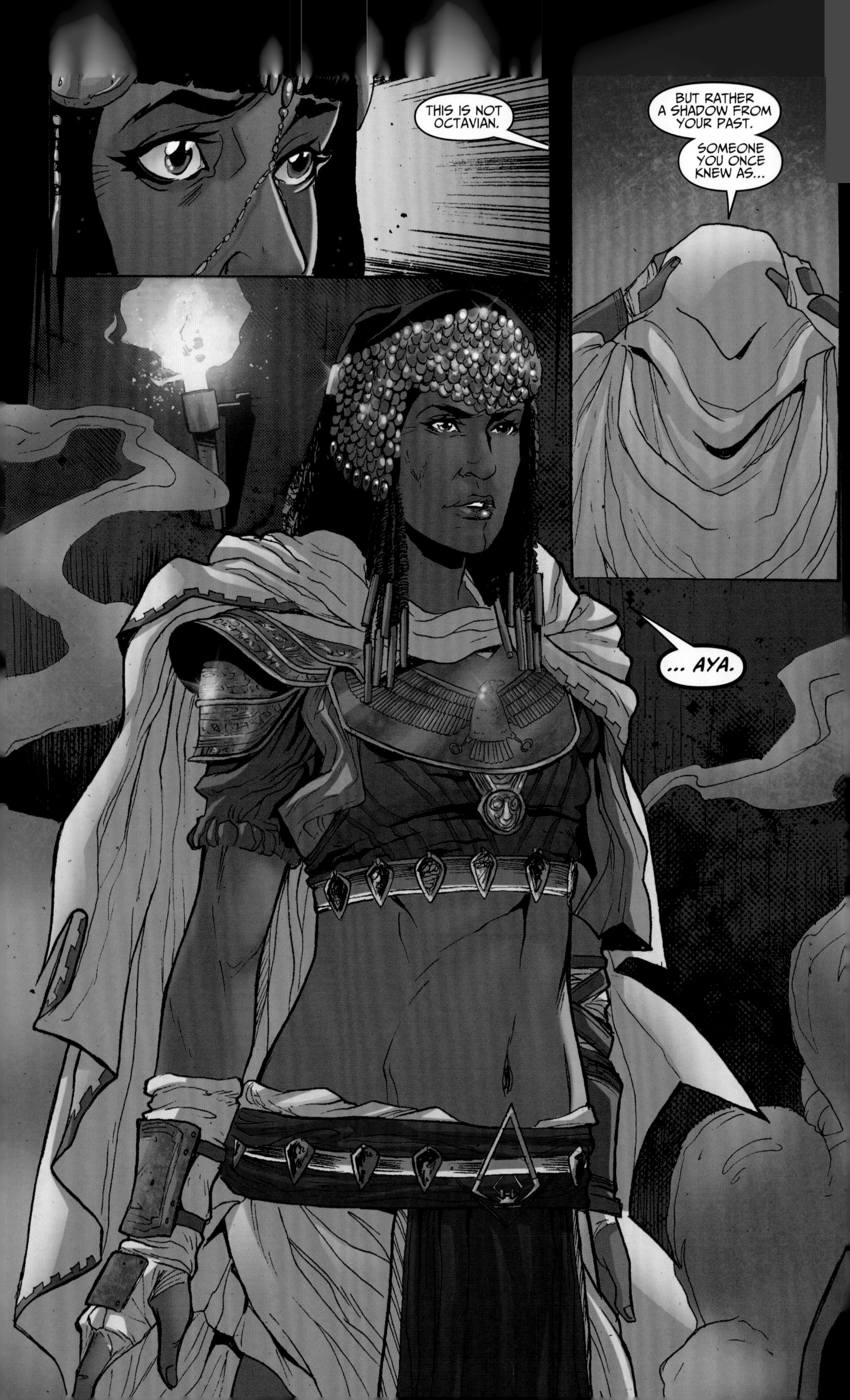
THIS IS NOT OCTAVIAN.
BUT RATHER A SHADOW FROM YOUR PAST.
SOMEONE YOU ONCE KNEW AS...
... AYA.

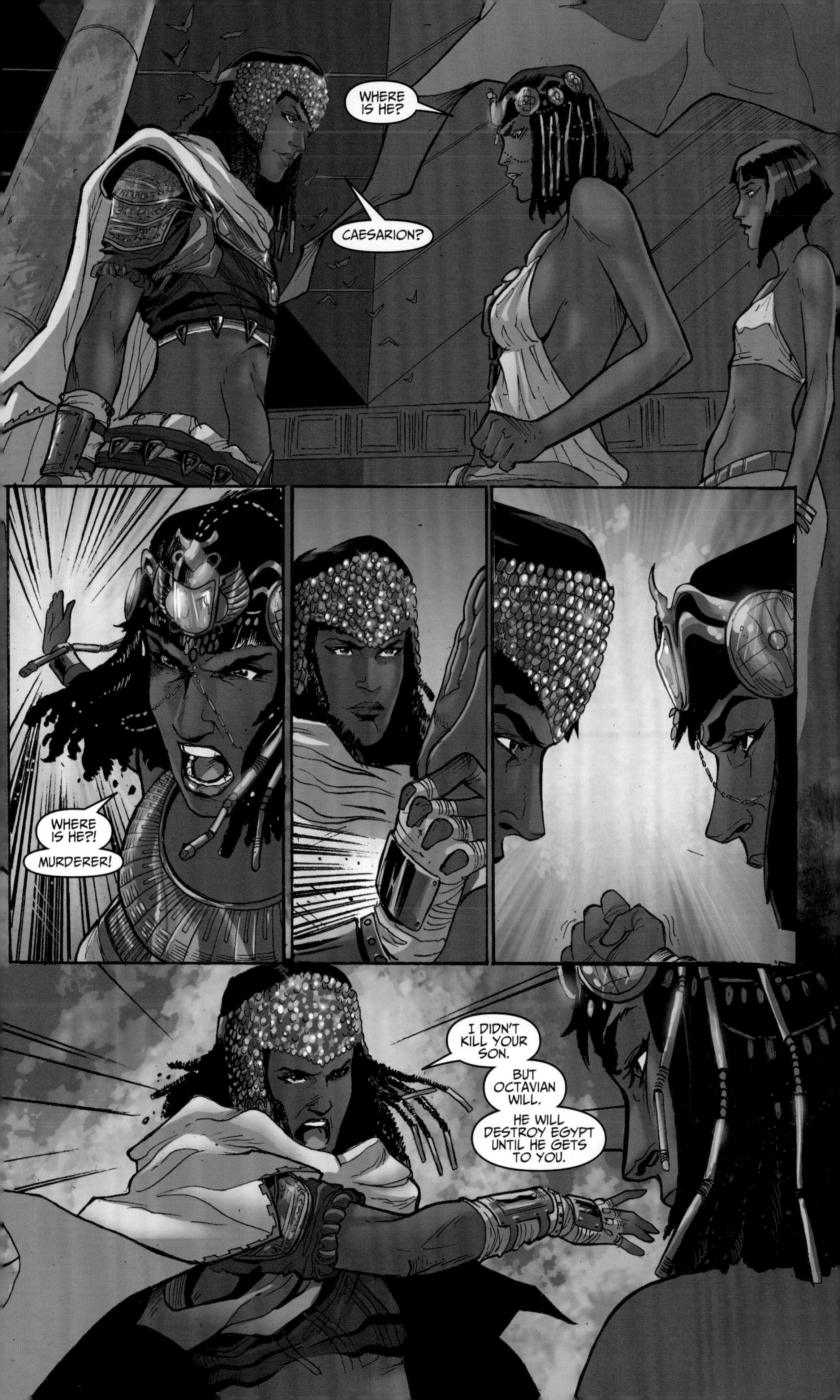
WHERE IS HE?
CAESARION?
WHERE IS HE?!
MURDERER!
I DIDN'T KILL YOUR SON.
BUT OCTAVIAN WILL.
HE WILL DESTROY EGYPT UNTIL HE GETS TO YOU.

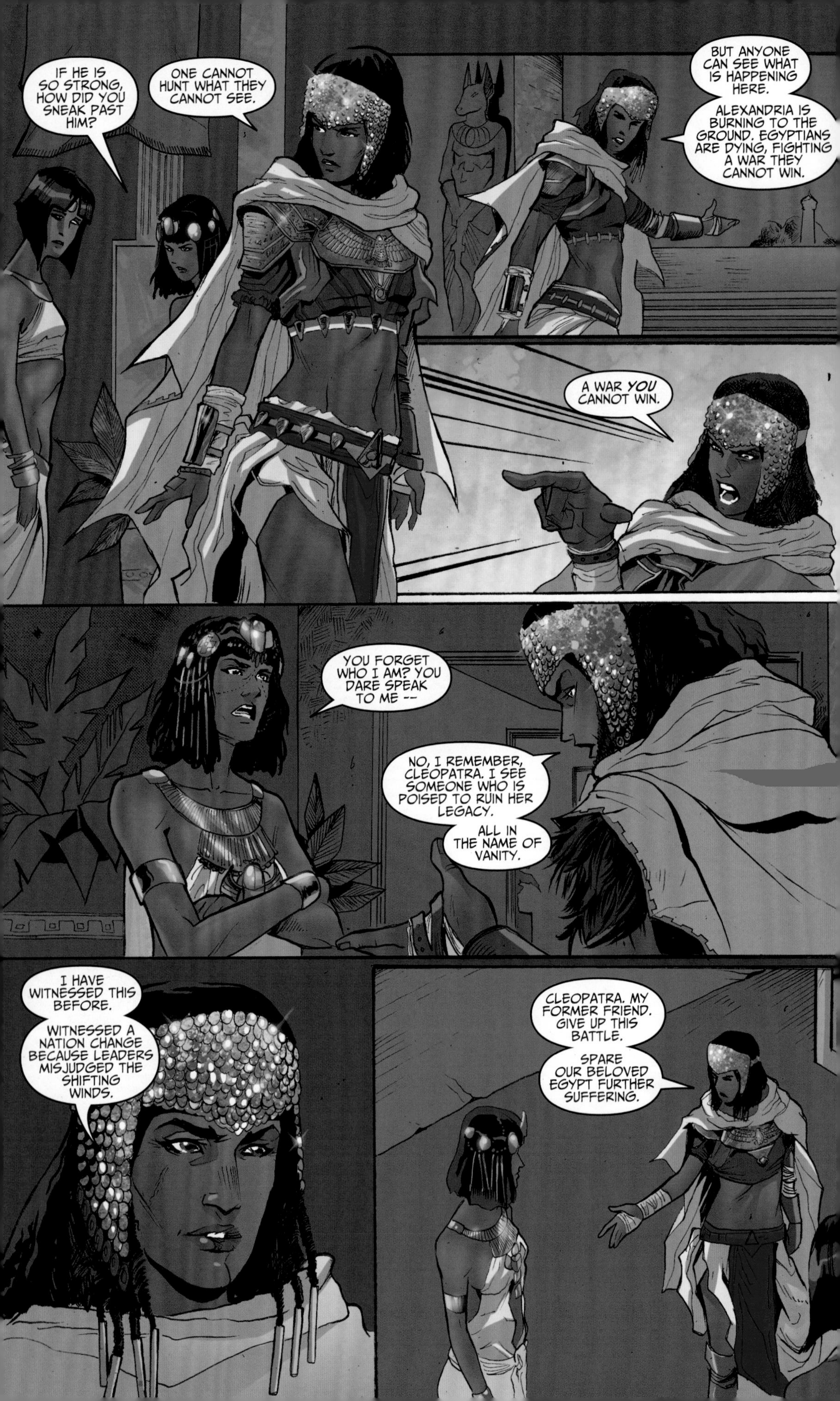
IF HE IS SO STRONG, HOW DID YOU SNEAK PAST HIM?
ONE CANNOT HUNT WHAT THEY CANNOT SEE.
BUT ANYONE CAN SEE WHAT IS HAPPENING HERE.
ALEXANDRIA IS BURNING TO THE GROUND. EGYPTIANS ARE DYING, FIGHTING A WAR THEY CANNOT WIN.
A WAR YOU CANNOT WIN.
YOU FORGET WHO I AM? YOU DARE SPEAK TO ME --
NO, I REMEMBER, CLEOPATRA. I SEE SOMEONE WHO IS POISED TO RUIN HER LEGACY.
ALL IN THE NAME OF VANITY.
I HAVE WITNESSED THIS BEFORE.
WITNESSED A NATION CHANGE BECAUSE LEADERS MISJUDGED THE SHIFTING WINDS.
CLEOPATRA. MY FORMER FRIEND. GIVE UP THIS BATTLE.
SPARE OUR BELOVED EGYPT FURTHER SUFFERING.

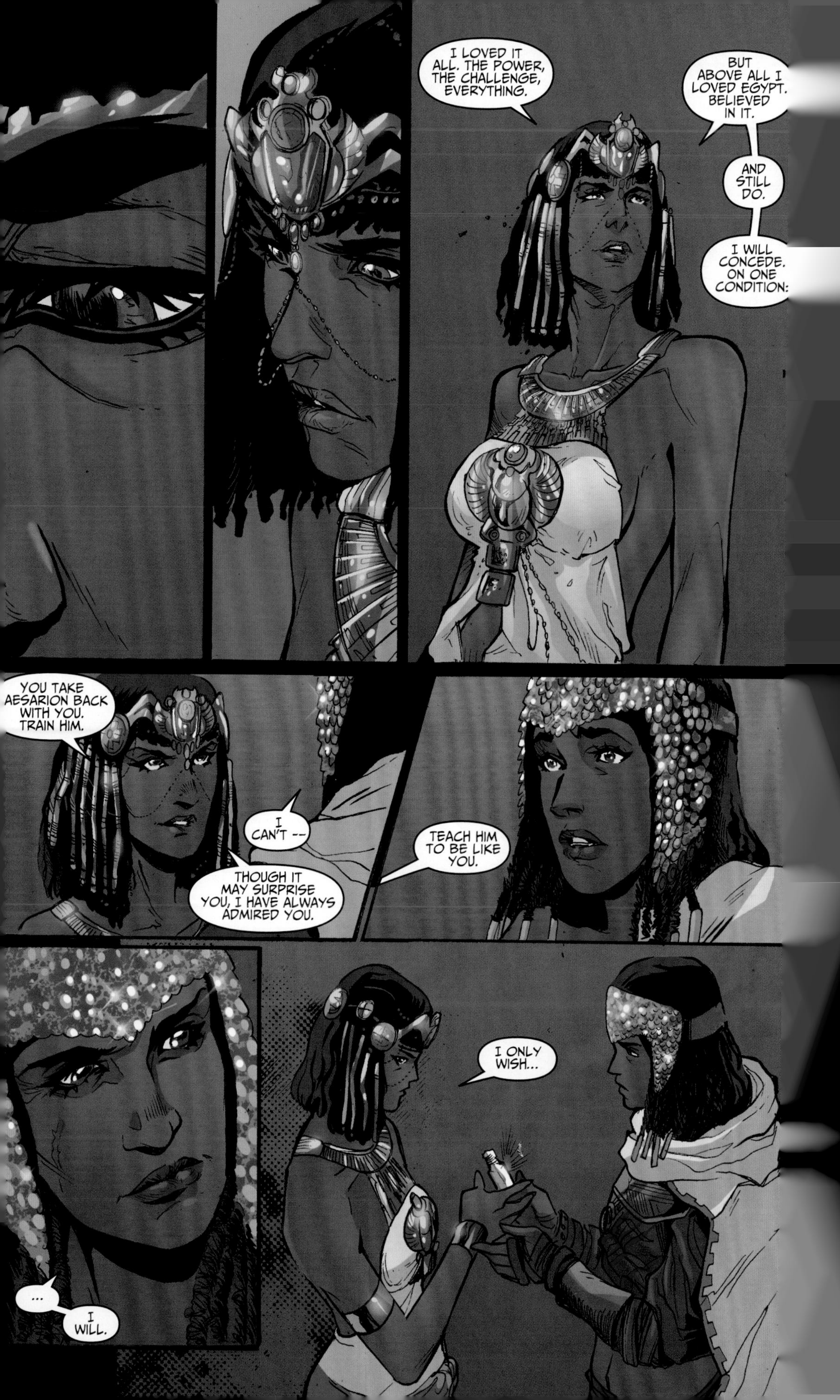

I LOVED IT ALL. THE POWER, THE CHALLENGE, EVERYTHING.
BUT ABOVE ALL I LOVED EGYPT. BELIEVED IN IT.
AND STILL DO.
I WILL CONCEDE. ON ONE CONDITION:
YOU TAKE AESARION BACK WITH YOU. TRAIN HIM.
I CAN'T --
THOUGH IT MAY SURPRISE YOU, I HAVE ALWAYS ADMIRED YOU.
TEACH HIM TO BE LIKE YOU.
...
I WILL.
I ONLY WISH...

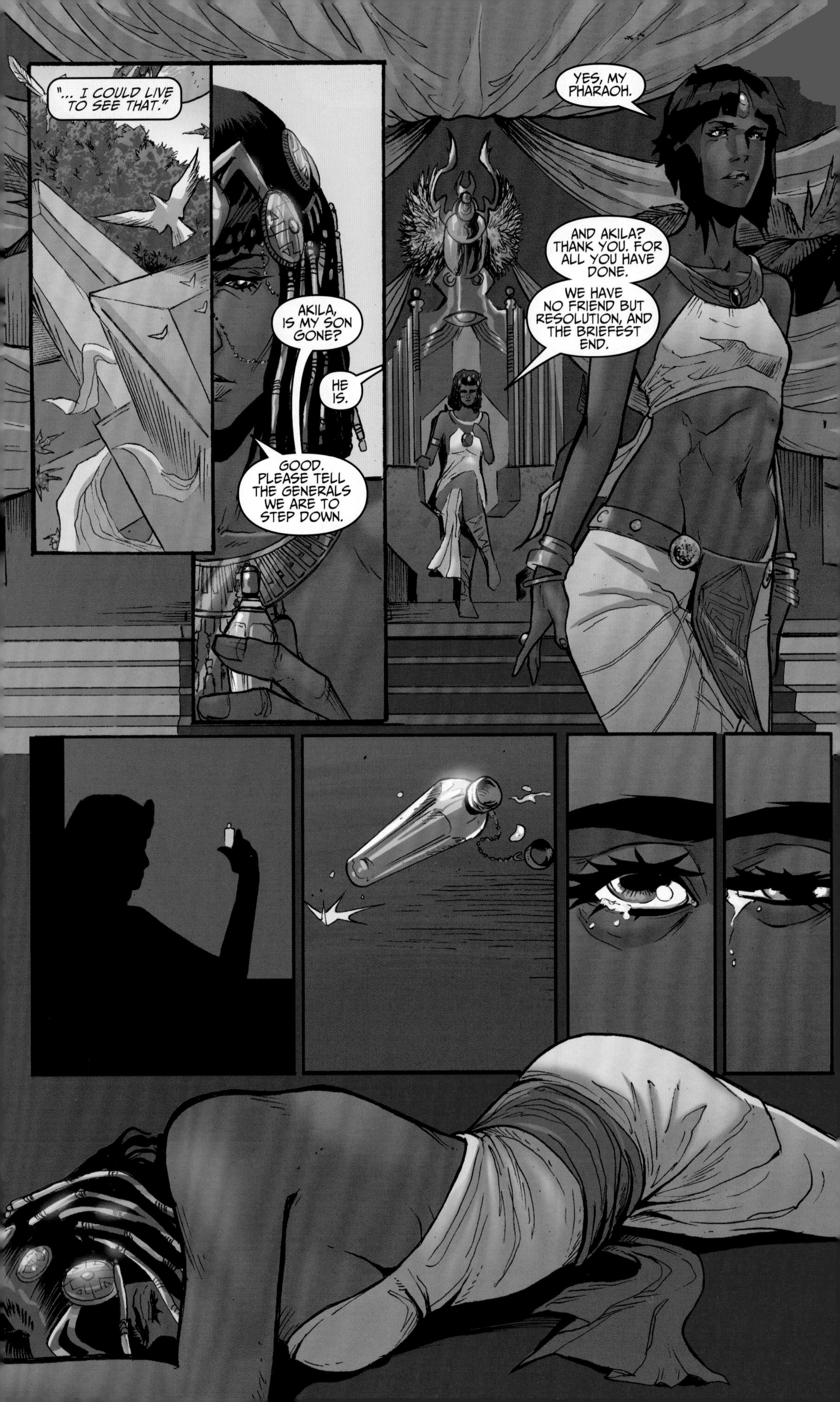
"... I COULD LIVE TO SEE THAT."
YES, MY PHARAOH.
AKILA, IS MY SON GONE?
HE IS.
GOOD. PLEASE TELL THE GENERALS WE ARE TO STEP DOWN.
AND AKILA? THANK YOU. FOR ALL YOU HAVE DONE.
WE HAVE NO FRIEND BUT RESOLUTION, AND THE BRIEFEST END.

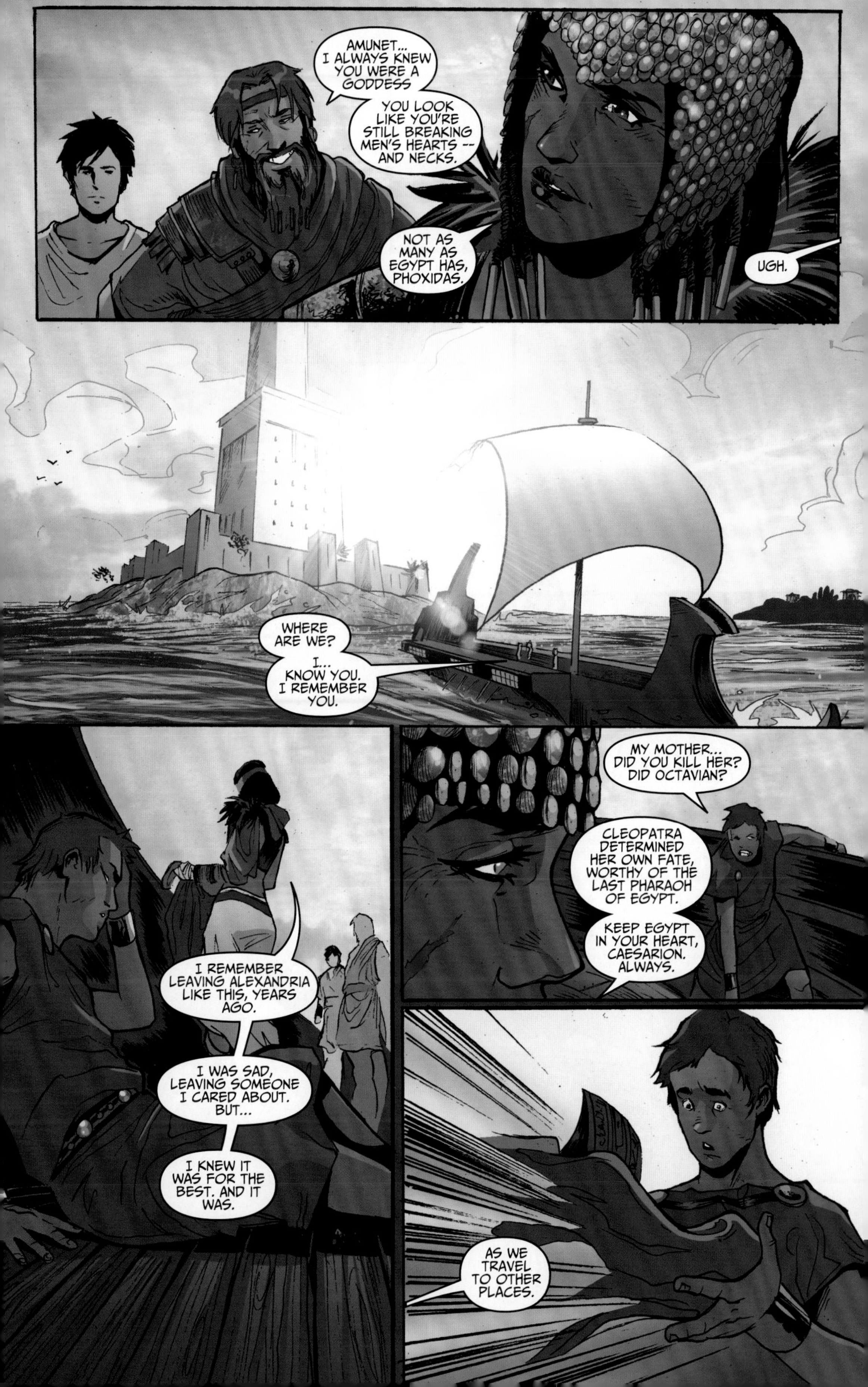
AMUNET... I ALWAYS KNEW YOU WERE A GODDESS
YOU LOOK LIKE YOU'RE STILL BREAKING MEN'S HEARTS -- AND NECKS.
NOT AS MANY AS EGYPT HAS, PHOXIDAS.
UGH.
WHERE ARE WE?
I... KNOW YOU. I REMEMBER YOU.
I REMEMBER LEAVING ALEXANDRIA LIKE THIS, YEARS AGO.
I WAS SAD, LEAVING SOMEONE I CARED ABOUT. BUT...
I KNEW IT WAS FOR THE BEST. AND IT WAS.
MY MOTHER... DID YOU KILL HER? DID OCTAVIAN?
CLEOPATRA DETERMINED HER OWN FATE, WORTHY OF THE LAST PHARAOH OF EGYPT.
KEEP EGYPT IN YOUR HEART, CAESARION. ALWAYS.
AS WE TRAVEL TO OTHER PLACES.

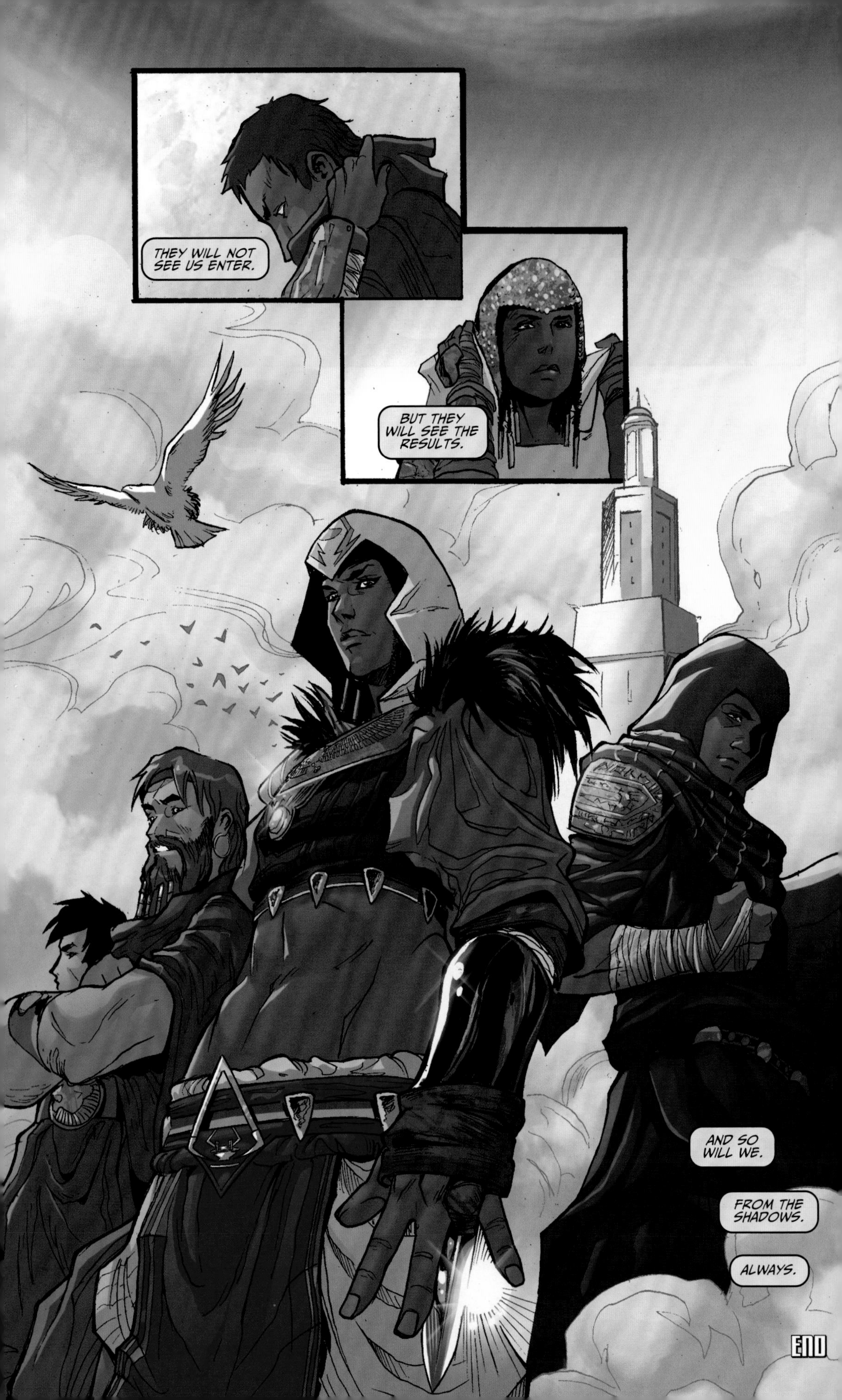
THEY WILL NOT SEE US ENTER.
BUT THEY WILL SEE THE RESULTS.
AND SO WILL WE.
FROM THE SHADOWS.
ALWAYS.
END

> COVERS GALLERY

ISSUE ONE

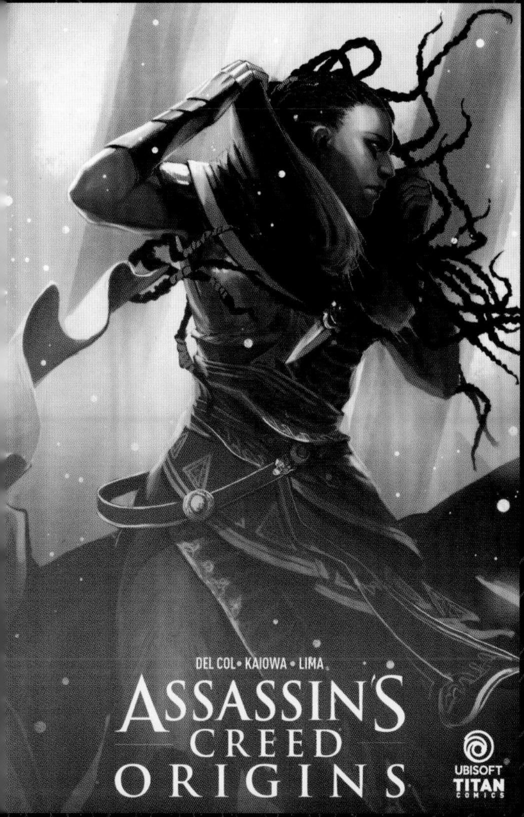
DEL COL • KAIOWA • LIMA
ASSASSIN'S
CREED
ORIGINS
UBISOFT
TITAN
COMICS

> COVER A / STEPHANIE HANS

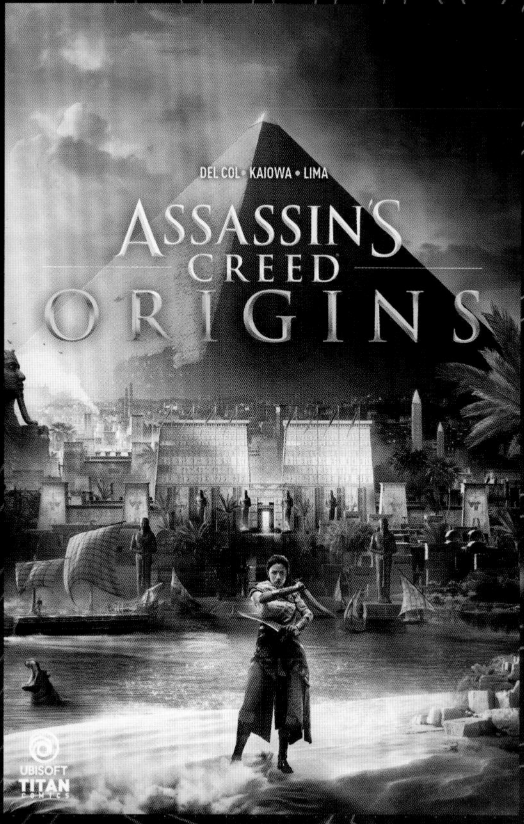
DEL COL • KAIOWA • LIMA
ASSASSIN'S
CREED
ORIGINS
UBISOFT
TITAN
COMICS

> COVER B / GAME COVER

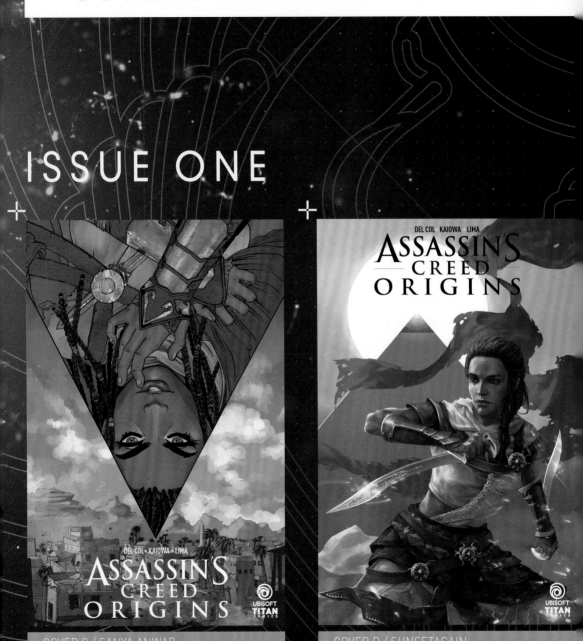

> COVERS GALLERY

ISSUE ONE

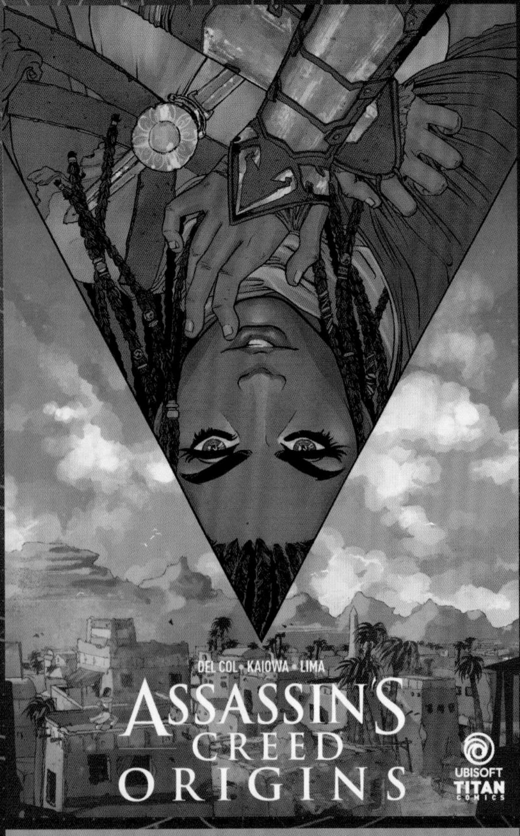

DEL COL · KAIOWA · LIMA
ASSASSIN'S
CREED
ORIGINS
UBISOFT
TITAN
COMICS

> COVER C / SANYA ANWAR

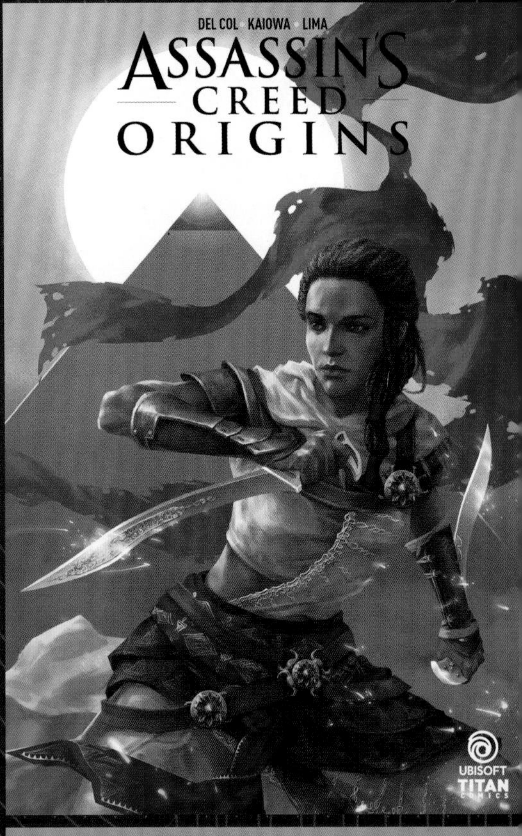

DEL COL · KAIOWA · LIMA
ASSASSIN'S
CREED
ORIGINS
UBISOFT
TITAN
COMICS

> COVER D / SUNSETAGAIN

ISSUE TWO

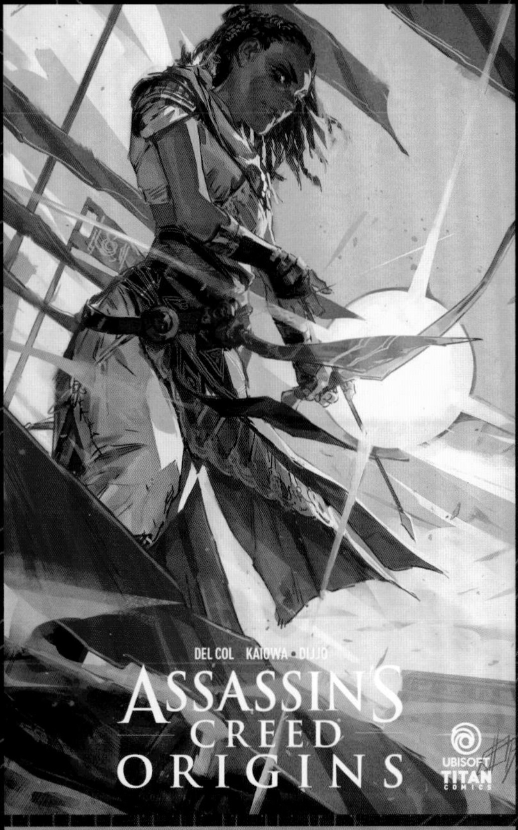
DEL COL · KAIOWA · DIJJO
ASSASSIN'S
CREED
ORIGINS
UBISOFT
TITAN
COMICS

> COVER A / TONI INFANTE

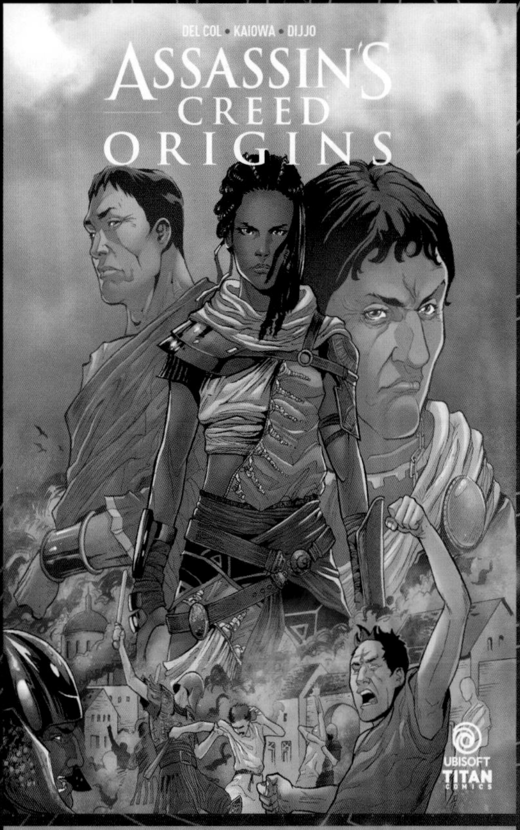
DEL COL · KAIOWA · DIJJO
ASSASSIN'S
CREED
ORIGINS
UBISOFT
TITAN
COMICS

> COVER B / PJ KAIOWA & DIJJO LIMA

> COVERS GALLERY

ISSUE THREE

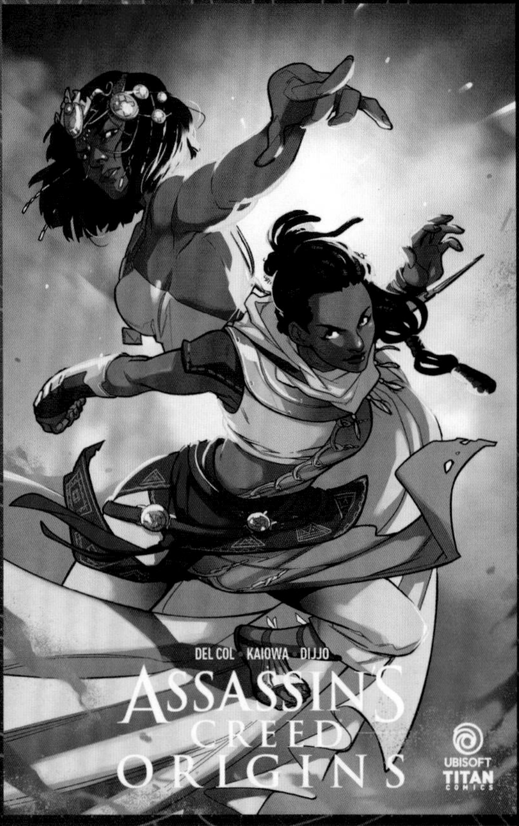

DEL COL KAIOWA DIJJO
ASSASSIN'S CREED ORIGINS
UBISOFT
TITAN COMICS

> COVER A / VALARIA FAVOCCIA

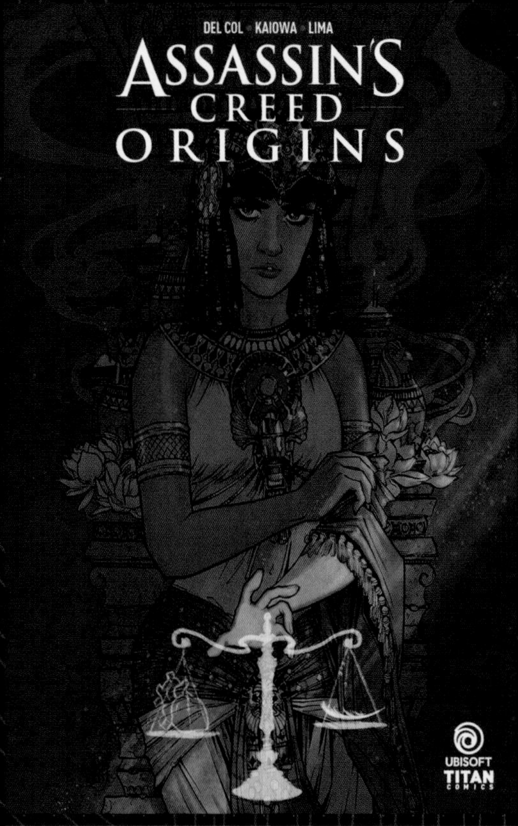

DEL COL KAIOWA LIMA
ASSASSIN'S CREED ORIGINS
UBISOFT
TITAN COMICS

> COVER B / SANYA ANWAR

ISSUE FOUR

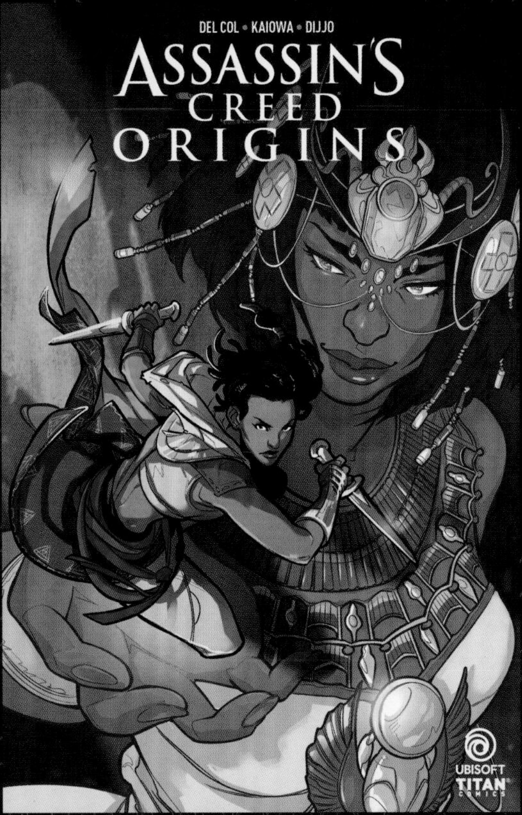
DEL COL • KAIOWA • DIJJO
ASSASSIN'S CREED ORIGINS
UBISOFT
TITAN COMICS

> COVER A / VALERIA FAVOCCIA

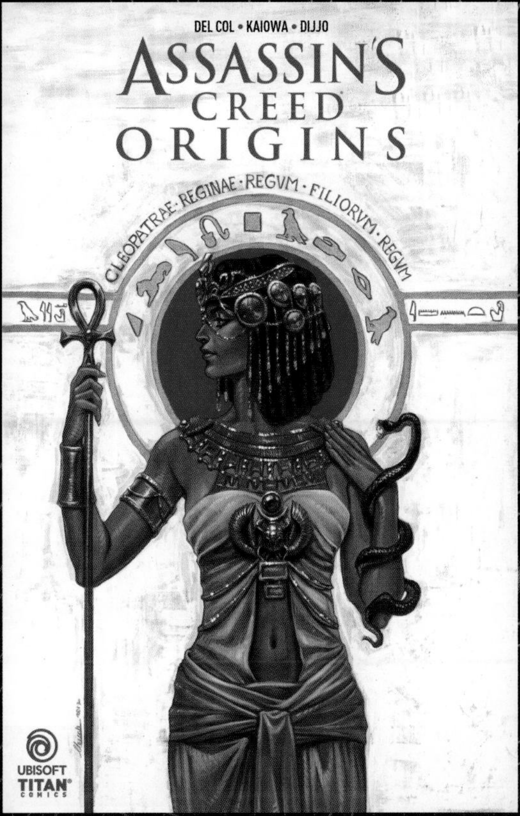
DEL COL • KAIOWA • DIJJO
ASSASSIN'S CREED ORIGINS
CLEOPATRAE · REGINAE · REGVM · FILIORVM · REGVM
UBISOFT
TITAN COMICS

> COVER B / CLAUDIA IANNICIELLO

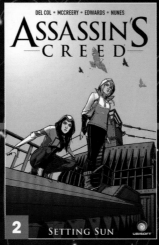

> READER'S GUIDE

Templars: Black Cross | $16.99
ISBN: 9781782763116

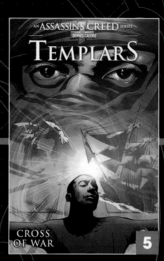

Templars: Cross of War | $16.99
ISBN: 9781782763123

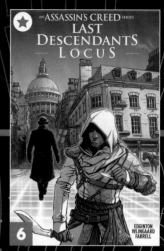

Last Descendants: Locus | $16.99
ISBN: 9781782763130

Uprising Vol. 3 | $19.99
ISBN: 9781785867941

Origins | $16.99
ISBN: 9781782763086

> THE
ADVENTURE
CONTINUES!

With so many amazing *Assassin's Creed* collections out on the shelves, it can be difficult to know where to start! That's where this handy guide comes in.

Follow the timeline to read the complete saga in our preferred order, or hop into any title marked with a star ⭐ for an accessible beginning to an arc, or a standalone adventure!

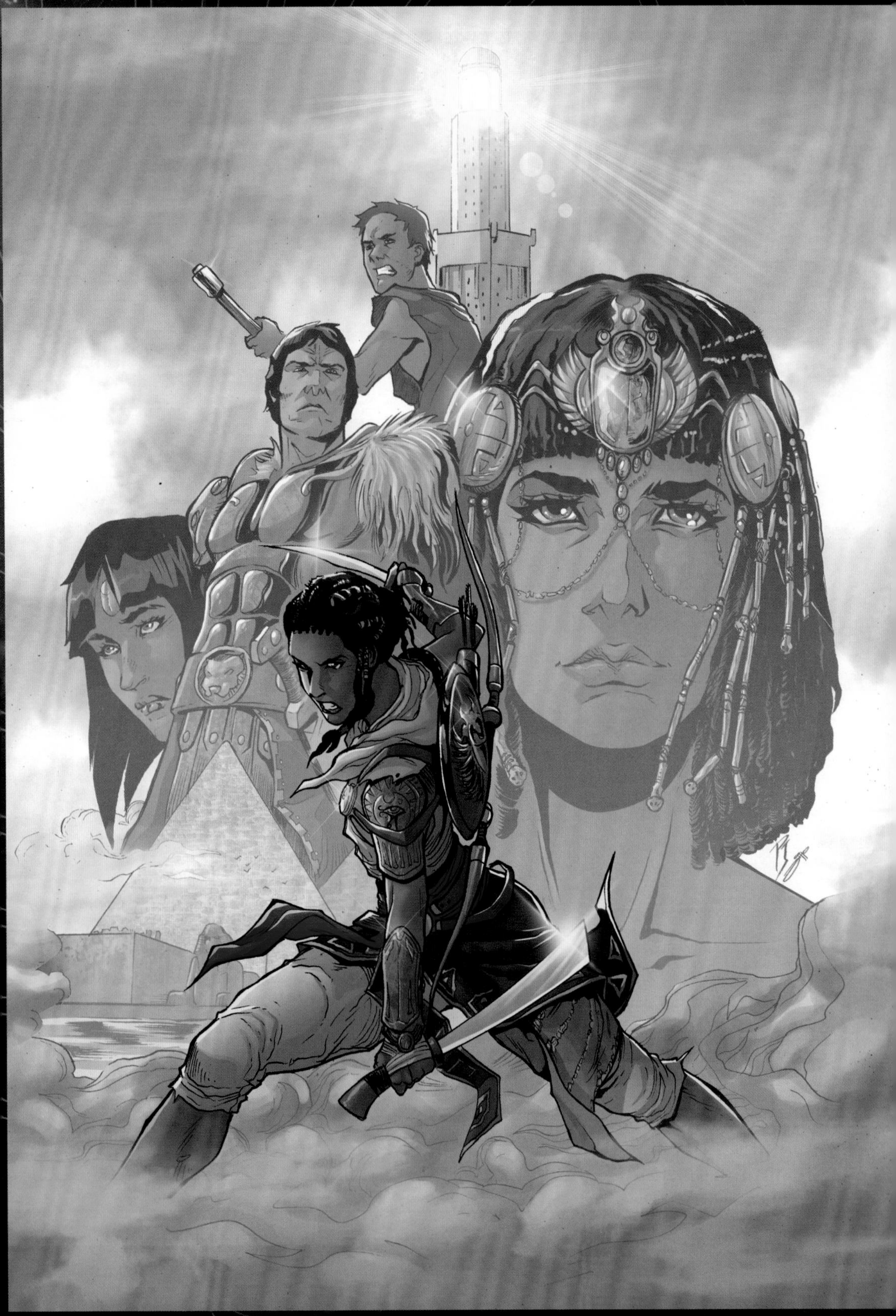

ORIGINS PINUP BY PJ KAIOWA & DIJJO LIMA

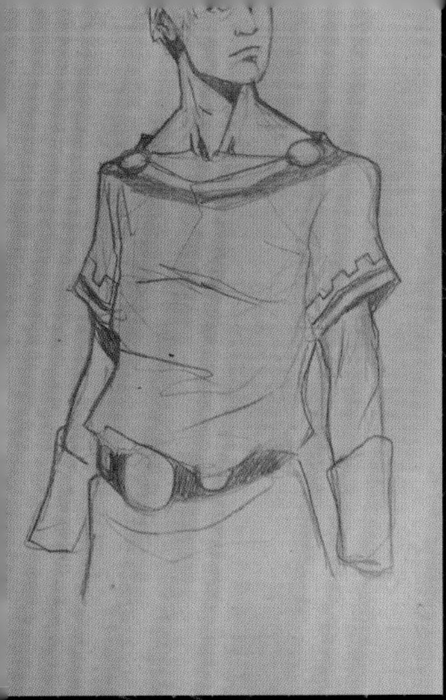

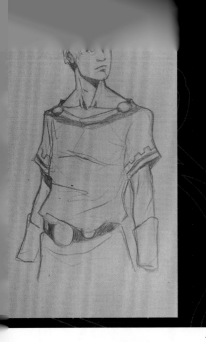

Akila sketch
by PJ Kaiowa

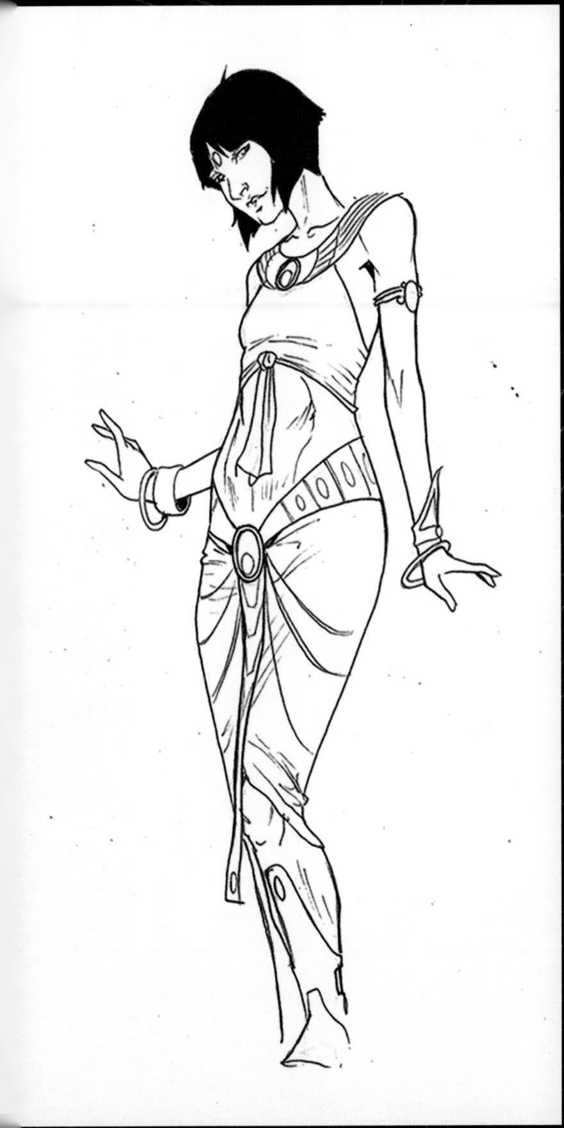

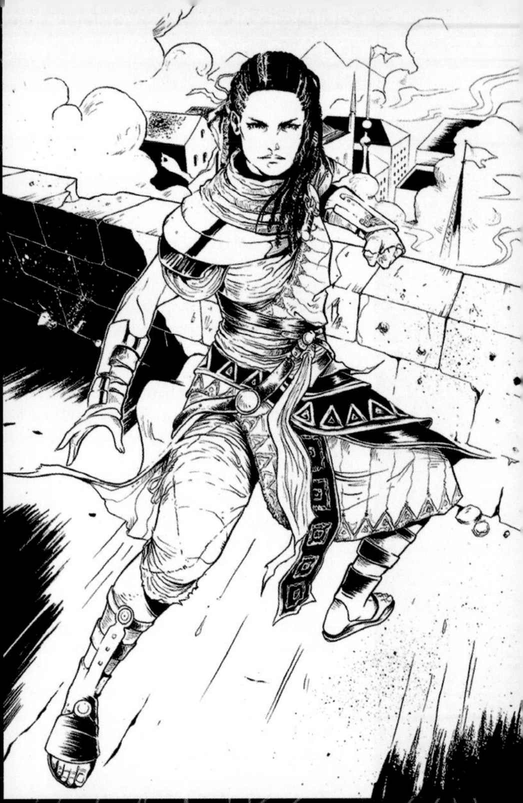

Aya pin-up
inks by PJ Kaiowa

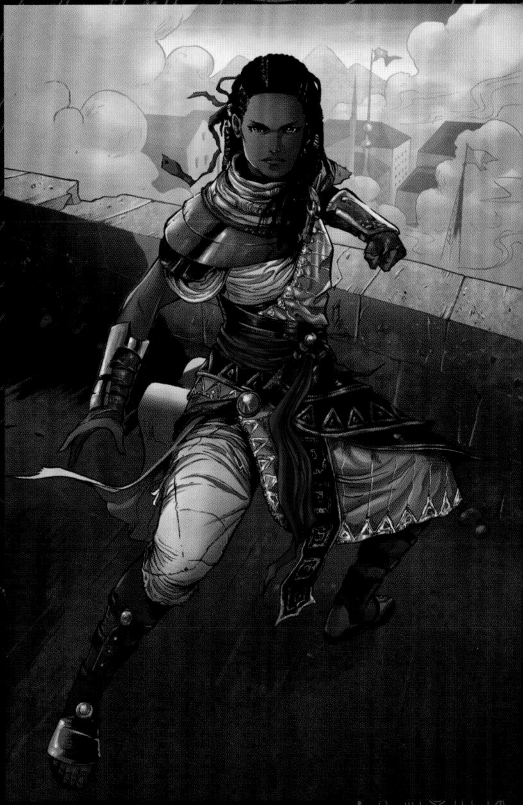

Aya pin-up
Colors by Dijjo Lima

<*SKETCHES* BY PJ KAIOWA>

> ART PROCESS

Here's a quick look at the various techniques and collaborative effort require
bring Aya and *Assassin's Creed Origins* from the screen to the page.

PAGE 4

Panel 1: A small panel. A close-up of our hero, AYA. She's running so let's see her focused and perhaps her hair flows behind her

(1) Cleopatra (caption): Where did you wind up, Aya?

Panel 2: A LARGE panel. This is an action shot of Aya stealthily walking along a Roman rooftop. She's in full gear so the outfit similar to the game, with box and the arrow on her back. Make her look like a true action hero.

But she's not alone. Just behind her is an older man… MARCUS JUNIUS BRUTUS (we'll just call him BRUTUS). He's not in full-out gear yet isn't dressed in the traditional Roman Senator garb we think of him in. Something in-between. He's pointing Aya just off to the side.

(2) Caption: Rome, 44 B.C. Fourteen years earlier.
(3) Brutus: He's over there.
(4) Aya (caption): By now, I know most of the city.
(5) Aya (caption): Thanks to Brutus.
(6) Aya (caption): Without him I would not have survived the journey here.

Panel 3: From an extreme angle below (we're looking right up), we see both Aya and Brutus jump across a small void between buildings.

(7) Aya (caption): Would not have been able to kill Septimius.

Panel 4: A medium-shot as Aya and Brutus hunch down, hiding. They both stare down, off-panel.

(8) Aya (caption): And would not be close to ending Caesar's madness.

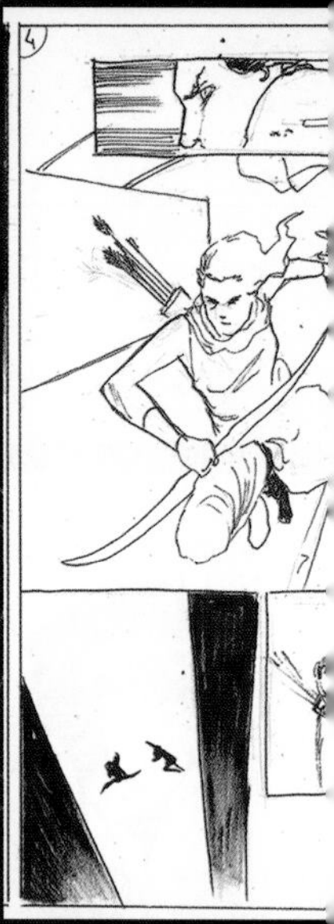

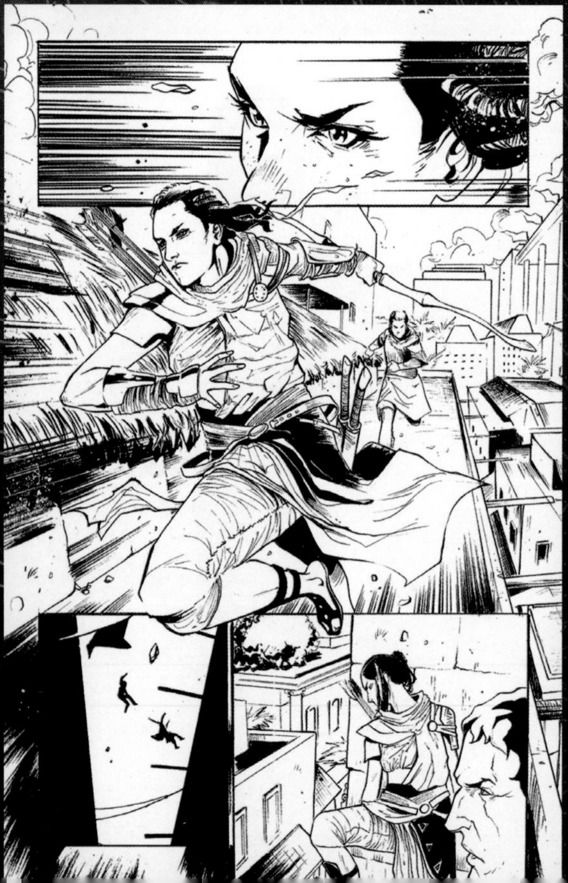

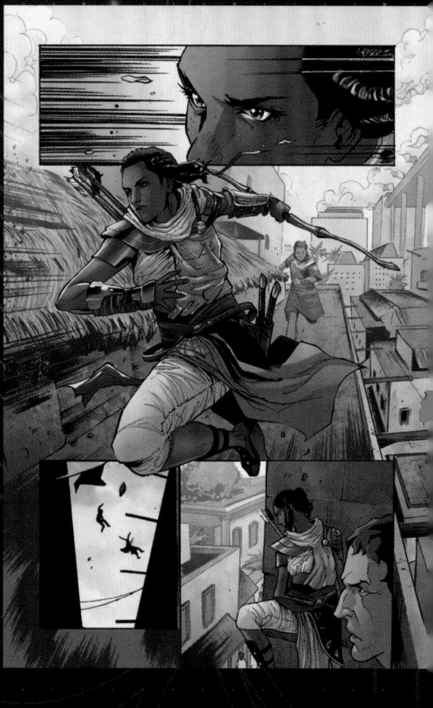

ISSUE #1, PAGE 04.
Script by Anthony Del Col
Layout/inks by PJ Kaiowa
Colors by Dijjo Uma